LADIES GET PAID

The Ultimate Guide to Breaking Barriers,
Owning Your Worth, and
Taking Command of Your Career

LADIES
GET
PAID

CLAIRE WASSERMAN

GALLERY BOOKS

New York   London   Toronto   Sydney   New Delhi

G

Gallery Books
An Imprint of Simon & Schuster, Inc.
1230 Avenue of the Americas
New York, NY 10020

First Gallery Books hardcover edition January 2021

GALLERY BOOKS and colophon are registered trademarks of Simon & Schuster, Inc.

For information about special discounts for bulk purchases, please contact Simon & Schuster Special Sales at 1-866-506-1949 or business@simonandschuster.com.

The Simon & Schuster Speakers Bureau can bring authors to your live event. For more information or to book an event, contact the Simon & Schuster Speakers Bureau at 1-866-248-3049 or visit our website at www.simonspeakers.com.

Interior design by Davina Mock-Maniscalco

Manufactured in the United States of America

10   9   8   7   6   5   4   3   2

Library of Congress Cataloging-in-Publication Data
Names: Wasserman, Claire, author.
Title: Ladies get paid : the ultimate guide to breaking barriers, owning your worth, and taking command of your career / Claire Wasserman.
Description: New York : Gallery Books, [2021] | Includes bibliographical references and index.
Identifiers: LCCN 2020029832 (print) | LCCN 2020029833 (ebook) | ISBN 9781982126902 (hardcover) | ISBN 9781982126926 (ebook)
Subjects: LCSH: Women—Vocational guidance. | Career development. | Sex discrimination in employment. | Equal pay for equal work. | Success in business.
Classification: LCC HF5382.6 .W37 2021 (print) | LCC HF5382.6 (ebook) | DDC 650.1082—dc23
LC record available at https://lccn.loc.gov/2020029832
LC ebook record available at https://lccn.loc.gov/2020029833

ISBN 978-1-9821-2690-2
ISBN 978-1-9821-2692-6 (ebook)

To my parents, who by their example and encouragement
showed me that it's possible to have a career of purpose.

To Ashley, for her infinite patience and support,
without which none of this would be possible.

And to the Ladies Get Paid community:
thank you for being on this journey with me.
This book is for you.

CONTENTS

Author's Note   ix

INTRODUCTION: How It All Began   xiii

PART ONE: Build Your Foundation

CHAPTER ONE: Get Aligned   7

CHAPTER TWO: Get Out of Your Head   29

CHAPTER THREE: Get Over Perfectionism   45

PART TWO: Game Time

CHAPTER FOUR: Get Connected   73

CHAPTER FIVE: Get the Job   101

CHAPTER SIX: Get Paid   117

CHAPTER SEVEN: Get Balanced   143

PART THREE: Level Up

CHAPTER EIGHT: Get Allies   177

CHAPTER NINE: Get Promoted   203

PART FOUR: Make a Difference

CHAPTER TEN: Get Your Company On Board   223

CONTENTS

CHAPTER ELEVEN: Case Study: Get Equal   239

CHAPTER TWELVE: Conclusion   249

Acknowledgments   251

APPENDIX: How to Effect Policy Change   255

References   273

Index   291

Continue the Conversation   300

AUTHOR'S NOTE

You may have found your way to *Ladies Get Paid* because you're excited about the future of your career, or maybe you're here because you're feeling stuck. Perhaps you're standing on the precipice of a big change, or perhaps you're itching to make one happen. Maybe you experienced something at work that was disappointing, frustrating, or downright infuriating. Or perhaps you're not satisfied with the status quo in your professional life or for the lives of all women. Whatever it is, you're ready to take your career into your hands. Welcome, you're in the right place.

This is a book about putting yourself in the driver's seat of your career. In it, I will ask you to declare yourself worthy of more, teach you how to set your sights on a goal, and push you to go after it.

Getting paid is about so much more than your paycheck. It's about respect and recognition. It's also about getting power, in all the ways you define it. Why "Ladies"? I chose the word as a nod to the image it conjures up: the well-behaved woman, the good girl. She doesn't disrupt and she's grateful for what she's given. But my question is, what happens when a lady takes up space? What happens when she is the one calling the shots? The phrase "Ladies Get Paid" is about pushing women to know their value and be unabashed to ask for more.

Writing about women in the workplace often invites criticism. There are those who argue that the wage gap doesn't exist or that the obstacles women (and in particular women of color) face have been overstated. I urge you to visit the References section in the back of this book. There, I believe you will find an abundance of research that shows the vast structural challenges and discrimination that persists despite some progress made in the last thirty years.

There are also those who call this corporate feminism, and say that it is performative at best and perpetuating systemic inequalities at worst. I hear you.

While I understand this criticism, helping women move up in their companies and make more money (which men have done since the beginning of time) is, on its face, not a bad thing. More money means more power. And hopefully a more balanced leadership, both in terms of gender and race, would yield a more inclusive and fairer workplace. I won't apologize for teaching women things that can improve their lives.

But does advocating for oneself address entrenched sexism and discrimination? No. That is why I include an appendix that lists a number of laws such as minimum wage, paid family leave, and universal childcare, which, if enacted, would greatly benefit women with an emphasis on low-wage workers and women of color.

And finally, there are those who will say that these are problems of our own making, that it is our lack of confidence or ambition that hold us back. I reject that. Yes, we sometimes hold ourselves back, but it is an internalization of how our gender is treated, whether it's how we are socialized or how we are paid.

This book will encourage you to question everything: your assumptions, what you believe you deserve (or don't), where you're headed, and what you think you're capable of. You'll meet nine real women (some names and identifying details have been changed) whose career challenges—from dealing with imposter syndrome to negotiating their salaries to navigating office politics—may resonate with your own. I hope their stories will inspire you, but most important, incite you to action. Change only happens by doing. Remember, small steps lead to big rewards, and by picking up this book, you just took the first one.

HOW IT ALL BEGAN

Before *Ladies Get Paid*, the book, came Ladies Get Paid, the organization. It was born from three pivotal moments in my life. The first happened at an advertising festival. Party after party, CEOs of major brands socialized (and drank) with those who wanted their business. It was mostly men. At the time I worked for a professional platform that connected creatives with jobs, and I was there to find clients. The festival opened with an outdoor cocktail party.

"Whose wife are you?"

He was tall, probably around sixty years old, dressed in an expensive-looking white linen suit. It had been barely five minutes since I'd walked into the party. I gritted my teeth and stretched my lips into what I hoped was a smile. "I'm here on business." This was going to be a long week. Around-the-clock networking is tiring.

And it was. But what was even more exhausting was the invisible (though sometimes obvious) imbalance of power between genders. Men greatly outnumbered women and their seniority dwarfed ours. I needed these men to send me their business, but so many saw me, and many of the other women there, not as valuable professional connections but as people to party with. Repeatedly, I had to wrestle the conversation back to a place that was relevant to my work or simply back to a place where I felt comfortable. It was draining, but I'd done this dance before. In fact, I'd been doing it my entire career.

Something profound happened toward the end of the festival. Needing to pee (and needing a break), I sought refuge in the women's restroom. It turned out I wasn't the only one. Crowded in there were women of all ages, huddled together, connecting and commiserating. They traded business cards and tips on who to avoid and who was actually serious about networking. These women had come to the festival to get shit done; it just happened to be getting done in the ladies' room. I spent some time there recharging, then took a deep breath and went back out, into the fray.

After the week was over, I slept for two days straight. I felt demoralized and a bit disgusted as I replayed each unsettling interaction over and over again, from Mr. Whose Wife Are You to the guy who slurred "You're hot" when I pitched him a business idea. Then my disgust turned inward. What had *I* done to attract this kind of attention? Was my dress too short? Had I been too friendly? This was an all-too-familiar loop, a constant refrain throughout my whole career, and maybe even my whole life.

But for the first time, something short-circuited my self-doubt. For years, I'd struggled to be taken seriously as a successful, ambitious woman, questioning *myself* in the process. One memory stood out in particular: I was at dinner with a man a colleague had introduced me to, thinking we might partner on a project. Toward the end of the evening, he grabbed my hand and pulled me in to kiss him. I snatched my arm back. "Excuse me?!" I said in disbelief. The man looked utterly confused.

"But you gave me your business card!" he sputtered. Besides the fact that it was a troubling misinterpretation of signals, what stayed with me was the fact that I was being perceived as a potential sexual partner instead of a professional one, despite every indication that I was there to do business. And as a result, networking with this person, who otherwise could have been valuable for my work, was an opportunity I would not pursue. It also made me feel like shit.

I had a realization: How many other times had I missed opportunities not because of a lack of ability or performance, but because I was a woman? How many hours had I wasted agonizing about how to maneuver among men like these in this world that they had created? I thought of all the energy I'd wasted seeking approval from the men around me. I couldn't continue like this; something needed to change.

I opened my laptop and googled three words: "women," "work," and "inequality." What I learned shook me to my core:

✦ The majority of today's college graduates are women, yet less than 22 percent of us make it past middle management.

✦ The wage gap, which is usually referred to as being 78–80 cents to the man's dollar, is not the reality for everyone. Depending on your race (and a myriad of other factors), it can be so much worse. Black women make between 63–68 cents on the dollar, while Hispanic women make a mere 55 cents on the dollar.

I was shocked. I felt angry. And on top of that, I was ashamed for not knowing it was that bad, and that reeked of my privilege. I'd grown up being told I could do and be whatever I dreamed of, that our workplaces are a meritocracy, and that the fight for equality was over and won by my mother's generation. I was finally understanding this was not reality. And I wanted to do something about it.

As I continued to research women in the workplace, I discovered an entire vocabulary that put words to things I'd always felt but hadn't known how to articulate. For example, I learned about emotional labor, the contortionism that women—especially women of color—perform to fit into and accommodate environments where they are not the status quo. All of this was enlightening, but it was also overwhelming. With such systemic, entrenched bias, what could I as an individual possibly do?

A year later, I was approached by an art director friend of mine, Leta. She'd recently found out that a male art director friend of hers was charging almost double what she was. This discovery made Leta realize how little she knew about pricing and how important it was for this to be a larger, more open conversation with our peers. She was also concerned that the lack of transparency might mean other people were underpricing themselves, which in turn could be bringing down wages for everyone.

Because I was the director of marketing for a platform that helped people find work, I was in a position to bring information and awareness to a large network of people. Leta wondered if there was something I could do to help women learn what they should be paid. It began to dawn on me that in so many ways, money symbolized much of what I'd been agonizing over in the past year. Money—and having the same opportunities to earn just as much as men—was about more than a number. It represented value, worth, and above all, power. All things that, as women, we have historically been denied.

This conversation with Leta happened during the lead-up to the 2016 presidential election. As I thought about organizing an event for women to talk about money, I became intrigued by the town halls the candidates were hosting and thought it could be a good alternative in lieu of the format of a typical panel. I envisioned one made up of women of different backgrounds and professions, trading stories and advice about money in an open forum, essentially democratizing a subject that had always seemed to be the domain of experts (men). More important, it could finally get us talking about a topic that was taboo, that was considered crass but that men seemed able to navigate with ease. Maybe if one of us spoke up, others would follow. All we needed was a bit of encouragement.

To get people to sign up, I asked six women I admired if they would be open to sharing their money stories. I also asked each of them to recommend a few women they thought should be there. For every woman I was introduced to, I asked if they could recommend another woman who might want to attend. This went on until we reached capacity. The day of the event, one hundred women came. They crowded together on couches, spilling out onto the floor, passing around bottles of wine, buzzing with energy. It reminded me of the ladies' room at the advertising festival.

It was my first public speaking experience and I knew I didn't have all the answers. I was there to learn just as much as they were. I told the room that we would get out of the event only as much as we were willing to give; to receive help meant we had to offer it. We raised our glasses to one another, and we began.

It was like a cork shooting out of a champagne bottle. One story begat another as these women opened up to one another and to themselves. They shared stories of disappointments and struggles, missed opportunities, denied promotions. There were lots of tears, but lots of high fives, too. One woman stood up and declared, "I'm an illustrator and make a *shit ton* of money." She got a standing ovation.

I was right; this conversation was about so much more than the dollars in our pockets. It was about solidarity. It was about self-worth. It was also about taking action to right the wrongs that we'd been laboring under. We would no longer wait (and hope) to be rewarded. Money was the first step, a tangible thing that could mark progress on what was sure to be a long road ahead. To close the wage gap, we could start with ourselves, by advocating for our worth. But for all of us to rise, we needed to work together.

Three hours later, the event was technically over, but no one was leaving. I was becoming antsy since the venue was charging me by the hour. "Go home!" I shouted as I turned off the lights. Everyone reluctantly shuffled out, and I could hear them discussing what bar to go to; they didn't want the conversation to end.

As one of the women walked out, she pulled me aside. "This," she said, motioning around the room, "you should do *this*." I didn't know what she meant, but something magical had happened that night.

On my way home, I felt electric. That energy in the room was coursing through my veins and my mind was racing. It had been over a year since I'd googled "workplace inequality," and I thought that maybe, just maybe, this could be the start of something big. Something that could lead toward making things right. While I didn't quite know what was next, perhaps the first step was simply for us to share our stories as we had done that night.

Over the course of the next twelve months, I organized 250 town halls in nineteen cities, bringing together thousands of women to talk about money, power, work, and self-worth. And every time a woman got up to speak, she discovered she was not alone. As I watched them, I knew there had to be a way to harness the strength we have when we come together. I wanted to see it move beyond those rooms and those town halls, to build an even larger collective that could allow us to learn from one another, encourage one another, and share practical advice and professional guidance to get us where we wanted to be. The town halls were our catharsis, but with no action afterward, all that inspiration and energy would be wasted. And nothing would change.

While organizing these events, I witnessed the power in peer-to-peer sharing, but I also saw that there was a great need for concrete tools to fix actual problems. One topic that kept coming up in the town halls all across the country was insecurity surrounding salary negotiation. Teaching more women how to negotiate their salaries wasn't a big-picture structural change, but it could at least start moving the needle in the short term. As I fit the pieces together, I knew there was something special happening, but what I didn't know was that a movement was being born. This one area of actionable change became the cornerstone of our movement, and a springboard for accessing—and improving—broader issues impacting women in the workplace.

As of this writing, the Ladies Get Paid community has grown to more than one hundred thousand women who are all working together to advance women in the workplace. In this book, I will share the stories of nine members (some names and identifying details have been changed). Each in their own way, these women battle internal and external struggles, pushing up against the bounds of what they (and others) expect of themselves, and are ultimately able to reach places of purpose, fulfillment, and power. For many of them, this meant undoing assumptions and rebuilding expectations, examining where they came from, and becoming clear on what direction they will go.

In their stories, I will highlight what they can teach us. In those moments, I hope you will reflect on your own life and how you'll use these tools to rocket *yourself* forward.

This book is organized into four parts. The first part explores the obstacles we may have in ourselves. We'll examine expectations we may have inherited from our families, the media, our communities, and other influences about what career success looks like and what we can achieve. From there, we'll learn to identify and evaluate opportunities to make sure we are headed on a path that's aligned with our values and goals. Then, we'll break down imposter syndrome and perfectionism, two major internal roadblocks (often resulting from systemic and cultural obstacles) that stand in our way of feeling and doing our best.

In the second part of the book, we'll broaden our focus: you'll learn how to build and leverage your network to get you where you want to go. This includes interviewing, securing, and negotiating for a new job. But getting the job is only the first step. You need to also set yourself up for success. That means educating yourself on how to develop healthy work habits for the long game—things like conducting an inventory of your energy and setting boundaries for yourself and others so that you don't burn out. You can't do well if *you* aren't well.

Then we'll explore how to navigate upward: cultivating a support system, increasing our visibility, and taking advantage of opportunities. The ultimate goal? To seek out rewarding challenges and do our best work in a place that recognizes and rewards us.

At a certain point, however, trying to do well in a system that was not made by or for us is not good enough; the system itself has to change. The final part of the book is about what we can do to make our workplaces more inclusive and supportive of women, including policies and practices companies can implement to make that happen. But for true systemic change to happen, we need updated and evolved laws. The appendix includes information on how to lobby your elected officials to enact laws that ensure wide-ranging and long-lasting progress.

Before we begin, I want to acknowledge that some of the lessons in this book come from a place of relative privilege. Being able to walk away from a negotiation or turning down a job are luxuries. And while as women we are bound together by our marginalized status, my experience in the workplace as a white cisgender woman is not the same as that of a Black woman, or a Hispanic woman, or a woman with a disability, or a trans woman, or any of the countless women in groups pushed to the fringes of society, who have been fighting these battles for generations. I firmly believe that we have progressed only as far as those who still struggle the most among us. If we're going to make meaningful change, it has to benefit *all* of us, not just some of us. And we have to do it together. Let's get started.

PART ONE

BUILD YOUR FOUNDATION

HOW DID WE GET HERE?

We teach girls to shrink themselves, to make themselves smaller.
We say to girls, you can have ambition, but not too much.
You should aim to be successful, but not too successful.
—Chimamanda Ngozi Adichie, *We Should All Be Feminists*

Before we can advocate for ourselves out in the world, we have to first believe that we are worthy of advocacy. This begins with examining our inner beliefs and the mindsets we carry into our lives and workplaces. Are they truly aligned with where we want to go?

In Chapter One: Get Aligned, we'll explore the cultural messaging we've received about women and work, and how that has impacted our career decisions. As millennial women, we were told growing up that we could achieve anything we wanted, as long as we were willing to work hard. On the one hand, this was incredibly encouraging: many of the women who came before us were told all the things they could *not* do. But creating equal opportunity for women is also more complicated than simply changing what young women are told.

As children, we learn that there is an "ideal" girl: she is nice, pretty, accommodating, gets good grades, and puts family first. We are rewarded if we become that girl and criticized if we don't. What that demonstrates to us is that our worth is contingent on the approval of others. This is further reinforced as we get older, so it's no wonder that we may start to contort ourselves to be whatever we think others need us to be. In turn, these messages can sometimes warp the expectations we have for our careers and make us lose sight of what fulfills us. Or, if we do know what we want but it doesn't line up with the norm, we may silence our desires in order to adhere to the safety of the status quo.

Just as there's an "ideal" girl, there's also an "ideal" career, with only so many paths to get there. This idea that there is a "right" path assumes that there is also a "wrong" one. Because as women, we've been brought up to please others, we of course feel pressure to do the "right" thing. The problem is, we might not stop to consider if that's truly the right thing *for us*. In Chapter One we'll talk about how to identify the societal, cultural, and familial messages that could be interfering with our judgment, and how to develop methods for tuning back in with ourselves and redefining what success really means to us.

Once you have an authentic vision of what success means to you, you have to believe you are worthy of it. In order to do that, you must confront any limiting beliefs that may be holding you back or keeping you small. Here's a thought exercise: When you think of a CEO of a Fortune 500 company, what do they look like? Did you picture a woman, or a person of color? Your mental image of a CEO is probably influenced by the fact that the number of female Fortune 500 CEOs has never risen above 6.4 percent. In fact, in 2018, *there were more Fortune 500 CEOs named John than there were women on the list.* (Beyond that, there are entire industries with barely any women in them.) When you don't see yourself represented in a certain environment, it is easy to assume that this is not a place you can access or a role you would excel in without changing something about yourself.

As women enter the workforce, this realization has an undeniable effect. Optimism can easily be replaced by doubt. Am I good enough to make it? It's also incredibly easy to turn that doubt inward, just as I'd done after the advertising festival: Is something wrong with me?

In the face of such doubt, many of us do what we've been taught to do: keep our heads down, work hard, and wait to be rewarded. But what I hear from women, over and over again, is that as they ascend in their field of choice, their male colleagues seem to be getting ahead while the promotions and raises for the women are harder to come by. This is not in our imagination. According to psychologist and organizational consultant Tomas Chamorro-Premuzic, studies show that men are more likely to be rewarded based on their potential, whereas women have to prove themselves again and again, solidifying our self-doubt even more.

Studies also show that men are paid more, and this is the final nail in the coffin of self-worth. That's the tangible proof of what we'd feared all along: that we are less valuable and must adjust our expectations of what we are capable of and what we deserve.

All of these factors—slower promotion cycles, lower wages, poor representation in positions of power—can come together and form a misguided foundation of how we operate in the workplace. This uncertain foundation is largely built on two core beliefs:

1. We are not as good as we present ourselves to be, and that people will find out, i.e., imposter syndrome.

2. Anything less than flawless is a failure, and in turn, we are the failure, i.e., perfectionism.

Imposter syndrome and perfectionism are like two sides of the same coin, both born from the belief that our worth is largely based on how well we perform (remember that childhood conditioning, where one's worth is contingent on doing the "right" thing as an "ideal" girl?) This can get in our way of embracing our self-worth, taking risks, and standing up for ourselves.

When we constantly play catch-up to what we think worthiness looks like, we risk expending energy, often to the point of burnout. Imposter syndrome and perfectionism also have the power to keep us small: not speaking up at a meeting for fear of looking dumb, or not applying for a job that we don't think we're 100 percent qualified for. These kinds of beliefs limit our expectations for what we can achieve, and even how we think we deserve to be treated.

We'll address each in turn in Chapters Two and Three, teaching you how to recognize these habits and thoughts and stop them from running the show. A lot of this work may feel uncomfortable at best and painful at worst. You may be undoing old habits and rethinking your choices. As scary as that can be, stick with it. I promise it will pay off (figuratively and literally)! Once we address these internal obstacles, we can clear the way to make real, unimpeded progress out in the world.

You've got this.

CHAPTER ONE

GET ALIGNED

By her senior year of college, Alisha had become seriously concerned about her future. She'd started her freshman year confident about what she would do after graduation. She always loved writing, being creative, and learning about other people. Growing up, Alisha idolized Barbara Walters and wanted to follow in her footsteps and become a journalist.

But over time, a little voice crept into her consciousness. Her parents had emigrated from Korea to the United States with very little, and here she was at Harvard, one of the world's most prestigious institutions. Shouldn't she be using this one-in-a-million opportunity to set herself up on a path toward success and financial security? Suddenly her dream of becoming a journalist felt frivolous, and even a little selfish. So, during her freshman year, Alisha switched her major from English to sociology, rationalizing that it was more "business"-oriented and therefore more practical.

As graduation loomed large and official adulthood crept closer, Alisha was feeling anxious, even panicked. She worried that she might have actually squandered her education by denying herself the chance to pursue what she was genuinely excited about. Now she feared it was too late to turn back. Her anxiety (or as she referred to it, "that sick feeling") grew and grew until Alisha was almost paralyzed by it, barely leaving her room except for meals.

Then the recruiters came. Descending on campus in droves, they represented hedge funds, consulting firms, and investment banks, pitching the students on careers befitting Ivy League graduates. These soon-to-be grads had gone to the "best" schools; didn't they deserve the "best" jobs (not to mention the enormous paychecks)? The recruiters assured them that starting their careers at such elite companies would put them on the fast track to guaranteed success.

But what exactly *was* success? Alisha wondered. Financial security? An impressive title at a big-name company? Or was it something more personal, and harder to describe? She banished that sick feeling and dutifully dressed up in what she hoped resembled business attire and joined the rest of the students who jostled to get into the right networking events in front of the right recruiters. Everyone was competing for the pot of gold that was promised at the end of the rainbow. All they had to do was follow it.

———

Whether it's silently modeled or explicitly stated, many of us are raised with a vision of what our lives will look like: stability, a spouse, kids. Certain professions are deemed serious, and others silly. As adults, we take that vision on as our own, even though it's inherited from those who came before us: our parents, schools, society; our churches, role models, and mentors. When we are faced with making critical decisions, we may orient toward that vision without question, choosing paths that will lead us to the "right" destination with the least amount of struggle.

Early on in my own career, I was very lucky to have been challenged to push myself past what I thought I wanted, to what I deeply needed. Just a few months after I'd graduated, I met Stephane, who was around fifteen years older than me and much wiser, and who would go on to become a mentor of mine. I vividly remember a conversation we had where he asked me what my definition of success was. As I began to answer, Stephane waved his hand, motioning me to stop. "Whose voice is that?" I was confused. I hadn't said anything. "Try again," he said. I'd barely uttered a sound when Stephane put his hand up again. "Try again." Now I wasn't just confused, I was annoyed. But before I could say anything, he smiled. "Is that voice your mother's? Your father's? Your school's?"

I then realized that what he was doing was pushing me to consider that there are infinite ways to imagine the future and that I was allowed to have my own, personal definition of success, not bound or limited by who may have influenced me, or what I'd been exposed to. He was also challenging me to be brave and think for myself. Coming up with my own definition of success meant that I had to question—and maybe even reject—what I'd always thought to be true and start fresh with my own ideas.

This is what Alisha had attempted to do during her freshman year when she set her sights on a journalism career. But her inner critic had quickly swooped in to protect her from taking a risk, and she changed her course. Four years later, even though she felt lost, Alisha actually knew more than she realized. That sick, anxious feeling was like a signal trying to alert her that she was headed in a direction that was unlikely to lead to purpose and fulfillment. Still, it would take some time (and real-world experiences) before she was able to heed the signs her body was sending her. In this chapter we'll see how Alisha, a high achiever most anyone would consider "a success," confronts the assumptions about work that she's carried her whole life, and how they've influenced the decisions she's made in her career—not always for the best.

Overcoming external expectations means recognizing that you have the power to define your own direction, no matter your circumstances. To change your way of thinking, you have to confront the assumptions you carry, where they come from, and how they've influenced your decisions, for better or worse. As you do this work, you may find that you begin to look at the unknown as exhilarating, not terrifying. There is no formula whereby you answer some questions and out pops your dream career. Instead, you'll learn how to trust your instinct over your inner critic and create a system to evaluate opportunities that are aligned with *your* values and goals. And while it will always be a little scary to stand up for what you want, you'll feel pride in taking control of your career. You'll also be more motivated, which in turn will help you do your best work, putting you in a position for rewards and recognition. You've earned it.

LISTEN TO YOUR INSTINCT

When Alisha received a job offer from a big consulting firm shortly after graduation, she took it immediately. While this wasn't what she would necessarily have imagined for herself during college, it would at least put her on a track where she knew she'd have financial and professional security. She assumed that sick feeling, still with her since college, would go away soon.

A few months into the job, it was still there, but Alisha was so busy that she barely noticed it. She was putting in long days at the office, so what little energy she had left was spent doing the minimal self-care necessary for survival: sleeping, eating, and showering. The workload was grueling, but it was the norm; everyone was in the same boat, so who was she to complain? This was the price you had to pay for a big paycheck.

No stranger to working hard in college, Alisha could handle long hours and taking work home on the weekends, but it was the office politics that really rankled her. After proving her competence on smaller projects over a few months, Alisha got the opportunity to lead a project for a high-profile client. She prepared for weeks, only to have the opportunity to present her hard work to the client taken away and given to someone else the day of the presentation. "I was laying out all the slides of our PowerPoint to do one final review. As I was walking the team through it, a senior executive walked in. She thanked me for my work and informed me that Paul would be presenting it to the client. I was stunned." Paul was a newer employee and from what Alisha could gather, a master at politicking. She, on the other hand, would describe herself as an introvert. She'd never considered this a liability before. It didn't matter whether or not you were gregarious, she thought; what mattered was how well you did the job, right? She'd been raised to believe that working hard would get her ahead. And it had, until then. But now something was off, and she didn't know what.

Like so many other women, Alisha assumed the problem was with her. She needed to not just work hard, but schmooze better, and be aggressive in the way that the company clearly rewarded. She never really considered that contorting herself into what the company needed her to be wasn't the only way to work. But it was hard to see any other way, given that most of her friends were having similar experiences. Clearly this was just what it meant to be a working professional.

Alisha hit her breaking point a year later when she returned from a major business trip. She'd gone to Korea, where, almost as soon as her team landed after a fourteen-hour flight, they rushed right into their first client meeting. For the next three days they ran around the city, gathering firsthand market research, talking to locals, and all the while Alisha (who is half Korean) was real-time translating from Korean into English for her teammates, then back into Korean. "A two-way language translation is incredibly draining mentally and difficult to pull off well, and doubly so when you are doing it for your direct boss. I was obviously sent on this business trip because of my language skills, and because it would save the company thousands of dollars (perhaps tens of thousands) rather than paying an external interpreter."

Upon her return to the United States, Alisha promptly got sick. She was able to hold it together for a client presentation, but the next day, jet-lagged and ill, she called in sick. She figured she could take a day to recover, given how hard she'd just worked. Wrong. Early that morning the phone rang: it was her boss's boss, calling to express his concern— not for her health, but for her absence. If she wasn't willing to put in the hours, he said, he was worried that she wasn't cut out to be a consultant. Alisha was taken aback. She'd been killing herself working around the clock! The conversation then spiraled into whether she was a good fit for the company. Similar to the time her presentation was given to Paul, Alisha was left feeling totally unsure and unsettled, not understanding where things had gone wrong.

As upsetting as the call was, it was the catalyst Alisha needed to be brutally honest with herself. Why *wasn't* she getting ahead at this job? Why wasn't she happier? It wasn't just the work-life balance that was exhausting, it was also constantly trying to twist into what she thought she needed to do and be in order to be successful. Alisha was starting to wake up to the possibility that as much as she needed to be right for the company, the company had to be right for her as well. The relationship needed to go both ways. This duality was something she had never really considered before. Instead of pushing the dread and discomfort away, Alisha needed to pay attention when things felt wrong and get to the bottom of it.

CHALLENGE YOUR ASSUMPTIONS

In the 1950s, psychologist Karen Horney identified a phenomenon that Alisha—and so many others—subscribe to: "The Tyranny of the

Should." Her theory posited that we have two views of ourselves: the "real self" (who we are) and the "ideal self" (the model of who we think we should be). If we feel our real self isn't living up to the ideal (hello to all the perfectionists and "imposters" in the room), we believe we are fundamentally flawed, and as a result, can have a hard time fulfilling our potential. Unless we challenge the assumption that there is some ideal self we should inhabit, we'll continue the cycle of self-doubt, self-flagellation, and dissatisfaction.

A way to replace those "shoulds" is to understand where they came from. That means digging into your past: how you were raised, the messages you received, how those around you influenced your opinions and choices about work, including whether or not it was gendered. For example, growing up, were you taught that certain jobs were or were not meant for women? It can be hard to imagine ourselves in industries and roles that for so long have been deemed "male" (engineering, construction, tech). With so few women at the top or in visible roles, we can feel even more cut off from those spaces. As the saying goes, "you can't be what you can't see." Throw some imposter syndrome into the mix, and our vision of what a career "can" or "should" be becomes even more limited.

Sadly, these limitations can be as much internal as external. I've heard from too many women who don't think they're good enough or deserving enough to have a job that brings fulfillment. It's not that they don't want it, it's just so far from their current circumstances that they can't even consider it a possible outcome.

If any of this sounds familiar, it's time for a gut check. How much have the "shoulds" dominated the way you've approached your career? How much are you guided by your voice, versus the voice of your parents, schoolmates, or the culture around you? Take some time to consider the following questions—you can write down your answers if you like or simply think them through, but allow yourself the space to really consider what has influenced the beliefs you carry about your career path.

UNDERSTAND YOUR INFLUENCES

✦ What career paths did you have exposure to growing up?

✦ Did the adults around you discuss their jobs openly? What was your impression of them?

✦ Did adults in your life ever explicitly share their expectations for your career? What did they say?

✦ Did anything in your environment influence what you thought of work in general, and the way you looked at your own career?

✦ What has been the major driver of your career choices? Has anyone commented on those choices and if so, what did they say?

✦ Have you ever done (or *not* done) something only because you thought it was the "right" thing for your career? What was the outcome?

✦ Have you ever regretted any of your career choices?

✦ Have there been times in your life where your gut told you something but you didn't listen to it? What do you think was stopping you?

✦ Are there any professions or roles that you feel are totally inaccessible to you? Why?

FIND CLUES

Alisha never actually felt pressure to follow any defined path. In fact, her parents encouraged her to pursue whatever she wanted; it was Alisha who put pressure on herself. She was acutely aware of how much her parents had given up to come to this country, so she never considered a job that might be associated with financial insecurity.

As you examine your assumptions, where they came from, and how they've influenced you, you might start to feel unmoored. You're in a sort of no-(wo)man's-land: you may have identified expectations you're ready to let go of but haven't yet landed on a new worldview that's consonant with your values, and what truly resonates with you. How do you get to that point? Let's begin by digging deeper into your past for the clues that will help orient you toward the future.

The best clues can be found in the things that energize you, or in other words, when you're "in flow." Coined by psychologist Mihaly Csikszentmihalyi, flow is defined as a state of complete involvement in an activity for its own sake. As he describes it, "The ego falls away. Time flies. Every action, movement, and thought flows from the previous one; in a way, it's like playing jazz. Your whole being is involved, and you're using your skills to the utmost." Think about times in your life when you've felt in complete flow: when you're fully engaged, all cylinders firing, time melting away.

As you examine those memories, go beyond just what you were doing; *where* you were doing it is just as important. Our environment has an enormous impact on how we feel and our ability to do our best work. Take into account things like what time of day it was, what the space looked like. What about people: What level of interaction did it require? Was it in front of a computer; did it require physical activity? There are dozens of bits of information to glean that, once you process them, can help you determine what is important to you in a work environment or field of work. This can also help you decide if there are things you want to negotiate for at your current position (such as flextime or remote working—more examples will follow), or if you're stuck in a situation that's never going to lead to job satisfaction, even with major changes.

On the flip side, what depletes your energy can also provide you with a ton of helpful clues. So much of knowing what you want comes from experiencing what you don't want. As Alisha learned the hard way, she hated the lack of work-life balance at the consulting firm and that being aggressive was a requirement for getting ahead. She also missed being creative. Because these factors were inherent to the position she was in, she realized that it would be nearly impossible to achieve "flow" in her current job.

Laying out clearly what elements enhance or deplete your energy can help you figure out if you are in the right position, or what you can do to improve your work environment. Here's a chart with Alisha's examples:

ENERGY +	ENERGY –
Being creative (specifically writing and designing)	Lots of travel
Collaborative work environment	Hierarchy/bureaucracy at work
Doing mission-driven work	Competitive culture

STRENGTHS

We often think that "work" automatically means "hard work," and anything that feels natural or comes easily doesn't really count or somehow shouldn't be taken seriously. Because of that, we spend so much of our energy trying to fix what's "wrong" with us, rather than cultivating and leaning into our strengths.

When you examine your strengths, it's important to go beyond the ones that have an obvious connection to your career and find things that are innate to you, qualities that you might not think would be related to that "other" life that happens at the office. Maybe you're great at organizing parties, maybe you're a masterful networker, or maybe you're the one your friends always confide in to help solve their problems. This isn't to say you should necessarily become a party planner or a therapist, but it does give you clues to use as you seek out and evaluate opportunities. It's about translating these soft skills into jobs that not only require them but put them front and center.

The following list of questions can be used in two ways. First, give yourself a chance to define your own strengths by thinking deeply about the questions below. Then, enlist the help of an outside perspective. It can be challenging to see yourself objectively, so enlist a few trusted friends or colleagues to answer these questions about you, too. Compare their answers with yours and see if there are patterns you discover.

ASK YOURSELF, AND YOUR WING(WO)MAN

+ What is my greatest strength?

+ What are things I do really well?

+ What do I do/say/think/see differently from other people?

+ If you were to describe me to someone else, what would you say?

INTERESTS

We're often encouraged to "follow your passion!" which sounds motivating at first but can become frustrating and confusing. Usually one of two things happens: you either have so many things you're passionate about that you don't know which one to pursue, or you have no clue what you're passionate about. I think a better way to orient ourselves is toward something that makes us curious, or a problem we want to solve.

DIG INTO YOUR INTERESTS

✦ What are topics or activities that I'm continually drawn to?

✦ What are things that move or motivate me?

✦ What are problems I want to solve?

✦ What things am I most curious about?

✦ (Bonus: Ask a friend): What do I never shut up about?

PUT THE CLUES TOGETHER

Once you've done the above exercises of finding your strengths and what gives you energy, it's time to identify patterns. The things that come up repeatedly are more clues you'll use to point you in the direction of new careers and opportunities to explore.

As I mentioned in the beginning of this chapter, it's difficult to know what options are out there if you've never been exposed to them before. When I graduated from college, my mother helped me define my strengths, experience, and values, as well as things that I liked and disliked, what I was great at, and what I was passionate about. Then she helped me brainstorm opportunities that might be a good fit. For example, in high school, I helped organize a campaign to raise money for an all-girls school in Afghanistan. Because it was something I did that was self-motivated (and that I enjoyed), it demonstrated a potential career path. My mom introduced me to this thing called "development," which is a fancy way of saying "raising money for nonprofits." I was extremely fortunate to have someone like my mom to guide and encourage me, otherwise I might never have known that that job even existed.

In order to connect the dots, let's take what you uncovered in your energy memories and combine it with your aptitudes. Like the exercise I did with my mom, this means writing out what you like and don't like, your skills and strengths, and things that you're passionate about or interested in. Even if it's not entirely obvious what jobs you want to apply for, you'll have a starting point to explore.

Here are some of Alisha's examples:

LIKE	DISLIKE	STRENGTH	PASSIONATE ABOUT OR INTERESTED IN
Time outside of work to live my life	Zero work-life balance	Writing	Building community
Ability to do independent work	Lots of public speaking	Attention to detail	Design
Supportive work environment	Competitive environment	Inspiring others	Sustainability

YOUR MOTIVATING VALUES

Exploring job fulfillment doesn't mean deprioritizing financial security. We all need to pay our bills. What I am asking you to do is to not give up on the possibility that you can both love what you do *and* make money from it. In fact, the more you love your job, the better you'll do, which hopefully, in turn, means making more money! What's important is understanding all of your values and then seeing how they fit together. I want you to identify what you want out of your job. Are you after a big fat paycheck? Having people think you're important? (No judgment!) Flextime? These are what are called extrinsic values: tangible, definable things that are the by-products of your job or occupation. In other words, what you get out of it, rather than what you put into it. Your intrinsic values are things that, when you use them at work, you find personally rewarding.

Putting these values into two columns will make it easier to see how they can translate into job opportunities. Here's what Alisha's two columns of extrinsic and intrinsic values might look like.

PUT IN (INTRINSIC)	GET OUT (EXTRINSIC)
✦ Connecting directly with an audience ✦ Helping others ✦ External recognition or praise	✦ Being a leader ✦ Stable paycheck ✦ Flexibility

DETERMINE YOUR PRIORITIES

It's important to remember that while the ultimate goal is to find the intersection of your interests, skills, and values, no one job can have it all. A good amount of career unhappiness comes from the misguided belief that it can. It's better to know your priorities and focus on opportunities that reflect them.

What are you willing to give up? What are you willing to fight for? In other words, what do you consider to be a "like to have," what falls under "I'd rather not," and what is a "need to have," otherwise known as a deal breaker? This is an opportunity to do a gut check and force yourself to be unsparingly honest as you consider what these things are for you. Remember that you are parsing out what *you* actually want and need vs. someone else's expectations. Here are some examples based on Alisha's experience:

I'D LIKE TO	I'D RATHER NOT	DEAL BREAKER
Be in media	Have office politics	Lack of work-life balance; being expected to work outside of normal work hours
Work in New York	Work autonomously (prefer team)	Not being creative
Make $100k	Make less than $85k	Anything less than $75k (bottom line)

As soul-crushing as the consulting job had been, it did something amazing for Alisha: it woke her up to her deal breakers. What her boss's boss told her on the phone that day she was sick verbalized what she'd been feeling (but ignoring) since she started the job. If she wasn't a good fit for consulting, she had to figure out what *was* a good fit for her. (Notice that I didn't say "what *she* was a good fit for.") For the first time, Alisha's own needs were setting the bar.

Evaluating the clues from her energy memories and digging more into her interests revealed to Alisha what her nonnegotiable priorities were: work-life balance and creativity. At the consulting firm, she was always interested in what the design team was doing. She subscribed to design industry newsletters and played around in InDesign and Photoshop. Alisha didn't consider it as a realistic career path (she was still stuck in the "shoulds" mindset), but she couldn't shake the joy she felt when she designed things. So, she kept turning toward it, finding networking groups to join, reading about the industry, and searching for as many free education resources as she could.

The more Alisha played with design, the more seriously she took it. When she worked on small personal projects, she felt "in flow" and she didn't want to stop. She began to pay attention to a growing desire to try her hand at doing independent design work. She challenged herself to learn how to use Photoshop and when she became proficient in it, she posted on Facebook that she was looking to do some pro bono work. Getting to experiment without the pressure of being paid would allow her to continue to learn and gain more confidence. Once she had a few projects under her belt, Alisha looked at her savings account and figured she had about a six-month runway to try to make it as a freelance designer. She decided that even if it went nowhere, she could use it to show a prospective future employer that she was self-motivated and willing to take risks. Alisha knew she had a lot to learn, but given how much she'd already taught herself, she was confident that she'd find a way to make it work. Shortly after that, she gave her two weeks' notice.

TAKE STEPS

Not everyone can quit their job, but we can all take steps, no matter how small, in a direction that feels right in our soul. Instead of trying to work backward from some predetermined end point (like the corner office or proverbial white picket fence and 2.5 kids), the goal right now is to gather as much information as possible about what lights you up and what makes you tick. Take a step in a direction—any direction—and see how it feels. Read a book, learn a new skill, watch a webinar. Too often we feel paralyzed when we've put in work but don't yet know the answer; taking action means you're making progress.

Signing up for a class? Progress! Showing up for the class? Progress! No doubt you'll be busy, tired, and at times uncertain (no one ever said making change was easy), and it will be tempting to quit and return to what you're comfortable with. Don't. From the beginning, set yourself up to be accountable. Put things on a calendar, designate a buddy to check in with you, or give yourself a reward when you accomplish something you set out to do.

That will help you get into the habit of feeling good and giving yourself permission to continue. By doing that, you've shown yourself that you can—and deserve—to take back control of your career. Just be aware that the voice of the "shoulds" may threaten to get loud again. That voice thinks it's protecting you from the prospect of failure that comes with veering off the "traditional" road map. Remind yourself that you're not throwing caution to the wind; you are being deliberate about moving in the direction of career fulfillment.

Learning to quiet the inner critic is getting more in tune with your instinct and allowing yourself to trust it. Tell that inner critic to hush if it starts to get loud again, but thank it first; it is just trying to protect you from potential pain and suffering. Ultimately, this is about learning to have faith in yourself, and it's a lot harder to do that if you always have this little voice inside that's telling you to be afraid. If you take one step and it feels good, take another. If it doesn't, try something different. The most important thing is to *keep moving forward.*

CASE STUDY

REINVENTION

THE SECOND WORKSHOP I organized for Ladies Get Paid was about how to get unstuck in your career. A friend of mine from college heard about it and reached out to tell me she'd be there. She was unhappy at her job in hospitality and needed a refresh. I was actually surprised to hear she hadn't gone in the direction of politics, since she'd been really civically engaged during college.

The workshop went well, and my friend felt encouraged to keep going. She hired Megan Hellerer, the coach from the workshop, and they worked together to come up with different things she could try to get a better sense of what lit her up. One thing Megan made sure to remind her was that a step in one direction or another didn't mean that it had to become her career. It was possible to be passionate about something and not make it your paycheck. Still, my friend soon realized that she might *want* to make her passion her paycheck . . . but she was concerned there wouldn't be much of one. She was headed back in the direction of political activism, and while it instinctively felt right, it might not pay off her student loans.

However, she wasn't ready to give up on a career path that fulfilled her, and she was determined to find ways to make it work. She needed more information. Also, if she was going to try to break into this field, she needed to get involved. Over the next few months, she participated in a number of progressive organizations, attended rallies, and even helped me brainstorm ways to get Ladies Get Paid members more civically engaged. By getting exposure and making connections, she was able to see that it actually was possible to make a living doing this work.

The next time I saw her was a year later, at a town hall I hosted on reinvention. The event featured women who'd done the hard work of digging deep and making brave changes in their lives and careers. There were over one hundred women in the audience, and at the end I encouraged them to share their own reinvention stories.

"I've always wanted to run for office," said one woman as she stood up. It was my friend. "But women like me don't run for office; people who look like me don't run for office," she continued. "But I'm going to do it. I'm going to run."

The room erupted in cheers. Here was someone publicly declaring her intention to do one of the most difficult and vulnerable things that anyone can do. The point wasn't that she might win, it was that she was brave enough to try, beginning by holding herself accountable. I was so happy for her, I cried.

And she did win. Less than a year later, she would go on to become the youngest congresswoman in US history. Her name is Alexandria Ocasio-Cortez.

KEEP REFINING

The first thing Alisha did when she quit the consulting firm was to join TheLi.st, a networking group that had been recommended by a fellow designer friend. She knew her limitations as a designer, so when she connected with prospective clients through the group, she set upfront expectations with them about her experience. Pretty quickly, Alisha was able to secure gigs creating basic assets such as logos or advertising banners; she also took on additional jobs like data entry and copyediting to have some money coming in during this trial period. A way she measured progress wasn't just by the number of new gigs she got but also by the new skills she learned. It made her feel confident enough to keep going.

Six months later, the financial runway Alisha had allotted for herself was coming up and she needed to make a decision. Did she want to keep freelancing or find a full-time job? Tapping into the same skills of reflection and refinement that she used to extricate herself from the consulting job, she assessed where she was now, and whether her original instinct about design was still right for her. It was; Alisha loved what she did for a living. But she wasn't quite sure about the isolation that comes with freelancing. She missed the camaraderie of being on a team (not to mention the steady paycheck). She also noticed that the work she particularly liked doing was for up-and-coming companies, usually consumer-facing and with a tech component.

Using all of those factors to guide her, Alisha began searching sites like PayScale and Indeed to discover companies that might fit what she was looking for. One opening caught her eye. It was for a designer role at a recently launched media platform. Alisha could not have found a better job: it combined her interests and strengths with an environment where she could thrive. An added benefit was that she'd be able to work closely with the engineering department, an area that Alisha was interested in learning more about.

She applied . . . and got the job! All the exploration, self-reflection, and self-teaching had paid off, and now Alisha was about to embark on an opportunity that never would have happened if she'd stayed at the consulting firm.

If you find yourself in a position like Alisha, where you feel stuck or are wondering what's next, consider how and where you can grow. Whether your next step will give you skills, exposure, access to a larger network, or a financial cushion to get you through leaner times down the road, or if you want to pick something that will build upon your last job. Consider the industry as well: what direction is it going, and do you see a place for yourself in it? If you're feeling good in your current job but looking for ways to grow, one way to envision how you might do so is to look at the career trajectories of your boss and other people who are high up in the company.

In Alisha's case, now that she was in a role and at a company that shared her values, the agita and insecurity she'd felt at the consulting firm evaporated. "When I started my new job, it was almost like entering paradise. It was like, I see the light now! Work doesn't have to make you feel small; it doesn't have to make you depressed. You don't have to work crazy hours. When I joined the company, I finally realized that, actually, there are other companies out there that care about their employees' lives and creating great camaraderie between employees. It was truly incredible."

When your work is aligned with your goals and values, everything feels lighter, just the way it does when you're in an environment that doesn't require some sort of contortionism. This isn't to say it's not challenging (it should be); it just shouldn't feel so difficult that you're having trouble getting yourself to do it. If you're going to put the work in, don't you want to be at a job where you look forward to each day, whatever it may bring? You deserve to do work that you're proud of, and you'll be more successful in reaching your career goals if you go in a direction that you've chosen with purpose.

CHAPTER TWO

GET OUT OF YOUR HEAD

For almost the entirety of her time in graduate school, Reece barely spoke. She'd gotten into the London School of Economics to earn her master's degree in global health. Before that, Reece attended a top university and interned at a prestigious microfinance nonprofit. However, once in grad school, Reece quickly began to feel she might be in over her head. Her class was filled with surgeons and physicians, many of them younger than her, and in her words, "some of the most brilliant people I've ever met." Reece's immediate thought was that she wasn't cut out to be part of this group. She was baffled by how she could've been accepted into the program and felt she was constantly playing catch-up to everyone else.

During class, she would take pages of meticulous notes, rehearsing what she might contribute to the discussion if the right moment presented itself. It usually didn't. Until one day her epidemiology professor asked a question that Reece felt confident she knew the answer to. But when she spoke up, the room erupted in gales of laughter. Apparently, her response was wrong, and hilariously so. This was all it took to "prove" her fear that she was less intelligent than everyone else, an imposter. And now everyone else knew she was, too.

After two years, Reece graduated with high marks in all her classes. But she was so scarred by her anxiety about not being good enough for the program that when she began her job search, she focused on applying for jobs that were not directly related to her master's degree. Unsure if she could deal with rejection, Reece narrowed her job search to roles she felt confident she was 100 percent qualified for, or sometimes over-qualified for; she felt the only way to protect herself was to set her sights lower. Despite evidence to the contrary, Reece had convinced herself she had failed in grad school. Her imposter syndrome followed her into her next phase of her life, weighing her down like a heavy stone in her pocket.

Imposter syndrome can manifest itself in imperceptible ways, which means often we don't even realize it's the thing that's holding us back. It is. We assume these feelings are inevitable and not related to a larger phenomenon. I've traveled the country speaking with thousands of women, and when I begin to talk about imposter syndrome or perfectionism they sigh and clap their hands, nod and snap their fingers. It's a profound experience to watch a room full of strangers lift the great weight of something they'd carried in shame for so long. Two things always happen: somebody cries, and after the event, I get emails from women who all say the same thing: "I thought I was the only one."

Knowing we're not alone can make us feel better, but it would be even better if we didn't have to feel this way in the first place. Releasing these feelings starts with understanding that having imposter syndrome is not our fault. Operating in a male-dominated system means the gender power balance is not in our favor and the kinds of disadvantages it spawns are embedded in the structure of society itself. Sadly, we often misinterpret this imbalance as a personal failing rather than a systemic flaw.

In this chapter we'll see how Reece, despite an impressive list of accomplishments, continues to carry the chronic self-doubt that characterizes imposter syndrome. Through her story, we'll look at ways to minimize the harmful consequences of this kind of internal struggle, explore how to reframe obstacles in the workplace, and learn to take risks without putting your whole sense of self on the line.

PRESSURE TO PROVE HERSELF

When Reece interviewed for her first job, post-graduation, she *nailed* it. She'd spent hours researching the company, preparing her talking points, and anticipating all the questions she might be asked. The interview was conducted over Skype, which was a relief; she could keep her notes in front of her in case she needed backup.

When Reece got the position, she was over the moon. But elation quickly turned to that familiar feeling of self-doubt: what if she'd presented herself as being better than she actually was? Because the interview hadn't been conducted in person, it felt easier for her to perform. If it had been in person, would she still have gotten the job? There it was, that rock in her pocket: imposter syndrome.

Reece had always felt pressure to do well, but now as she embarked on her new job—one she felt like she didn't deserve to have in the first place—she started every day with dread. She felt as though there was no way she *wasn't* going to mess up today, and when she did, her employer would uncover her "secret": that she wasn't as smart or as competent as they thought she was. From the way she talked to how she dressed, Reece did what she'd always done: contort herself into a version of what she thought they needed to see. Emails were a particular point of stress for her. She spent hours obsessing over them, trying to balance sounding smart but not too serious. She would write a draft and then rewrite it, eliminating any words that might sound too "fun," then she'd backtrack to ensure her diction didn't come across too "terse." Then she'd review for logic and again for the flow of her writing.

For so many of us who deal with imposter syndrome, it starts young. Reece learned these contortion tactics back in elementary school. She was self-conscious about being "smarter than the boys" and noticed that when she acted deferential and even apologetic, it made her less threatening. Through school and into college, Reece adopted a sort of bubbly and almost ditzy outward persona, which she was now working hard to undo. It was tough for her to remember a time when she didn't change her voice to fit what she thought others needed. (Hence the obsession over her emails.)

Attempting to appear deferential is one of the hallmarks of imposter syndrome and a primary way we keep ourselves small. Since the "ideal" woman puts others' needs before her own and makes everyone else feel good, she has to be careful not to step out of line, lest anyone think less of her. For Reece, this came across in her constant apologizing. She began way too many emails with "I'm sorry for [FILL IN THE BLANK]," peppering her writing with smiley emojis and exclamation points. It was exhausting, but—in her mind—necessary, and at this point, it was so second nature, Reece didn't even notice how long it was taking her (or that it was emblematic of her insecurity).

CRITICAL FEEDBACK

Reece was working so hard to be who she thought her boss needed her to be, and so it was extremely difficult for her when he questioned or disagreed with her ideas. Even a simple "I'm not sure we should do that" was enough to send her into a spiral of self-doubt. Once, when he didn't give her the go-ahead on an initiative she presented, Reece saw it as a referendum on her intelligence. She quickly jumped to all-out catastrophizing: Had she lost a relationship with a very senior person? Should she quit? "I doubted myself so much I thought, maybe I'm just not cut out for this." She'd been working so hard for approval, that to get this kind of response wasn't just disheartening, it was devastating. Just like in school, Reece viewed critical feedback as confirmation that she was, in fact, an imposter. Because Reece felt unworthy of her position, anything negative was enough to derail her, triggering sweeping generalizations about who she was and what she was capable of.

When we tie our identity and self-worth to the expectations of others (or rather, what we *perceive* those expectations to be), making a mistake can feel like stepping on a landmine. We take critical feedback incredibly personally, because *we have made it personal*. For example, when Reece's classmates laughed at her, she wasn't able to distinguish between a misstep and her overall intelligence. In her mind there was no way she could be smart *and* make a mistake. As you'll see in the next chapter when we talk about perfectionism, the result is a vicious cycle of working harder, self-flagellating, and sometimes even self-sabotaging.

The healthier and more constructive thing Reece could have done was filter the feedback through the lens of what she could learn and actually do something about it. Turning feedback into an opportunity for growth reclaims the experience as something with purpose—and the potential for a positive outcome.

HOW TO DEAL WITH CRITICAL FEEDBACK

✦ **Welcome it.** Critical feedback is a normal part of any workplace. The issue is not whether you receive it, it's what you're going to do with it. Look forward to the feedback and embrace it as a growth opportunity.

✦ **Designate dwell time.** If you find that negative feedback or making a mistake triggers a highly emotional reaction, don't deny it. Allow yourself a space for that emotion to exist. Alison Gilbert, a business coach, likens emotions to a beach ball on the surface of a pool. No matter how many times you push it down, it always pops back up again. When something doesn't go as planned and you're feeling the swell of self-flagellation, give yourself an allotted amount of time (say, five to ten minutes) to sit and stew. Once that's done, it's back to work. You've got shit to do.

✦ **Reframe failure.** The best way to turn criticism into something useful is to try to learn as much as you can from it. It doesn't have to be the end of the world; it can be used as a springboard to actually get better at whatever skill has been called into question. This means that you need to break down the situation in question and filter it through what you can do differently moving forward. How can this information inform what you do next? If there's nothing you would've done differently, then accept that you did the best you could, which includes acknowledging that sometimes things are beyond our control. How can you make this work for *you*? (You also should consider the source. Is this a person whose feedback can help you in the first place? Do you even agree with them?)

✦ **Remember that you are not what you do.** What you do can be a large part of your life. But to tie your entire identity to your work can set you up to feel like an imposter. Failing at something should not be a referendum on your worth. Even if you started your own company and are a one-woman show, it was born from who you are, but it's not *what* you are.

TURNING POINT

For some time, Reece had been noticing in meetings that her male colleagues—and even her boss—often made broad and definitive generalizations about things they had no real expertise in. In fact, sometimes they even repurposed others' ideas as their own, including hers. The second or third time this happened, Reece felt something shift within her. If her ideas were good enough to be used and repeated by others, why was she the one feeling like an imposter? Maybe she'd had the whole thing backward. Maybe *they* were the imposters.

This realization didn't feel good at first. It made her question how she'd been operating her whole life, and all the ways her imposter syndrome had affected her. Had she actually held herself back without even realizing it? What had she missed out on or lost because of it?

Reece had read somewhere that journaling could be a good way to process and release her negative self-talk. She'd never kept a diary (she never seemed to have any time), but now she committed to writing every day for at least two weeks. She forced herself to be brutally honest about the times she sold herself short or held herself back, and the consequences it'd had on her career.

As simple as it seems, writing things down can lead to major discoveries. James W. Pennebaker, a social psychologist at the University of Texas at Austin who is considered the pioneer of writing therapy, says that keeping a journal is not only cathartic, it also helps to organize an experience in our mind. In other words, it can help you make sense of something that feels out of your control. Articulating your thoughts enables you to take what's swirling around in your head and make it objective. This is particularly important when dealing with chronic self-doubt that has begun to spiral; writing it down gives you the space you need to get perspective. Only then can you properly examine and work through the behavior that stems from it.

Reece's journaling began to pay off. Reflecting on her own behavior led her to evaluate her work environment; maybe something was causing her to feel this way. She realized that the company culture (which was very male and competitive) had in fact made her imposter syndrome worse. She was startled: this was the first time she'd ever considered that her imposter syndrome was connected to external circumstances and was not something that was wrong with *her*. Not only that, imposter syndrome wasn't innate or inevitable.

It can be difficult to discern imposter syndrome from simply not knowing something. Maybe you've never done it before or maybe others really do know more than you. How can we feel more comfortable in these situations, and not misunderstand them to mean that we are surely more ignorant than everyone else?

First, you shouldn't *want* to be the smartest person in the room. If that's the case, you won't be challenged, which in turn means limited growth and/or progress. The key is finding a way to see the knowledge of others as a source of inspiration and not intimidation. People are wells of information and as long as you stay focused on how you're improving, you can take solace in the fact that you're doing a great job.

But knowledge alone isn't everything. It's also about how you present that knowledge. Remember that no one is you and that the unique perspective you bring and the way you articulate it inherently has value.

TAKE UP SPACE

Priortizing what we think others want, instead of honoring what feels natural to us, can have negative consequences on our careers. It can lead to being discounted, overlooked, and talked over, which in turn means fewer promotions, smaller raises, and missed opportunities.

If you've spent most of your life orienting yourself to what you think others need you to be, it will take a little practice to reacquaint yourself with yourself. The following tactics are a beginning; growing past minimizing behavior takes time, but the first step is recognizing these patterns of behavior and experimenting with new ways of being.

TAKE UP SPACE

✦ **Stop hedging.** One of the primary ways that women express deference is by softening their language; for example, "I just have a question" or "I actually have a question" instead of "I have a question." This includes apologizing (as we saw with Reece). Instead of beginning emails with "I'm sorry," try using "Thanks for your patience." Perhaps you're running late on a project and need an extension. Unless you're really behind, try something as straightforward as "This is taking longer than I expected and I want to make sure it's the best it can be. I'll have it for you first thing tomorrow. I appreciate your understanding."

✦ **Take credit.** Because we're socialized to be humble, even just taking credit for our achievements can feel like we're bragging. And so we downplay or discount ourselves, chalking our wins up to luck, timing, or a team effort. When you get a compliment, do you sit with it? Do you believe it? Even the desire to quickly reciprocate the praise speaks to the discomfort we have in accepting it. So next time someone congratulates you on a job well done, you can simply say, "Thank you! I worked hard."

✦ **(Wo)man spread.** The idea of taking up space can even be applied literally. The cultural ideal of femininity is petite, and so without even noticing it, we can fold into ourselves, trying to take up as little physical room as possible, whether this means getting out of the way when someone passes us, sucking in our stomachs, or crossing our legs. Commit to observing and then undoing ways you make yourself small. Make the choice to expand your body and see how powerful you feel.

✦ **Flex.** Trying to contort yourself to always be agreeable can become a habit. One way to unlearn this behavior is to find ways to push back or engage in what I like to call "small acts of resistance." Women, particularly those of us who crave approval, tend to be the ones always willing to do the "housework" in the workplace—the thankless and time-consuming tasks that don't necessarily pay off. Try flexing the muscle that doesn't need that instant hit of approval: this includes not *always* volunteering to take on extra work or taking on tasks like cleaning the kitchen or being the default note-taker.

STOP IMPOSTER SYNDROME IN ITS TRACKS

In order to undo your imposter syndrome, you have to first understand it. Information is power, so treat yourself like an empirical study: every time you can feel the telltale signs of imposter syndrome creeping up—like when you experience negative self-talk or avoid speaking up—write down everything about it. Where were you? What were you doing? Who was there? Keep a journal of this for at least two weeks. By doing this, you should be able to see patterns of what (and maybe who) triggers you. With this insight, you can make a plan to do something about it.

MAKE A PLAN

1. **Stay grounded.** If the negative script in your mind is louder than everything else, try to identify something that stops the script in its tracks. Be ready with something on hand—an image, mantra, an email you've saved of someone singing your praises—anything that will remind you that this is your imposter syndrome taking over, so you can let it go and get back to your work. For example, Reece carried with her a keychain from her

alma mater, UC Berkeley. It reminded her of her ability to persevere; she'd originally been rejected, but after two years at a community college, she applied again and got in.

2. **Shift the focus.** Instead of making your work about what you're trying to accomplish, shift the focus to the value you're providing or the things you're learning. In other words, focus more on the process, and less on the outcome.

3. **Phone a friend.** Having someone to reach out to when your imposter syndrome is kicking in will give you the support you need to get out of your own head and back in the game. If you don't already have someone like this in your life, we'll teach you how to cultivate this kind of relationship in Chapter Four: Get Connected.

4. **Reframe the imposter.** The only way to grow (and succeed) is by challenging yourself to do things you've never done before. An inescapable part of this experience is feeling vulnerable and being aware of your inexperience. That means you may always be in a position to feel a little bit of that imposter syndrome. Instead of letting it hold you back, look at these feelings of vulnerability as an indication of your courage and your growth.

EXPERIMENT IN VULNERABILITY

Reece knew that she couldn't just snap her fingers and make her imposter syndrome disappear. But she felt determined enough to start chipping away at it. Just like she might use a series of exercises to build physical strength, Reece devised some mini challenges that, done enough times, would hopefully help her achieve her goal. She called these her "experiments in vulnerability." Her first experiment was doing something she never would've dared to before: she told people that she was struggling. She admitted to her family and friends that she was afraid she wasn't as talented as she might appear to be and that she lived in constant fear of messing up. Not only did everyone respond with kindness and empathy, they shared their own struggles.

As she grew more comfortable sharing, Reece sought out women's groups on social media, searched through their event listings, and gradually allowed herself to open up to people who weren't in her immediate circle. It was enormously helpful to see other people letting go of the veneer of "having it all together." By putting herself out there, she found it wasn't just cathartic for her, it was also a source of comfort for others.

Reece's next experiment was to make herself speak up at least once in every work meeting. Even if she looked stupid (her greatest fear), she knew that by keeping her ideas to herself, she would never grow, or be recognized. She had to learn how to not take it personally if she didn't get the reaction she hoped for. (In Chapter Nine: Get Promoted, we'll talk about ways you can command the room when you speak up.) Reece was also able to motivate herself by thinking about the other people in the room who might also be intimidated to speak up and that if she did it first, it might inspire them to join her.

By pushing herself to speak up in meetings, Reece gave herself the chance to see what she was capable of, and in the process, she began to trust herself. As Reece's confidence took hold, her coworkers noticed, and it changed the way people interacted with her at the office, including a VP with whom she'd been working closely. One day he stopped her to let her know that he'd noticed her speaking up more and welcomed "this new audacity" in her. It was then that Reece realized she had turned despair into vulnerability into power. The VP's feedback was a vote of confidence she needed to realize she was moving in the right direction.

Her "new audacity" led to what Reece considers her proudest moment at work. It was during a meeting where she was the youngest person and the only woman in the room. Her boss (the one who'd shot her ideas down months earlier) sat across the table from her. As the group brainstormed, he kept bringing up a roadblock he was adamant about. Reece thought he was wrong to be factoring it in in the first place and she had the knowledge to back it up. She spoke up.

In response, he drew a crude graph on a sheet of paper, held it up, and proceeded to explain the basics of economics to her. The London School of Economics graduate. Reece could feel the blood rush to her head; she was furious. Before he finished, Reece took a breath and raised her hand to stop him, "Patrick, I understand the basics of economics. That's not my question. My question is why this is relevant to what we're talking about at all." He shut his mouth and said nothing.

Letting go of imposter syndrome means flipping the script from one of scarcity ("I'm not good enough, I'm faking it") to one of growth ("I'm learning and evolving"). It requires learning to have a little more faith in yourself. You were hired for a reason. You're in the room for a reason. Who are you to doubt that?

Just as Reece learned with her experiments in vulnerability, there is a level of surrender you need to achieve, plus an acceptance that our perception of others may be totally off. For Reece, it was her discovery that while she'd spent all of this time worrying about being an imposter, it turned out her boss and male colleagues didn't always know what they were doing either (and presented as if they did).

It's hard to reach your full potential if you're always debating your worth. And if you're always debating your worth, you'll expend precious energy that you should be directing toward doing things that serve you, not limit you. As you saw with Alisha and now Reece, changing yourself based on what you think others need or will approve of is a dangerous path. It redirects energy that you could be giving to yourself, taking you further away from your desires, your truth.

Moving away from chronic self-doubt, and toward experiments in vulnerability, will help you emerge with a boldness—an "audaciousness"—that will push you to seize opportunities in your career, further building your confidence and your resilience when you encounter obstacles.

Because that's what a big life and career is—overflowing with all kinds of obstacles. It is up to you to navigate around and through them. And the only way to do that is with a deep belief in yourself and your capacity for greatness, which may be even larger than you realized. You essentially have two choices: focus on how you're falling short of the image you've projected—or that has been projected on you—or turn your attention to what you've learned and feel proud of your growth.

CHAPTER THREE

GET OVER PERFECTIONISM

Kate had been in business for only a few years when she was invited to speak at her industry's preeminent annual conference. She was flattered but there was no way she was going to do it.

Part of it was the size—Kate had only spoken in front of small local groups before, and this would be an audience of hundreds—but it was also the preparation. Kate didn't mind how long it would take to prepare; she liked working hard. It was the inevitable obsessing that was going to be the challenge. A self-proclaimed perfectionist, Kate knew that she'd spend countless hours doing, undoing, and redoing her talk, consumed by everything from the color scheme of the slides, to what font to use, to the spacing between them.

Being a perfectionist was practically in her job description. Kate was a Certified Professional Organizer, helping families and businesses clear out the clutter in their homes and offices and setting up systems to make things run more smoothly. Taking a mess and making it organized gave

Kate a gratifying sense of completion, and the reactions of her clients, in her words, gave her a "high."

Speaking at the conference in front of her peers and prospective clients would definitely level up her business. It was also a ton of pressure; there was zero room for mistakes. She had four months to prepare, which was enough time; in fact, it was *too* much time. The more time Kate had, the more time she had to obsess.

It was Kate's husband who eventually persuaded her to do it. He reminded her that she'd wanted to attend this conference for a long time (free ticket!); plus, the opportunity to attract new clients was too good to pass up.

For years, Kate had a sign hanging above her desk that read, "Done is better than perfect." For years, she'd been ignoring it. But this time, she hoped, things might be different. Maybe she'd be able to pull herself from the vortex of overworking that always threatened to consume her in the pursuit of perfection. Maybe.

———————

Being a perfectionist is not the same thing as having high standards. It's having unachievable standards. At the root of perfectionism, similar to imposter syndrome, is the belief that our worth is contingent upon what others think of us and how well we perform. Anything less than flawless is a failure; and failing at a task really means that *we're* the failure. Rather than being motivated to do well for the sake of doing well, perfectionists work from a place of fear: What does it say about us if we fail? What will people think? Because of that, the stakes always feel high and we'll do everything we can—overwork, overcommit, and obsess—to avoid that devastating consequence.

We rationalize that if we are (over)prepared to perform exceptionally, it will prevent us from making future mistakes. We rationalize that if we are overly critical of ourselves in the process, it will soften the blow if the unthinkable happens and others criticize us. But by convincing ourselves that having unreasonable standards is in our best interest, we risk getting stuck in the never-ending cycle where we're pushing ourselves too hard and then being too hard on ourselves for any and every misstep.

In this chapter, we'll follow Kate's journey as she prepares for the conference and grapples with deeply rooted perfectionist tendencies that slow her down, and even threaten to derail her completely.

To release perfectionism, we have to shift our worldview. It requires us to redefine what doing well means and reframe what it takes to get there. We have to be willing to be vulnerable, dig deep, and be truly honest with ourselves about how perfectionism may be holding us back, despite our belief that it's what's preventing us from messing up.

To be clear: letting go of perfectionism does not mean lowering our standards. It means operating from a desire to do well, not so we can escape judgment but so we can grow. We need to find new ways to motivate ourselves, draw the fine line between working and overworking, and learn how to encourage ourselves to strive for the best and forgive ourselves when we stumble.

OVERWORKING

Making the plan was the easy part. But when Kate started to actually work on the presentation, it was clear that her usual habits were going to make things difficult. Soon Kate was working ten hours a day, spending much of her time on minor details, like formatting. She'd be satisfied with her work for a little while, then she would inevitably find something she didn't like. Changing one detail wasn't enough; usually it meant an entire overhaul. Because things were never good enough, Kate started over more times than she could count. Anything could trigger it. Figuring out what clothes she was going to wear could mean a whole new set of edits, because the colors had to match, of course. The fact that most people wouldn't notice didn't matter. Kate noticed it and any imperfection would distract her. Even though Kate was technically working, obsessing over things like what font to use was actually her way of procrastinating. She was cocooning herself away with the most minor details so as to avoid the real work and the potential judgment that goes along with it.

Constantly finding ways to "improve" meant adding so many new things to the presentation that it quickly ballooned into something so big it no longer resembled what Kate had originally set out to do. Part of the difficulty of curbing herself from overworking was that Kate didn't see it as overworking to begin with. To her, it was just working. Plus, she enjoyed it. Throwing herself into a project, poring over the details, gave her a sense of control. The problem was that spending so much time on the small stuff made her lose sight of her bigger goals and where this presentation fit. It pulled her away from other things that required attention, many of them critical to the financial health of her company.

If every aspect of a project requires the same amount of (extreme) attention, it's difficult to prioritize. Soon Kate was running behind on how far along she meant to be with her presentation, now juggling both the pressure of perfectionism as well as the fear of not finishing on time.

But because her hard work usually paid off—and because of the rush she got from the sense of achievement and the approval from others that came with it—Kate could never seem to get off the hamster wheel of overworking. However, she wasn't blind to its negative consequences (and its unsustainability), especially on her relationships. As she tells it, "I drive my family crazy, along with myself. My quest to catch every problem before it becomes a problem can make it hard to live with me. Getting out the door is a daily series of verbal checklists and walkthroughs in my house to make sure we have everything we could ever possibly need on our current trip. No joke—I have food, Band-Aids, and a tape measure in my purse at all times, because I must be prepared for any emergency."

If you struggle with perfectionism and time management, it's important that, before you get started, you make a plan of your goals and what you want to accomplish. Start by breaking things down into smaller tasks and give yourself deadlines on how long, realistically, you think it will take to complete each one. That way, when you start to go down the path of overworking and subsequent scope creep, you'll have something to hold you accountable. It can act as both a reminder of the big picture as well as a guardrail to keep you from going overboard.

STOP YOURSELF FROM OVERWORKING

+ **Establish scope.** If you're working on a project for someone else, establish parameters with them from the outset. What is the goal of your assignment and who is the audience or recipient? How do you define and measure success? Put time on the calendar to check in and review priorities along the way with your boss (or yourself).

+ **Prioritize.** The most important thing you can do is understand the difference between what's important, what's urgent, and what can be delegated, and then have a hierarchical system where you know what needs to happen when (or whether you're the right person to do it!). Later on in the chapter, we'll discuss how to delegate and, in Chapter Seven, how to prioritize.

  + **Is it important?**

- ✦ It will affect many people or projects if it's incomplete

- ✦ Other tasks depend on its completion

- ✦ It contributes a lot of value

✦ **Is it urgent?**

- ✦ It's due

- ✦ It's overdue

- ✦ It demands immediate attention

- ✦ The consequences of not doing it are immediate

✦ **Manage your time.** Identify the most important components of the project, and then estimate how long they will take. If you're delivering to someone else, talk to them at the outset to establish priorities for the project. (We'll talk more about this in Chapter Eight: Get Allies). Look back at your past experiences with various kinds of tasks and ask yourself how you think they went. Did you *really* need to spend as much time on them as you did, or could you have worked more efficiently? (Don't be overly ambitious—that's only setting you up for frustration.) If these tasks are new to you, who can you ask for guidance on how long they might take?

✦ **Check in with your timeline.** Be ready to adjust as you go along, but if something is taking a very long time, consider whether it actually requires that much, or if you're overworking, or if it's an issue of how you are managing your time.

Oftentimes we feel—or are made to feel—like everything is urgent. Because it is literally impossible to get everything done at the same time, you have to know when something needs to be done now, scheduled for later, delegated to someone else, or deleted entirely. President Eisenhower came up with a helpful system to help prioritize all the things he had to do each day as the commander of the armed forces during World War II and as president. Called the Eisenhower Matrix, it's still helpful to this day.

URGENT + IMPORTANT	IMPORTANT BUT NOT URGENT
Do it first	Schedule it
URGENT BUT NOT IMPORTANT (FOR *YOU* TO DO IT)	NEITHER URGENT NOR IMPORTANT
Delegate	Delete it

A great way to let go of perfectionism is to show your work before you think it's ready. Share something when it's in the draft stage, when no one expects it to be perfect, with a trusted source who can give feedback. Call upon the people you may be delegating tasks to, so they can make the project their own.

GET PERSPECTIVE

✦ **Get a draft down quickly.** If you get through everything as fast as possible, you'll have a better sense of how much time you have to make things as best as they can be and where your energy is best allocated. Be confident that the magic happens during the editing phase.

✦ **Have someone check your work before it's "perfect."** They will help you practice not being publicly perfect. They can also help pull you out of the weeds.

✦ **Take whole-body breaks.** Get up and physically walk away; go outside or do some stretching. You can then come back with fresh eyes.

✦ **Ask for it.** Remember that in order to get better, you need feedback. There's only so much you can accomplish on your own without the input of others. See them as a source of improvement, not judgment.

RUMINATION

Kate's desire to make the presentation a slam dunk was, yes, motivated by her desire to bring helpful information to conference attendees, but it was also driven by the fear of criticism. Kate couldn't shake the last time she'd made a presentation. She'd received a ton of great feedback, with the exception of two "blah" comments: one person said "I knew this stuff already" and another noted that Kate "seemed nervous." On a logical level, Kate recognized that these weren't all that negative, but her desire for perfection made her feel as though the talk had been an utter failure. Anything less than stellar was a total disappointment and often triggered tunnel vision where anything positive she did evaporated and any imperfection was all that mattered—and what she obsessed over. Kate was aware that she was being irrational, which then triggered *another* wave of frustration; now she was mad at herself for being mad at herself.

Perfectionists seek control. Unfortunately, no matter how hard we try, how others react to us is something we simply can't dictate. What we can count on, though, is that beating ourselves up for the past or projecting perfection into the future is a surefire way to get stuck. The best thing we can do is to see room for improvement as an opportunity to learn and grow. Ruminating won't make us better; being resilient will. It's better to focus on actionable things we can do in the here and now and take solace in any step forward—no matter how small.

STOP RUMINATING

✦ **Don't make assumptions about what others are thinking.** We've all been there: reading into small things people say (or write over email) and then making leaps about what they mean. All of a sudden, you're imagining/assuming how others feel about you, and it's usually wildly different from the reality. Try not to make leaps from a specific situation to a generalization about someone's entire belief system. Also, if you want to know what someone is thinking, just ask them. That being said, if you're intimidated or concerned that by asking you may in some way be jeopardizing the relationship, seek an ally at work who can advise you. (We'll go over that more in Chapter Eight.)

✦ **Watch your words.** If you want to preserve your self-esteem, you can't take on external events as an indication of how good or bad you are. Your worthiness is not up for debate. So, the next time you hear yourself say "I'm bad at my job," reframe it as "Right now I *feel* as if I'm bad at my job." Recognize that this is one moment, not your entire existence.

✦ **Focus on the present.** Pay attention to your internal monologue and what you are telling yourself about your job performance. One of the most obvious words to watch out for is "should," since that signifies the past or projects into the future, two things you have no control over. For example, "I shouldn't have done that" or "I should do better" can be replaced by "What can I do differently?" Focusing on what you can do *right now* gives you next tangible steps that will lead to progress, rather than spinning your wheels, which can leave you paralyzed.

✦ **Forgive yourself.** We often beat ourselves up because we think we could've done better. The truth is, there is only so much we can know at any given time and therefore only so much information to act on. I repeat this almost every day to myself: "I did my best with the information, experience, and resources I had at that time." Trust that you don't need to beat yourself up in order to improve.

✦ **Be kind to yourself.** Find a way to step back and see yourself from the outside as a way to silence your inner critic. Imagine what you'd say to a friend if she told you someone said to her the things you've said about yourself. Or you can carry a photo of yourself as a child, and the minute your inner voice turns into a mean girl, take out that picture. Look at it. You may not completely recognize her, but you're still that little girl. Would you ever speak to her that way? I hope not.

DELEGATE

Because perfectionism is about control, delegating often doesn't even feel like an option. "If you want something done right, it's better to do it yourself" is practically a perfectionist's anthem. Scientific research confirms that among the reasons that managers *don't* delegate is something called the Self-Enhancement Bias, the (incorrect) belief that the greater their own involvement in a task, whether they do it themselves or manage someone else who does it, the higher the quality of the outcome.

This rings true for Kate both at work and at home. She shoulders most household responsibilities, coordinates calendars, and manages her two sons' soccer practices. She's the mom who shows up with the snacks and the Band-Aids, taking pride in being the one that everyone can count on. In her mind, if other people can count on her, that means they think highly of her, and therefore she has worth. Her husband is the polar opposite. He's "completely scattered, relaxed, and unconcerned if mistakes are made" (which of course drives Kate nuts).

Kate is not the only one: despite the fact that we make up half the workforce, gender norms persist, and in heterosexual households women end up being the default for all things caretaking. According to studies done by the Bureau of Labor, women spend an hour more per day than men on housework, and an hour more on childcare. Besides the exhaustion and stress this can often cause in a marriage, it does real damage to our careers; it's often cited as a leading cause of the gender gaps in pay and promotion at work.

If we're going to fight for wage equality at work, we have to seek equality in our personal lives. If you're partnered with children, that should mean a fair division of labor. Not only do you benefit, it also demonstrates behavior that your kids can model. It's important that they see equal participation in household responsibilities, regardless of gender, otherwise they may perpetuate those inequalities in their own future relationships.

In other words, we *have* to delegate! And when we do, we have to be okay when things aren't done exactly the way we would have done them. Delegating is not dictating, nor is it micromanaging; it is asking another person to do a task, equipping them with the tools to do so, and then letting them actually do it. Ironically, this is what Kate teaches her clients: how to involve the whole family in organizing and maintaining the home. In fact, it was the topic of her presentation. But it's always easier to give advice than take it.

Trying to delegate as a perfectionist means striking a balance between holding people accountable to do great work and not making them feel like there is a guillotine waiting if they make a mistake, no matter how minor. Because Kate is so hard on herself, it can be intimidating to work with her. She admits that she finds it "offensive" if someone else's fumble affects her ability to be perfect.

But as Kate started to work on letting perfectionism go, she realized that a reason her husband is so relaxed is precisely because she's the one taking care of everything! He doesn't worry because he doesn't have to; she does this for both of them. And that is an unfair burden, even if it's one she's willingly taken upon herself.

Whether you're delegating at home or at work, at its core, it's all the same. It involves being clear about expectations, checking in, and then learning to let go. And because delegating requires trust, it's imperative that whomever you're delegating to is set up for success.

HOW TO DELEGATE

1. **Be clear about expectations.** Express the importance of paying attention to details, but also make it clear that this is a learning experience for both of you. Encourage them to come to you if they run into any challenges.

2. **Set designated check-ins.** If they know when you're going to be checking in, you don't need to micromanage. When you meet, you can give them constructive feedback and ask if they need more support.

3. **View delegating as teaching.** If they've never done something before, they may make a mistake. That's okay (assuming it's not a life-or-death situation). The goal is *progress*, not perfection. Stay focused on the big picture. Even if they didn't do it the way you would, it's about the fact that it got done. Who knows, maybe they can teach you!

4. **Remember that this is a process.** The first time you want another person to do something, you may need to have them shadow you so they can learn what your expectations are. You're probably not going to go from doing everything yourself to outsourcing all of your tasks. Gradually delegate responsibilities so you can adjust as needed.

REFRAME WHAT MOTIVATES YOU

As Kate continued to work on the presentation, she was aware that she was making things more difficult for herself. As much as she wished she could quiet her perfectionist tendencies, she was afraid that without them, the presentation wouldn't be as good. In fact, she attributes her achievements to her unrelenting perfectionism ("I'm more accomplished than anyone I know") and worries that if she were to let her standards slide, the quality of her work would suffer, not to mention that her clients might not see her as credible. But this standard of work comes at a cost, one that is increasingly at odds with how Kate wants to live her life. "I feel like I'm in fight-or-flight mode all the time," she says, "almost as if I'm combatting myself to relax more. I know that I need to let go more." The pressure to perform won't allow Kate to be at peace with herself, just as she is. It's as if she's looking through a window to where she wants to go but has no idea how to get there.

The first step is understanding why we're holding on to perfectionism in the first place. We do things we think are helping us. But the flip side of that is, what are we afraid will happen if we let it go? Whatever fear you uncover, keep pushing to get to what's going on underneath the surface. These kinds of fears are usually instigated by deeply ingrained beliefs that we carry about ourselves (usually rooted in childhood), which we've since adopted as absolute truths and immovable personality traits.

To get to the core, whatever you come up with, ask yourself why you believe that. And if it were to come to fruition, so what? For example, if you're afraid of "being mediocre" (and you believe perfectionism is helping you avoid that), the question becomes, why? And if you were mediocre, so what? This might be a time to examine where and how you developed this mindset and if there are things—other than being perfect—that you can do to achieve it.

HOW I THINK PERFECTIONISM IS HELPING ME	WHAT I'M AFRAID WOULD HAPPEN IF I LET IT GO
Detail-oriented	Let things fall through the cracks
Get a lot done	Be lazy
Accomplish big things/Be impressive	Wouldn't reach my goals/Be mediocre

Now I want you to do an honest assessment of what being a perfectionist has done to you, emotionally, logistically, mentally, physically, and spiritually. Because perfectionists believe that their worth is defined by their (perfect) output, they're all too willing to sacrifice their own well-being in the pursuit of it.

Ask yourself: What price am I paying for my perfectionism? Do I really believe that perfectionism is the main reason I've been successful? That if I were no longer a perfectionist, I would no longer do excellent work? The *Harvard Business Review* did a meta-analysis of ninety-five studies on perfectionism in the workplace, and among the many conclusions was that "performance and perfectionism were *not* related to each other—perfectionists are not better or worse performers than non-perfectionists. Even employees high in excellence-seeking perfectionism were not better performers." So what are you holding on to?

Letting go of perfectionism is about coming up with another way to get to your desired outcome without offering yourself up as collateral damage. For example, the consequences of Kate's perfectionism were:

- ✦ Anxiety

- ✦ Exhaustion

- ✦ Low self-esteem

- ✦ Fights with her husband

- ✦ Stress on the family

And she is far from a minority. Medical research has overwhelmingly found that perfectionism is a risk factor for obsessive-compulsive disorder, eating disorders, self-harm, substance abuse, clinical depression, all flavors of anxiety, and life-threatening medical conditions like heart disease and chronic stress.

Because perfectionism is about control, we try to control situations we don't trust will work out well. And so, letting it go means learning to trust ourselves. We have to believe that we're capable of excellence without pressure and that we can be motivated by the desire to expand our life experiences without the fear of self-flagellation when things don't go our way. Letting go of perfectionism means learning to be brave.

LET IT GO, ONCE AND FOR ALL

- ✦ **Step back.** Yes, details are important, but did you accomplish what you set out to do? Was the big picture achieved? That is the most important thing.

- ✦ **Look for evidence.** Think back to a time in your life when you didn't reach perfection. What happened? How much does it matter now? Is there anything positive that came from it? For example, I used to have a total meltdown whenever there was a spelling error in the Ladies Get Paid newsletter. I was afraid that it made me look sloppy and unprofessional, and that people would judge me for it. I realize now that at the root of it was perfectionism but also imposter syndrome, as well as an outsized assumption that people cared a lot more about me than they actually do (barely anyone noticed). But more importantly, I learned that when I made those errors—and I would make them, despite how much I obsessed over them—the world didn't end.

✦ **Expect to stumble.** The pressure to be perfect can actually make it harder to perform. How can you expect to do well if you're under constant threat of punishment? It's almost a guarantee that you will make mistakes. When your reaction becomes "Ugh, that's annoying" instead of "You suck," you're freeing yourself up to learn from that mistake and improve.

✦ **Don't beat yourself up.** When things don't go as intended and you can feel the harsh voice of perfectionism start to get louder, stop and ask yourself: "Is my reaction proportionate? Is beating myself up making the situation better or helping me improve?" In other words, keep your eye on the prize.

MAGIC IN THE MESSINESS

The night before the conference, Kate probably practiced her speech at least ten times. She didn't just speak it out loud, she also wrote it out by hand—over and over—hoping the act of putting pen to paper would burn the words deeper into her head.

Finally, it was the Big Day. Kate was nervous, maybe more nervous than she'd ever been in her life. She was about to stand in front of hundreds of her peers and prospective clients, her reputation at stake. Walking onstage, it was an out-of-body experience to see her Power-Point looming large on the screen, all the fonts and formatting she'd spent countless hours on. Kate was terrified she wasn't going to be able to remember the speech despite how much effort she'd put into memorizing it. She took a deep breath and introduced herself to the crowd. The audience was engaged right from the beginning, raising their hands to ask questions throughout her speech. At first Kate was flustered, worried that pausing to take questions would make it impossible to re-create the phrasing that she had worked so hard to get just right. She managed not to panic, and realized that the more she interacted with the room, the looser she got. And the looser she got, the better the presentation was. By going with the flow, she let her personality shine through, overriding the rigidity of the script she'd planned out. She began to trust that she knew the major points she wanted to cover and as long as she did that, she could be as spontaneous as she wanted. To her surprise, she found herself making jokes, and even more shockingly, she was actually having *fun*.

Breaking away from the perfection of her preparation allowed Kate to be open, to show her real spontaneous self, and to really connect with people rather than put up a wall between her and her audience in the form of a perfect speech whose every word she had memorized. By letting herself be genuine, it allowed people in the room to feel comfortable enough to share more of themselves. Throughout the presentation, people were murmuring things like "Me, too," or "I'm there with you" and by the end, there was a line of people at the microphone waiting to ask a question.

When the session was over, Kate was swarmed. There were so many people wanting to talk to her, they had to be ushered out as the next session was beginning. As she made her way to the elevator, more people stopped her to congratulate her.

Kate was on a high, but not for the reason she'd expected. Of course, the external validation felt good, but that was fleeting (as it usually was). What stuck with her was seeing the power of helping others and how that—not the perfect presentation—was what mattered. She realized that what was special about her talk was her willingness to be real and even reveal her vulnerabilities. That made her relatable, which in turn allowed the audience to see themselves in her. This was way more profound and did so much more than any perfectly formatted piece of advice could do. For Kate, it was a whole new way of looking at success.

If being more herself was a good thing, then that meant her imperfections were something to be embraced, not beaten away. Kate didn't need to work so hard to be accepted, she could just *be*. As a little test (or as Reece would have called it, "an experiment in vulnerability") she posted more of her "messy" side on social media. Instead of detracting from her credibility, as she'd feared, Kate got feedback from her clients that they enjoyed—and appreciated!—it. Now that she'd experienced, for the first time in her life, how good it felt to relieve the pressure to be perfect, Kate didn't want to go back. Her happiness and sanity were priorities over perfection. It was no longer just about doing a good job; now it was also about feeling good.

But what if her speech had bombed? Or if it went well but no one congratulated her? Yes, it would have been harder to stomach. It also would've required her to do some more work to get to a place where her definition of success broadened to include her own well-being. Regardless of how the speech went, the courage to give it in the first place was a win. Pushing herself out of her comfort zone to grow was a win. Even learning how her perfectionism was hurting and not helping her was a win. This entire experience, no matter the outcome, is part of Kate's journey.

You have a say in how you treat yourself. Whatever the outcome—whether it's a presentation or a negotiation—it's just one part in a larger story. It's how you handle it that matters. It's up to you to move in a direction of limitless possibilities or stay small in the pursuit of perfection.

A WORK IN PROGRESS

A few months later, Kate was invited to speak again at the next conference, as well as to be on the planning committee. Extremely flattered, she immediately said yes. Kate threw herself into the job and, per usual, got sucked into the vortex of overdoing, overanalyzing, and overworking. Kate wanted to go the extra mile to make sure that the organizers didn't regret asking her. It didn't matter that she was overcommitted (she was still managing her two sons' soccer schedules!); her drive to be the best meant she simply had to buckle down and push through.

Kate's *aha* moment after the presentation the year before was a first step on a longer road of letting go of perfectionism. While she'd shifted her mindset, she now had to learn how to make decisions that were aligned with it. Fortunately, Kate was learning to catch herself when she began to cross the line from working hard because she wanted to do a good job into overworking because she wanted to be perfect. It's not bad to take things on and work hard; it just should not be at the expense of your health and other priorities.

This is particularly important for women of color, who often overextend themselves in order to prove their worth and be validated. In her study entitled *Superwoman Schema: African American Women's Views on Stress, Strength, and Health*, Professor Cheryl L. Woods-Giscombé at UNC Chapel Hill writes about the expectation to be a "Strong Black

Woman." Dr. Woods-Giscombé discovered in her research that Black women of all age groups and educational backgrounds reported feeling overwhelmed by multiple roles and responsibilities in their families, community, and church organizations. She attributes that in part to the refusal to be "another statistic," a response to a history of oppression. It's not just about overextending, it's also about the suppression of emotions. Dr. Woods-Giscombé writes that, originally born from the necessity of survival, Black women work hard to not allow themselves to be vulnerable or dependent on others. All of this is compounded by the disparities in healthcare (and lack of mental health resources) faced by African American communities, as well as the fact that many of these women are single mothers with little to no help. (We'll address the consequences of these factors in later chapters.)

Remember, no one but you is going to know your actual capacity or how to best prioritize your well-being. Before saying yes to anything, evaluate your bandwidth for it. See where it fits into your other commitments and if you can give it proper attention without getting overwhelmed. This is a prime opportunity to delegate. Who else could take this on? Who else might be *better* than you at doing this? Suggesting someone else is a good way to maintain the relationship without overextending yourself. (In Chapter Seven, we'll go over how to set boundaries.)

AVOID OVERCOMMITING

✦ **Evaluate.** Before you say yes, consider the commitment, ask questions, and assess your bandwidth. Compare this to your goals and priorities: How much will this benefit you? For example, will you learn new skills or expand your network or add something new to your résumé? Consider what you may have to give up in order to take this on. You can't do everything at once without burning out or dropping the ball, so it's better to focus on things that you have the time, space, and desire to dedicate yourself to. If the only reason you're doing it is because you'd feel guilty not doing it, it probably means you shouldn't say yes.

+ **Set proper expectations.** If you decide to say yes but are concerned about your bandwidth, be honest with yourself and with them. For example, say "I'd love to help but have limited bandwidth right now. Is it possible for me to contribute [INSERT SMALL THING] and then regroup next week? I don't want to overcommit or leave you hanging!" It's better to give them a heads-up before you (potentially) drop the ball. And if you do drop the ball, don't beat yourself up. It happens; you're human.

By the time the next conference rolled around, Kate was still (somewhat) of a perfectionist, but she had made a lot of progress. She knew how much she'd improved when she received the results of the feedback survey that was sent out to all attendees. She obviously scrolled straight to her name, and there it was, that negative comment. "You didn't look happy to be there." Kate could feel her blood rising, at first angry at the woman who wrote that, but then angry at herself: she should have smiled more! Why didn't she spend more time psyching herself up beforehand?! She was starting to spiral.

As a conference committee member, Kate could access all the speaker feedback. Curious, she looked through the other comments. A pattern quickly emerged. No speaker had a perfect score. In fact, there seemed to be at least one Debbie Downer in each section, no matter how many other rave reviews were received.

Kate remembered when she was an art major in college and she used to crumble when her professors critiqued her work. She'd let that override the joy she felt when she created things, leading her to eventually abandon something she loved. Ironically, Kate's favorite part about being an artist was the process; getting to experiment, to be messy, to watch things take shape independent of what others might think. Like her presentation, Kate's best work always emerged when she freed herself from unattainable expectations.

Kate now understood that she could choose how she reacted to criticism and how she framed her own experience. She didn't have to be a perfectionist and suffer everything that comes with it. Once Kate liberated herself from the pressure to be perfect, she found herself actually looking forward to the conference rather than dreading it. She made the conscious choice to be patient with herself, stay focused on the bigger picture, and maybe even enjoy herself.

Pursuing perfection isn't so much about trying to achieve excellence as it is about avoiding failure. Ironically though, perfectionism gets us closer to failure; perfectionists view life through a binary lens— if it's not perfect, it's a failure—which means we're always just one step away from it. As you saw with Kate, and perhaps in your own life, that means overworking, obsessing, self-berating, self-sacrificing. Perfectionism is like a merry-go-round that we can never really get off; it ultimately doesn't take us anywhere and just results in disappointment and frustration.

When we seek perfection, we put up walls around us. It's hard to connect with others when we're trying so hard to control how we're perceived. It also takes away precious energy from simply being ourselves, and as Alisha learned in the first chapter, that can be a dangerous thing.

Letting go of perfectionism is similar to letting go of imposter syndrome in that it requires reframing how we view success. What if success wasn't about how well we did, but rather about the effort we put in and what we learned? What if it was about pushing beyond anything we've done before, inviting in mistakes instead of trying desperately to avoid them? Like Reece learned in the previous chapter, experiments are not the same thing as tests. As Kate discovered, there is magic in the messiness. In fact, when Kate posted videos on Instagram about the chaos of being a working mom (and her messy home!), she got a lot more engagement.

If there is one thing you take away from Kate's story, it is to forgive yourself. It's forgiveness that will allow you to snap back from setbacks and move freely, and without fear, toward the future.

PART TWO

GAME TIME

Lord, make me so uncomfortable
that I will do the very thing I fear.
—Ruby Dee

You've arrived at Part Two, congratulations! You've done much of the tough stuff: confronting the limiting messages you may have internalized, letting go of what doesn't serve you and shoring up what does. You've come to understand that obstacles are opportunities for growth and with that, your world has expanded. You've learned to prioritize what *you* want your career to look like, not what someone else has told you it should be.

All of your work thus far has helped strengthen your inner foundation so you can confidently take your first steps along the path you've chosen.

Part Two is about those first steps. Networking with people you don't know, applying for the job you want, and negotiating for the salary you deserve. All of these things will require you to do what, as a woman, you may have been told not to. Like ask for more money, talk about your greatness, and be unabashed about building wealth. You'll also learn to ask for help and to give it to yourself. The last chapter in Part Two is about how to pace and protect yourself from the demands that are put on us and that we all too readily put on ourselves. It's important that as we accelerate our careers, it does not come at the expense of our well-being.

You'll meet Phoebe, Amy, and Giselle (we'll also catch up with Reece from Chapter Two), who built their networks from nothing, went after dream jobs, negotiated big paychecks, and took steps to protect their mental and emotional health. None of this was easy. It required them to adopt new ways of viewing themselves and what was possible, and a new language for how to articulate their needs. They stepped out of their comfort zones and so must you. Remind yourself that you have the strength to stand by what you want and what you need. You deserve the best. So, go get it.

CHAPTER FOUR

GET CONNECTED

Networking, much like business in general, has been the domain of men. For hundreds of years, women weren't allowed into the spaces where decisions were made and where power was wielded. The "Old Boys Club"—born from colleges, secret societies, and country clubs— has always given men immediate and extensive access to networks that help them get ahead. Women were often legally barred from joining these networks, and even when they did make headway into these institutions, to be accepted they often had to behave like "one of the guys."

Whether it's how we're socialized or that men have gotten a head start on us, women often feel uncomfortable referring business to one another; many of us may feel that by personally gaining something from a relationship, we've somehow tainted the authenticity of it. There's also a vague sense of unfairness; if we get a leg up by a connection, it's not playing by the rules that everyone else is supposed to follow. Plus, we'd never just outright *ask* someone for a favor—we don't want to be a burden.

Networking also requires us to do another thing that pushes the bounds of how we're socialized. We have to talk about ourselves and our accomplishments, which sounds a lot like bragging, another no-no for women.

Networking isn't easy but it doesn't have to be painful. Part of learning to network is being mindful about how you present yourself but not at the expense of authenticity. It's also about being strategic about where and with whom you connect. It's asking for help while paying it forward and shooting your shot even when you're pretty sure you won't get a yes. There will always be an element of vulnerability inherent in meeting new people or asking for help, so part of networking is also developing a thick skin so that when someone says no thanks, you don't take it as an indictment of your worth. Finally, networking shouldn't feel transactional; if it does, there's a better way to go about it.

In this chapter, you'll get to know Phoebe, who has to learn to overcome her anxiety around networking so she can move into a new industry. She quickly realizes how powerful networking can be; it offers her entree into worlds of opportunities, many of them lucrative.

I'll show you how to lay the groundwork to expand your network, and then how to activate it when the time is right. My goal is to show you how networking doesn't have to be a necessary evil, but an opportunity to build community. If done right, it's as much about helping others as it is helping yourself.

FIND YOUR PEOPLE

Phoebe was getting restless. She'd been at her company for three years and it was becoming increasingly clear that there wasn't anywhere for her to grow. Her role was to organize fundraising initiatives for an educational nonprofit, and as much as she enjoyed her work, things moved slower than she would have liked. Plus, the limited resources—and her limited paycheck—were starting to get to her.

As Phoebe reflected on the past few years, she realized that the part of her job she liked the most was producing and marketing events. Just as Alisha, from Chapter One, had done in her own career, Phoebe put in the time and effort to make an intentional step in a direction aligned with her values. The more research she did, the more marketing and advertising seemed like it might be that direction. The problem was, Phoebe didn't know anyone in those industries. If she wanted to make a move, she would need to network.

The very idea of networking made Phoebe's skin crawl. It brought up a lot of emotions, including some of the resentment she'd experienced back in college. Though Phoebe admits that she had a privileged upbringing as a white middle-class woman, she'd felt really out of place when she got to college. It was the first time she was around wealthy people who had summer homes and were considered "legacies" (meaning their parents—and often their parents' parents—had also attended the school). Phoebe's mom hadn't gone to college, and her dad drove a UPS truck to put himself through school.

Networking was a foreign concept to her, and it seemed to buck the values she'd grown up with. Phoebe was raised with the belief that you don't burden people by asking for help. Anything she got she was expected to get on her own. But in college, it seemed like everyone around her was landing plum internships and jobs simply through family connections. Whether or not it was fair, this was how the world worked, so she knew she'd have to set out to build her own network.

To get started, Phoebe researched events and meetups related to the marketing and advertising industry. She looked through Eventbrite listings, Instagram hashtags, and Facebook groups and quickly became overwhelmed. Phoebe lived in New York City, where there were literally hundreds of events to go to every night of the week. In order to whittle things down, Phoebe realized she needed to be more specific about what she wanted to ultimately achieve.

She started by defining areas of the industry she was most interested in learning about. She came across organizations like the Art Directors Club of New York, which supported people in visual communications, as well as groups such as the Association for Women in Communications, which catered to a more specific demographic.

The more targeted Phoebe got about what she was looking for, the better the opportunities her search yielded. She scoured LinkedIn, signed up for event listings, and asked people for recommendations.

Like Phoebe, to refine your focus, you need to be clear about your goals. The following questions will help.

EXPAND YOUR NETWORK

+ Why do you want to expand your network?

+ What information and access are you seeking?

+ What are you passionate about?

+ What do you want to learn?

+ If you walked into an event, what kind of people would you want to be there?

+ What are benchmarks you can create for yourself to hold you accountable? For example, is there a certain number of events to attend or people to reach out to?

EVENT NETWORKING

Phoebe challenged herself to attend at least one event a month and created a calendar to hold herself accountable. It was sometimes difficult to find someone available to go with her, and Phoebe was unaccustomed to flying solo. The thought of showing up to an event alone and approaching a group of strangers felt really awkward. Actually, excruciating. Phoebe isn't alone: social anxiety is the third-most-common mental health issue in the United States. (And that's based on just the people who self-report.) There are probably countless more who may not suffer to the extent of having panic attacks but can feel the heart palpitations and sweaty palms when put in an environment where they don't know anyone. So, the next time you get nervous, remember that you're not the only one. Not by a long shot.

Walking in without a plan doesn't help. If you're going to an event, a way to feel more comfortable (and be prepared) is to reach out to the event organizer a few days beforehand and ask what you can do to support them. Offer to check people in, which is a clever way of getting to meet (albeit briefly) everyone who comes to the event. Plus, volunteering will give you something to do so you don't spend the whole evening in the corner. Getting to know the organizer will also help you down the road since they're probably someone with a large network that you may eventually be able to tap into.

When you first arrive, center yourself and take it all in. What's the vibe? Where are people congregating? Who looks friendly? Being a good networker means being able to read the room, and the best way to do that is to be present and observant. If you've come by yourself, don't be afraid to go up to a group of people and ask if you can join them. (Even if it's a group of people who already know one another, they share the same goal as you: to meet new people.) After getting a sense of the group dynamic, try to find a way to piggyback off what someone says. Whether it's mentioning an article you just read, or posing a question, don't wait too long to participate a little, otherwise you'll be the silent lurker.

Take the pressure off yourself—you don't have to try to meet as many people as possible. In fact, if you do that, you'll end up with a bunch of business cards but probably not a whole lot of meaningful connections. So instead, aim to have at least two to three of those more in-depth conversations; quality is better than quantity.

Remember that if you're going to an event that's specific to a certain industry, cause, or affiliation, there's context to why everyone is there. You've all come for the explicit purpose of meeting each other and if you're the first one to initiate the conversation with someone else, they'll probably be relieved. It's useful to have some openers prepared so you don't have to come up with something at the spur of the moment.

A FEW OPENING LINES

✦ "Hey, I'm here alone. Do you mind if I hang with you guys?"

✦ "Networking events can be really awkward, so I'm just going to introduce myself!"

✦ "How did you become interested in design/engineering/publicity/ etc.?"

✦ Give a compliment. People put thought into what they wear and so complimenting their bag or earrings will make them feel good and is a great conversation starter.

Having a conversation at a networking event is a little like doing a dance. The steps of this dance come from taking something the other person has told you about themselves and then finding a way to organically connect it to something about you. However, you want to be cognizant of how much airtime you're taking up; the biggest faux pas in trying to establish a real connection is to monopolize the conversation. Better to err on the side of asking them questions. Besides, part of this is about winning other people over and the truth is most people like to hear themselves talk. Plus, the more you know about them, the more commonalities you can find between you.

There is only one rule to networking: no shit-talking. No matter how friendly the other person is, don't use that as an indicator that you can bad-mouth anyone, whether it's about your job, boss, coworkers, or an ex. (Well, maybe that one's okay.) But still, it's a small world . . . so be careful. If the other person is doing the shit-talking, don't pile on. You can either change the subject or simply say, "I wasn't aware of that." Then move on.

Have a few stories in your back pocket that showcase something interesting about you—or that you're interested in. For example, maybe it was a recent concert you went to or a trip you took; maybe it's a side hustle you have that you're hoping to turn into a full-time job. If you're really struggling with what to talk about, focus instead on things you're passionate about. Sharing something that lights you up will make you memorable and inspiring.

Don't like what you do for a living? It can feel tough to network if you're out of work or less than enthused about your job. Come prepared with what you'll say when you're inevitably asked what you do for work. Talk about the challenges you like to solve or the things you enjoy. You can also be candid about what you're looking for since you never know what connections the person you're talking to might have, or their willingness to help.

What's more important than anything you could say about yourself is making the other person feel good. The way to do that is simple: give them your undivided attention. That means eye contact, asking questions, and then actually *listening* to the answers. Don't look over their shoulder to scan the room for who else to talk to; it will make them feel like a layover on your way to meet someone more important, and it can signal that you're not trustworthy or sincere.

Another way to make them feel good is to bring positive energy. Think about the kinds of people you're drawn to. They probably have open body language, smile often, and freely gesture; all things that radiate positive energy. *You* can be that person. If this means you need to get yourself hyped up before the event—listening to music, doing jumping jacks, power posing in the bathroom—do it. If you're not feeling particularly confident, square your shoulders and plant your feet. Rooting yourself will make you feel strong and take up more space, which projects power.

The quickest way to bring someone positive energy is by an enthusiastic handshake. According to studies, it takes only seven seconds to make a good first impression—no pressure!—so it's important to give a good one. Think about the handshakes you don't like (limp, sweaty), and think about the ones you do (firm, medium-to-strong squeeze), and make sure you're doing the latter. A way to ensure that is to practice with a friend beforehand.

Eventually, make sure to move on, otherwise you won't meet enough people to make it valuable. At events, I'm usually the one stuck in the corner learning someone's entire life story, which may accomplish the goal of having at least one meaningful conversation but doesn't really broaden my network. I know all too well how hard it can be to exit a conversation gracefully (especially when they've only gotten halfway through their childhood); here's the line I always use: "I'm sure you have other people you want to meet, I don't want to monopolize all your time. Can I have your contact information? I'd love to continue later." Or the "I need to get [insert food, bathroom, whatever]" line always works. But before you do that, don't forget what you came for: make sure to get their contact information.

Some controversial advice for you: don't bring business cards. You read that right. When I used to bring mine, I noticed that whenever I met people, they'd ask for my card and move on before I could get theirs. They never followed up, which meant all that networking went to waste. Now, when people ask for my card, I tell them I don't actually have one, and would they mind putting their information directly into my phone? I send them an email on the spot so they have mine. Easy.

CASE STUDY

BETH COMSTOCK

A S NERVE-WRACKING AS it can be to go up to a complete stranger, you have nothing to lose and everything to gain. I consider myself an excellent networker, but even I get periodic stage fright. Thank goodness for my cofounder, Ashley (I brought her on board around seven months after I launched Ladies Get Paid). Over the course of the year, Ashley had gotten to know another business owner (through Twitter!) who invited us to a small gathering of female entrepreneurs and investors at her office. It wasn't your typical happy hour; we sat in a circle where we went around and introduced ourselves. We were told to ask the room for something and then offer something. A woman in the back stood up. "Hi, I'm Beth Comstock," she said. Ashley elbowed me in the ribs. Beth continued, "I just ended a long corporate career and am about to publish a book. I don't really have an ask; I'm just here figuring out what's next." Ashley whispered in my ear, "Holy shit, Beth is a *legend*. We need to meet her." (Beth is the former vice chair of GE, and one of the key players in the creation of Hulu.)

This might have been the most powerful woman I'd ever been in the presence of, and I had the chance to introduce myself. My heart was racing, but I couldn't move. The stage fright had taken over. I told Ashley I couldn't do it; I couldn't bring myself to go over to her. Ashley threw me a disapproving look and strode over to Beth while I stayed by the wine and cheese table (which isn't a bad place to be, by the way, since most people stop by). I watched as Ashley waited in line to meet Beth (yes, there was a line), and watched as she handed her a Ladies Get Paid business card. After maybe ten minutes, Ashley came bounding over to me. "Let's go outside, I'll tell you *everything*."

Apparently, when Ashley mentioned Ladies Get Paid, Beth totally lit up. Turns out she was a fan and not only that, she had gone so far as to find the woman who designed the homepage of our website and hire her! (The artist, Leta Sobierajski, was the one who inspired me to hold that very first town hall that led to the founding of Ladies Get Paid and she designed our much beloved Money Scrunchie icon.)

To keep the relationship going, Ashley offered to help Beth by promoting her book to the Ladies Get Paid community. She sent a prompt follow-up message with a suggestion to meet for coffee. They grabbed lattes the next week.

Since then, Beth has become a sort of business godmother to us. She's made introductions that have led to major brand deals, she was the keynote speaker at our annual conference, and she even hired us to do some consulting. (She also wrote a blurb for this book!) When we pitch ourselves, whether it's for a brand sponsorship or attracting an important speaker, having Beth in our corner is hugely helpful. She lends validity through her star power and is a good person to bounce things off of. The relationship has been beneficial because, yes, we can help each other, but also, we genuinely like each other (well, we adore her; I think she likes us!). No matter how hard you network, if it isn't authentic, it won't work.

To this day, I'm still mortified at myself for what I did (or rather, didn't do) at the party. If Ashley hadn't been there, or if we'd decided to stay home that night, Ladies Get Paid wouldn't be what it is today.

COLD OUTREACH

As nerve-wracking as it was, going solo to networking events forced Phoebe to meet new people. By consistently showing up at events held by the same organizations, she began to recognize other people who were also regular attendees. Some of them also tended to come alone, and eventually they all banded together and became their own little crew, sharing new events they found and meeting up beforehand.

Phoebe got a lot more comfortable talking to strangers, and so when she found herself on a flight next to a friendly-looking guy named Brett, she struck up a conversation. It turned out he owned a marketing company that specialized in in-person brand experiences, the exact kind of thing Phoebe was interested in. Phoebe told him about the fundraising events she'd organized and the things she wanted to learn. She was upfront about wanting to make connections in the industry and asked if she could keep him updated. He gave her his contact info and encouraged her to stay in touch.

Phoebe felt emboldened to keep putting herself out there. She'd gotten lucky with her seat assignment but wasn't able to wait until her next plane ride. She needed to create more opportunities for herself now. Just as she had at the beginning of her networking journey, Phoebe turned to LinkedIn. She went through all her connections, seeing if they were connected to anyone in a field or a job that she wanted to learn more about. She looked at various groups to see who frequently posted and if they might be someone to reach out to. She researched industry conferences to find potential speakers to connect with.

Phoebe also reached out to her existing network. She posted on all of her social media channels asking about the best female speakers that they'd heard at marketing conferences. A number of people responded with great suggestions; she now had a robust list of people to email.

But Phoebe knew that she wasn't going to get someone to agree to connect with her simply because she asked. She had to give them a reason to want to. Phoebe was aware that as someone new in the industry, she didn't have much to offer. But she had her enthusiasm, a hunger to learn, and a willingness to offer any help if they needed it. Surely they'd been in her place at some point, and if she crafted her outreach thoughtfully, they just might say yes. What did she have to lose?

Phoebe came across a podcast episode that featured Nisha Dua, the cofounder of Built By Girls Ventures (BBG), a New York–based venture capital fund that invested in women-led technology companies. Nisha talked about the importance of networking in her career since the more people she knows, the more potential deals she can make. But because Nisha constantly receives pitches from hopeful entrepreneurs who want her to invest in their businesses, she had a lot to say on the etiquette of the cold outreach. "Something that really bugs me is when people aren't direct. There's no context of 'I work for this company; we focus on X.'" When doing cold outreach, emails that provide no information other than you'd like to meet are almost guaranteed not to get a response. Instead, you need to use your email as the opportunity to introduce yourself, explain your intent, and give them everything they need to fulfill your request with as little time investment as possible on their part.

When it comes to cold outreach, the rule of thumb is to put yourself in their shoes: What would make *you* say yes?

Phoebe boiled down her outreach into a step-by-step strategy. First, she had to show them that her reaching out wasn't entirely random. She needed to demonstrate what they had in common and where she'd learned about them. Phoebe knew how valuable their time was, so she had to be as clear and focused as possible about what she was looking for. Saying she wanted a job or a mentor would come across too strong and a bit vague; she had to build the relationship first. Also, saying she wanted to "pick their brain" was too general (and quite frankly, kind of gross-sounding). She had to ask for something that respected their bandwidth and was specific to who they were.

COLD OUTREACH 101

Places to find people

+ Podcasts

+ Conference speaker listings

+ Facebook and LinkedIn groups

+ Post on your channels about who you're looking for

+ Hashtags on Instagram and Twitter

Before you reach out

✦ **Define your ask.** Even if you ultimately would like them to hire you or help you get a job, you need to build the relationship first. Be clear about what you're asking for: Advice? A connection?

✦ **Consider the appropriateness of it.** Are they the right person? Is there someone who is more junior whom you should reach out to first? People who are just above your level may be more likely to respond.

✦ **Is there anyone who can make the introduction for you?** You're much more likely to get a response if someone can vouch for you by making the connection.

The outreach

✦ **Express a commonality.** Whatever research you did on them, mention it both in the body of the email and the subject line. For example, "I saw you speak at [INSERT NAME] conference," or "I read this article about you." If you have a mutual acquaintance, put that in the subject line.

✦ **Make it personal.** After you do your research, reference things you uncovered about them that motivated you to reach out. Flattery never hurts (as long as it's genuine!).

✦ **Be compelling.** Get them excited about responding to you by telling them (briefly) about things you've done in the past that are relevant to your outreach, the origin of your passion for the subject matter, and express a desire to learn from them.

✦ **Be specific.** Send them no more than three things that you want to learn from them, making it clear why you specifically reached out to them (it'll show that you did your homework). That way, they know how they can help you. Once you've gotten to know them (one call or a few email exchanges will suffice), don't be afraid to ask them if there's anyone else they know who might be interested in connecting with you.

✦ **Respect their time.** When you invite someone to coffee, you're asking for a lot of their time and energy, which they probably don't have much of. That doesn't mean you shouldn't ask to meet in person, but also give them the option of connecting by phone or Skype. Tell them you just need fifteen to twenty minutes of their time and be specific about what you're looking to learn. (If the two of you click, you'll probably get more time.)

✦ **Be (politely) persistent.** If you don't hear back from them, reach out again within seven days. Then send another email five days later. Last year, Nisha had 100,000 (!) unread emails in her inbox. She had to deal with what was most important or time-sensitive, and she figures that if something is really important, the person will email her again. "I strongly encourage people to follow up with polite persistence. Still, the worst thing you can do is be aggressive in your email when you're following up—watch your tone. Also, don't be passive-aggressive if the other person has not responded to you. And do not just reforward an email to someone and expect them to read an entire chain. You can say, 'I'm sure your inbox is really full. I just thought that I would bump this up and reiterate it; I would love the opportunity to—' Basically, how do you make this the easiest, lightest lift possible for the person you're emailing?"

✦ **Don't get discouraged.** Don't be discouraged if the person you email doesn't have time to chat with you. Often, it's a matter of timing and just because it doesn't work out today, that doesn't mean it won't in the future. However, if you keep getting no's, you might want to consider *why* you're getting a no. Ask someone else to read your email and give you feedback. In short: make things personal, but don't take it personally. This is business.

When you finally do connect, whether online, on the phone, or in person, send a prompt follow-up note thanking them and letting them know what resonated with you from the conversation. Keep them periodically posted with your updates, especially if you implemented something they suggested. They'll feel good to know that they helped you.

Also, if you haven't already, don't be afraid to connect with them on LinkedIn, Facebook, Instagram, and Twitter. It's a great way to get to know someone—and stay peripherally in touch—so that by the next time you see each other, you'll have a better sense of who they are and how to connect with them.

CONNECT THROUGH SOCIAL MEDIA

The people you reach out to will most likely google you, so you want to be in command of what they find. Look at how other people in the industry are using social media to present themselves and put time into building your own profile. Get active on platforms like LinkedIn, Instagram, and Twitter. That way, people looking for information about you online have a sense of who you are and what you're all about.

What kind of content should I post?

Start by clarifying your goals. This will help shape the kind of things you post, as well as where you spend your time engaging. Be explicit about those goals by putting them in your Instagram and LinkedIn profiles. For Phoebe, her goals were to connect with other companies and freelancers doing experiential marketing.

Don't be afraid to show who you are, and not just what you do for a living. Let go of trying to be "perfect." In fact, the more real your content is, the better. (Remember Kate from Chapter Three?) It will humanize you and in turn resonate with more people. That being said, anything you put online should be viewed through the lens of what your boss or prospective boss might think. So, unless you're a party promoter or a fashion influencer, it probably means no photos of you partying on a yacht in a bikini (though you could create a private account just for those kinds of posts). Also, be careful about oversharing, complaining, or anything that might alienate people. Instead, share things you're excited or passionate about, things that can help or inspire others; in short: things that provide value. Pay attention to what content gets the most engagement and do more of that.

Where should I post?

There's no one-size-fits-all content; different online platforms are used in different ways. What you put on Instagram is usually not what you would put on LinkedIn. The most important thing about representing yourself online is being consistent, so be realistic upfront about your bandwidth and focus on the platform that is most relevant to your goals.

For most industries, LinkedIn is that platform (unless you're in a creative field like design, fashion, or even marketing, in which case Instagram is probably your best bet). Twitter, on the other hand, is a primary networking platform for people in fields like journalism and comedy, however, it can also be used as a discovery tool, whether it's to find thought leaders, news, or general things happening in the zeitgeist. If Twitter doesn't feel natural to you, look at it as a way to keep up to date with what's happening in the world without the pressure to participate.

In terms of how often to post, networking through social media follows the same principle of networking offline: the more you give, the more you get.

ENGAGE, ENGAGE, ENGAGE!

✦ **LinkedIn.** Add people with whom you are trying to build a relationship so your content starts to show up in their feed; comment on people's posts, and tag others who you think are relevant.

✦ **Twitter.** Follow people you admire, ask them questions, reply to their tweets.

✦ **Facebook.** Join groups of like-minded people, ask and answer questions.

✦ **Instagram.** Start by commenting on people's posts, reposting to your Stories (crediting them, of course), and then send them a direct message (DM), following the same rules of etiquette as you would with cold outreach by email. Make sure your bio is clear about who you are and what opportunities you're interested in.

CULTIVATE RELATIONSHIPS

Building her online profile helped Phoebe get in touch with people in experiential marketing (she would often repost photos of activations they did), and with all these new connections she was making, Phoebe needed to keep track. A relationship doesn't happen by meeting once or twice; it's built by consistently staying in touch. But given how busy we all are, that can be a near impossibility. That's why companies spend millions of dollars on customer relationship management platforms; they know that a lost relationship means lost revenue. Same thing goes for you. Any lost relationship is a missed opportunity. To make sure that doesn't happen, you have to organize your contacts.

CREATE A "ROLODEX"

1. **Get organized.** Create a spreadsheet or use a template from Airtable and export your LinkedIn contacts, email addresses, or whatever digital rolodex you have, getting everything into one place. List each person's title, where they work, how you know them, and the information and access they might have.

Yes, this will take you a fair amount of time. But stick with it. Having everything organized and in one place will help you easily and quickly tap into your network when it matters.

2. **Make a short list.** Now that you have an overview of your network, it's time to get strategic about who you want to know better. Judy Robinett, author of *How to be a Power Connector: The 5+50+100 Rule for Turning Your Business Network into Profits*, suggests targeting 100 influential or potentially helpful people as the ones to cultivate relationships with. If this sounds like a lot, you can start smaller. And this doesn't have to be accomplished in one week or one month—this is a long-term strategy. These don't have to be people you already know well; in fact, there is *more* value in acquaintances such as those who you've worked with briefly or maybe met through a friend. Known as "weak ties" (a phrase coined by Stanford University sociologist Mark Granovetter), these people give you access to more diverse opportunities precisely because you don't travel in the same circles. These people should also be as diverse as possible in seniority, industry, and location. You never know what you may need in your career—or in your life—and this will increase the chances you'll find someone who can help you.

3. **Identify the Portal People.** From your short list, highlight those who are themselves the most networked. I define them as a Portal Person: someone who is at the intersection of a lot of people, a community builder, the person who everyone seems to know. Because they have access to a diversity of information, they are the people you can go to first when you

need help with finding something or someone. (In Phoebe's case, Brett would turn out to be that Portal Person.)

4. **Stay in touch.** If you don't follow up and maintain your connection after meeting, contacting them out of the blue to ask for a favor is rude. One of the best and most efficient ways to stay on someone's radar is by sending periodic emails. Whether it's a quick congrats on something you saw about them on LinkedIn or an article you thought they'd find interesting, your goal is to show that you're thinking of them. Also, include an update about you—things going well at work, a conference you attended, or a new job.

5. **Hold yourself accountable.** Create calendar alerts to remind you when to reach out (I suggest at least once a quarter). Karen Wickre, the author of *Taking the Work Out of Networking: An Introvert's Guide to Making Connections That Count*, recommends integrating it into a preexisting habit. "My morning ritual of checking email and my news feeds is a way to limber up for the workday. As I scan the headlines, I'll share a story or two that I know are of interest to people I haven't been in touch with along with a short note: 'This made me think of you. What's your take? And how are you?'" If there's someone you want to reach out to but haven't been in touch with for a while, don't hesitate to email them anyway. Just acknowledge that some time has passed, and then jump to the present.

BE A CONNECTOR

Phoebe would send Brett periodic updates about what she was up to, inviting him to events she was organizing, inquiring about how he was doing, and always offering her support. In turn, he would invite her to events he was attending, and once there he would integrate her into conversations by asking, "Have you met Phoebe?" He also started to make introductions to people in his network.

Connecting people to each other can be very powerful. In fact, it was making connections that allowed me to start Ladies Get Paid. Remember that first town hall I hosted? I invited six women whom I admired (and knew to be Portal People) to think of at least three women they thought would enjoy the event. I asked if they'd be open to either connecting me or forwarding the invitation on to them. Every one of them made the introduction and when I was connected, I asked those women if they could suggest at least three other women to invite. I continued that until I reached 100 women. The event was really special, in large part because everyone there had someone in common, which made it instantly feel intimate and welcoming.

Being a connector establishes the behavior you want to see. When you do it, others will, too. It's a simple act that can do so much—not just for them, but for you as well. Being a connector builds goodwill with both parties, something you can never have too much of. Imagine how many people each person in your network knows. If everyone were connected to one another, it would create an incredibly strong web. It would create community.

When I meet new people and learn about what they do or are looking to do, I usually start thinking about my network and someone I should introduce them to. (This is another reason why it's important to have your contacts organized in one place.) However, never connect people for the sake of connecting; the connection has to be truly beneficial for everyone. And the only way to know what someone is looking for in a connection is to ask them. Connections need to be meaningful, and it's an important responsibility to connect people in a way that is respectful of everyone's time, energy, and interests. Here are some rules to follow to safeguard your relationship with people you are connecting:

CONNECTOR ETIQUETTE

✦ **Get the "double opt-in" first.** It's crucial to ask both sides for permission before making an introduction, otherwise it can get really awkward. Nisha, whom we met earlier, knows this well. In her opinion, if you don't ask someone if they are okay with being connected to another person, you can come across as a bit of a jerk for presuming that they will have the time and interest to engage. "I want to look like a good guy. I want to look like I went to the trouble of making this introduction. What you fail to realize is that in winning points with the person you're making the introductions for, you could lose points with the person you made the introduction to."

✦ **Make the introduction as clear as possible.** A pet peeve of mine (besides not being asked before someone makes an introduction) is when I'm introduced to someone, and the reasons *why* we are being introduced are unclear or confusing. I've been on email chains where the introduction was simply "you both do lady stuff, you should meet," with not just one, but multiple people! None of us knew where to start, so none of us followed up.

GOOD EXAMPLE:

Ashley <> Michelle

Ashley Louise (ladiesgetpaid.com), Michelle Krisel (gmail.com)

Ashley <> Michelle

Hey ladies, I'm excited to connect you two. A bit of context:

Ashley is the co-founder of Ladies Get Paid, an organization that seeks pay equity for women by helping them strategically navigate their careers.

Michelle is an advisor to female-companies who are making a difference.

I can see lots of ways for you to team up. Feel free to keep me cc'd as you continue the conversation.

x Claire

--

Claire Wasserman
Founder, Ladies Get Paid

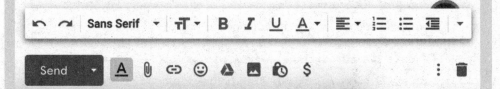

NOT SO GOOD EXAMPLE:

Ashley <> Michelle

Ashley Louise (ladiesgetpaid.com), Michelle Krisel (gmail.com)

Ashley <> Michelle

Hey Ashley! Hey Michelle!

You're both awesome women and I thought you should know each other :)

I'll let you two take it from here.

x Claire

--

Claire Wasserman
Founder, Ladies Get Paid

✦ **Consider the optics.** When you're the one who is asking to be
connected, it's important to consider the appropriateness of
the request. Do you want to be connected to a CEO? Maybe
go for the assistant first. When you ask for the introduction,
acknowledge that you know this is a favor. When people make
an introduction, they're spending their social capital; how this

introduction plays out will reflect back on them. You also want to make it as easy as possible for them; it takes a lot of effort to write a thoughtful introduction about someone else, so provide them with a note they can forward on your behalf. When Nisha asks for an introduction, she writes something short and sharp that gives her contact enough ammunition to feel good about the introduction that they're making. "I basically preload one to two paragraphs that are specific to the person or the company they're introducing me to and explain why I'm interested in getting to know them and what my relevant experience is."

If you are the person who is being connected, you want to be gracious. Do two things: thank them and follow up after you've made the connection. If you don't, it not only makes you look bad, it also reflects poorly on the person who connected you. Whatever happens next, keep the original person updated so that they know you followed through and what the result was.

SHOOT YOUR SHOT

Phoebe saw how crucial connections were in opening up opportunities, as well as giving her access to knowledge about the industry and what jobs were available. Because she'd created a system to organize her contacts, whenever she met someone, the wheels would start spinning in her mind of who *she* might introduce them to. (She made sure to follow the connector etiquette.) The more her network expanded, the more valuable her contacts were. Soon she was the one connecting Brett! When one of her introductions became his client, Phoebe had a realization: she could do this for living. She'd learned a lot about the marketing industry and could use her newfound networking skills to do business development or sales.

She decided to pitch Brett on why he should hire her. To him, it was a no-brainer. Phoebe was clearly a go-getter, a fast learner, and willing to hustle. Without missing a beat, he said yes.

It had taken Phoebe less than six months of being proactive and consistently putting herself out there. It showed her that she didn't have to wait to make things happen. That, yes, there was always an element of fate or luck but she was the master (mistress?) of her fate. Now, she was up and running, and whatever happened next, she had a network to rely on.

Remember, connections can be made anywhere, anytime, and with anyone. Never underestimate what you and those you're connected to can do for each other—if not today, then in the future.

We must seize every opportunity we have and create them when we don't. You may not get a yes every time but that's okay; remember, you've already done the important inner work to be able to withstand it. And one yes is all you need. The doors will open. Now all you have to do is walk through them.

CHAPTER FIVE

GET THE JOB

The thought of applying to a new job was terrifying. While Reece (from Chapter Two) had made a lot of progress with her self-esteem, she was still grappling with her imposter syndrome. She knew she deserved a better work environment than her last job, but she dreaded the job-hunting process. She wasn't sure she was ready for the emotional roller coaster; how was she going to convince others of her value when she had only just begun to believe in it herself?

Reece needed to protect herself from getting stuck in the self-limiting thoughts that had held her back in the past. She also needed to do what Alisha in Chapter One did: find work that aligned with her values and stay strong until she found it. Taking a job out of desperation would be a step backward. She also knew that when she eventually did get a job, she was going to do something she'd never done: she was going to have to negotiate her salary. And that made her feel sick to her stomach.

CLAIM WHAT YOU DESERVE

The process of getting a job and negotiating your salary is the ultimate form of self-advocacy. It requires us to confront and reconcile all the ways we've been socialized to remain small. We have to sing our own praises (*"don't brag!"*), we have to believe we deserve it (*"you should be more grateful!"*), and we have to be willing to put ourselves out there (*"it's better to not take risks"*). Negotiating makes us push up against the biggest fear of all: we might not be liked and we might be told no. If they offer us less than what we expected, isn't that hard proof that we're not good enough? Negotiating can induce dread in even the most confident among us.

No one teaches us how to negotiate. It's a process shrouded in secrecy and filled with jargon; on top of that, money carries with it a ton of emotional baggage for many of us. Women have told me that they'd rather not do it just to avoid the terror it brings.

But to not negotiate is to give up your power. Because it's about more than today's salary, it's the interest it gains, the generational wealth it accumulates. Men have been doing this since the beginning of time. When we ask for more, we normalize a woman's right to stand her ground and have her worth taken seriously. It's normal to doubt yourself, but when you do, remember that this is greater than you.

In this chapter, we'll catch up with Reece, who learns to articulate her worth all the way from the first job interview through to the salary negotiation. She learns that nailing the interview is about telling a story, filtered through both the job description and the company culture. It's also about more than just experience; it's about who you are and your enthusiasm for the work.

As much of an emotional roller coaster as job hunting can be, I want you to hold strong in the belief that you *will* find a job and when you do, they'll be lucky to have you.

GET IN THE DOOR

Reece knew her deal breakers. After quitting her job, she'd spent time digging into her values and realized how important collaboration and inclusion were to her. Now as she began her job search with purpose, she came across a company on LinkedIn whose description seemed to match those values. She scanned the list of their employees, hoping she had a mutual connection. Reece knew that the chances of getting a job improve immeasurably if you know someone at the company. What she needed was an in, someone at the company who could let her know about job opportunities before they were publicized to the rest of the world; someone who could advocate on her behalf.

Fortunately, Reece found someone she knew who had a connection there, and following good networking etiquette, reached out to her to ask if she'd feel comfortable making the introduction. Reece positioned it as an informal interview, expressing a desire to learn about the company culture. She first needed to get more intel about the company in order to be the strongest candidate possible if she did eventually apply for a job there. Her friend agreed and introduced Reece to her colleague, Ruth.

When Reece and Ruth spoke on the phone, they instantly connected. At the end of their conversation, Ruth mentioned that while there weren't any jobs currently open, Reece was a good fit for the company and that she should send over her résumé anyway. Reece thanked her (and updated their mutual friend to let her know how it went—remember, connector etiquette!).

To not miss any job postings, Reece set up a LinkedIn alert for the company and four months later, an opportunity opened up. Reece immediately reached back out to Ruth to ask for advice on applying. It turned out Reece had already passed an important hurdle: Ruth informed her that before a potential candidate gets recommended to HR, they have to go through a screener interview. Because of their earlier meeting, Reece was already past the first round.

Reece was then introduced to a recruiter. The conversation went really well, but he leveled with her—she was overqualified for the position and would be a better fit for another role. Unfortunately, there were none available at the time, but he encouraged her to reach back out in three months. Reece was disappointed, but she marked the calendar and tried to distract herself.

Reece waited impatiently. Exactly three months later, on January 1, Reece wished him a happy New Year and reminded him of their earlier conversation. Crickets. Ten days went by. Reece decided she had nothing to lose and reached back out again one more time. Almost immediately she got an apologetic response and an invitation for an interview the following week.

Reece's work experience helped her get the interview, but what clinched it was that she was proactive. It started with making a connection inside the company, staying up-to-date online, and being diligent in her outreach. It had taken a few months, but Reece's persistence had paid off.

DO YOUR RESEARCH

If you've made it to the interview stage (congrats!), the recruiter is confident you have the right work experience. Now what they need is to understand *who* you are. They want to be assured that you can learn fast and be a team player. In other words, they want to see if you're a culture fit. In order to demonstrate that you are, you first need to do research on what their culture is. That could include LinkedIn articles they've published, events they've hosted, or press they've received. The best way to know what it's like to work there is to reach out to a current employee in the department you're applying to and simply ask.

When you get to the interview, take what you've learned about the company and connect their needs and their goals to your work and your values. For example, one of the values listed on the company's site was "Adventure," and so in her interview, Reece talked about having traveled to over thirty countries and what she learned about herself in the process.

But as we learned in Alisha's story, the relationship you have with your job goes both ways. Just as the company is trying to determine whether you're a good fit for them, you need to do the same for yourself. During the interview, don't be afraid to inquire about specific examples of how they're living up to their values and confirm they're not just listing them on their website.

UNDERSTAND A COMPANY'S CULTURE

✦ What's their mission statement?

✦ Do they have employee resource groups (ERGs)?

✦ How long do people stay at the company?

✦ What does the path to promotion look like?

✦ What's the composition of their leadership?

✦ Are they committed to diversity and inclusion initiatives? If so, what are their metrics for success?

✦ Do they have professional development opportunities?

✦ Do they encourage work-life balance? (Look for and ask about concrete examples beyond stating "we have work-life balance!" For example, what are their approaches to flextime and working from home? What is their paid family leave policy?)

✦ What are the Glassdoor reviews? (Take this one with a grain of salt; people love to complain online!)

TALK YOURSELF UP

The interview process was intense for Reece. Five rounds of interviews gave her a lot of practice in talking about her wins, something that had always felt uncomfortable to her. When you struggle with imposter syndrome or perfectionism, it can be tough to even recognize your professional accomplishments in the first place, let alone talk about them. In order to articulate your competence, you'll need a strategy for identifying the elements of your experience that demonstrate why you're the right person for the job.

KNOW YOUR WINS

✦ **Revisit the original job description of your last role.** Now write a job description of what you actually did. Whether you created new initiatives or covered for an employee on leave, chances are you did a whole lot more than what was expected of you. That change in scope is a good place to focus when trying to identify your accomplishments, especially if you did things that were self-motivated or went above and beyond. You'll see what *you* brought to the job, how you rose to challenges, and what impact you had.

✦ **Think about your obstacles.** Companies are looking for people who are resilient and learn fast. What are the various challenges you encountered this year and how did you address them? For example, were you able to do big things on a small budget? Or maybe your team didn't have a solid project management process and you created one. Other areas to focus on are programs, processes, or products you created, or any bumps in the road and how you got through them.

Besides the impact of your work, an important thing to establish is how high the stakes were. Even if you feel like you have a mundane job, there are always people relying on you, and what you do affects them. Whether you were given minimal resources, had limited time, or had little experience, contextualize your accomplishment in a way that makes the person interviewing you impressed and invested.

Your wins are only as compelling as how you choose to talk about them, and adding context—i.e., establishing the stakes—is crucial. This is not the time to be humble. A great way to tell an engaging story is to approach it as if you're writing a movie script. You, of course, are the main character. I encourage you to structure your story according to the STAR Method, a framework that will help you lay things out in a clear, concise, and compelling way.

STAR METHOD

1. **Set the scene.** Start by giving some context (the who/what/ when/where/why), laying the groundwork, and demonstrating high stakes.

2. **Task or target.** What were you asked to do or what did you take on?

3. **Action.** What did you do? How did you do it? Traits to highlight include resourcefulness, the ability to learn fast, and resilience.

4. **Result.** What happened? What was the impact? What did you learn? Quantify as best as you can. For example, number of attendees, social media impressions, or money made or money saved, which includes time saved, because time is money.

Assuming you've done lots of great work in your career, be strategic about which examples you decide to talk about. Select the accomplishments that best correspond to what this new role requires—use language that's in the job description—and don't talk about more than two or three (though you should have more in your back pocket). Only highlight the work you actually *want* to do moving forward. For example, maybe you had great success with creating a more efficient project management process . . . but maybe you hated doing it. Leave that one out.

REECE'S EXAMPLE

1. **Set the scene:** I had just graduated from graduate school and begun my job as a social entrepreneur in residence in food security. The organization had just set a three-year strategic plan in place, and the number of people they wanted to reach in food security was more than bold, it was unprecedented—unrealistic, honestly. There was a lot of pressure.

2. **Task or target:** We had to come up with different strategies to reach the number (it was in the millions) of people they needed to serve by 2020. My job was to create new and innovative ways to help increase people's food security status. We had a number of challenges, including no preexisting relationship with manufacturers, plus the cost of making healthy food affordable. Because we couldn't guarantee a large order, I had to persuade manufacturers to take a risk and run a small-scale operation at least to begin. If I didn't find one I would either not hit my quota for the year or have to start from scratch and scramble up a new idea before December.

3. **Action:** I started by cold LinkedIn messaging as many random people in the food business as I could. One worked out, the founder of Territory Foods.

4. **Result:** Over the course of eighteen months, I developed a prepared meal product for low-income older adults, a segment virtually priced out of the market. I spent time learning the motivations, attitudes, and behaviors of our prospective

consumers, gaining deep empathy around issues of dignity and pride that they navigate every day. After extensive market analysis, building evidence and supportive data, ideating, and prototyping in partnership with Territory Foods, the product was projected to serve 150,000 people two years from launch. The three biggest things I learned were how to make a compelling case to manufacturers, translating market research into a product, and being nimble in our need to pivot. Need did not translate to demand for this segment, and to overcome the stigma of "handouts," the design required an opportunity for the consumer to show self-sufficiency with their purchase.

SUPERPOWERS

Remember, in your interview, a prospective employer is not looking for you to recite your résumé; they already read it. You want to focus their attention on the things that make you *you*. Things you bring to the table that may not be quite tangible but absolutely have an effect on the people around you. I call them Superpowers. Oftentimes they're things that come so naturally to you, things that are so ingrained in who you are, that you may not even realize them. (This is when it's good to seek the perspective of your colleagues and friends, just as you did in Chapter Three: Get Over Perfectionism.) These demonstrate not just what you can do, but who you are. Companies aren't just looking for candidates who have the right skills for the job; they're also concerned with finding the right culture fit. How will this person perform? Will they fit in with the team?

Don't assume the person interviewing you will know what your superpowers are. You need to articulate them and, most importantly, how they impacted your work. For example, in Reece's case, she might say, "My drive to make connections and establish productive partnerships made the company's goals possible in a way that we could not have achieved with internal resources alone."

EXAMPLES OF SUPERPOWERS

✦ Leadership (*People value my input and enthusiastically implement directives.*)

✦ Positivity (*By being super positive, I keep morale high, which I've seen motivates the team.*)

✦ Empathy (*I help people feel heard, which helps them do their best work.*)

✦ Good communication (*We work together more efficiently.*)

✦ Detail-oriented (*Things don't fall through the cracks.*)

✦ Unique skills and expertise (*I'm the go-to person for everyone in the office.*)

✦ Team builder (*I help people collaborate better.*)

✦ Large network (*I easily find vendors, clients, and prospective hires.*)

✦ Client connector (*I generate more business.*)

+ Fast learner *(I get a lot done and can quickly pivot if needed.)*

+ Institutional knowledge *(I accomplish things efficiently and help others navigate how the company operates.)*

+ Values diversity *(I foster an inclusive work environment that helps people do their best work.)*

You can start identifying your superpowers by asking yourself questions such as: What feels effortless? How would someone describe me? What is my role in the team dynamic? This is similar to what we did in Chapter One when we identified our strengths. This time, we want to explicitly tie those strengths to the impact they had.

If you're a recent graduate, you may not have traditional work experience yet, so spend a little extra time focusing on your superpowers—especially emphasizing your ability to learn fast. You can also demonstrate your potential by sharing research you've done on the company and ideas you'd bring to the table if hired.

If you're pivoting between industries or roles, or you're coming back to work from time off, the framework of telling your story still applies. If you can, take courses (like Alisha did) to demonstrate you have the core competencies needed for this new type of job. Get as much intel as you can about the role, ideally from someone who has or had the role, as this will help you preemptively speak to any potential concerns the company might have about your level of experience. Emphasize why your unique perspective as an "outsider" is actually an asset.

THE INTERVIEW

In her career as a recruiter, Nissa Booker—formerly the head of talent acquisition at BuzzFeed, and currently the vice president of talent at Moda Operandi, an e-commerce luxury fashion platform—has vetted hundreds of candidates. She has no-nonsense advice for ways to ace the interview.

ACE THE INTERVIEW

1. **Talk about your career trajectory.** Explain how you made decisions about your roles, what led you to them, and your general thought process from job to job. Or as Nissa describes it, "the connective tissue between all the roles that you've had is going to be the narrative that carries you into the interview."

2. **Be aware of a conversational give-and-take.** You should be able to talk about yourself and your wins, but also be mindful so you avoid the trap of talking so much that you're not listening to what the other person is saying. Nissa sees lopsided conversations as a red flag: "It makes me wonder if this person is going to allow space for other voices to be heard." If you're feeling nervous, take a beat and breathe.

3. **Get up to speed on what the company is doing and use it.** Nissa says being informed on company specifics showcases enthusiasm: "If someone sends me a note saying, 'Hey, I just read this really cool article about the new things that you're doing. Here's why I think my experience ties into this,' I think that's impressive. That means that you, as a candidate, are

really interested in this role. You're making a concerted effort to keep learning about this organization."

4. **At the end of the interview, understand expectations.** If it hasn't already been covered, don't be afraid to ask what the timeline is and what the sequence of communication is going to be. Nissa suggests these two questions to use as part of your script: "'How long will it be before I hear from you? When is it appropriate for me to follow up?' Any good recruiter will set up a timeline for you in that initial phone call about how long this process is going to take, what the interview loop is going to look like, and then when they're going to get back to you. The onus is on the recruiter to share that information with you, but if they don't share it with you, you have every right to ask."

Remember that the interview process goes both ways; you are also interviewing them! Just as much as they're trying to determine if you're the right fit for them, you also need to make sure that they're the right company for you. Pay attention to your instinct here. How personal—or impersonal—was the communication? Did they make the process clear? Did they put pressure on you to say yes immediately? Like any relationship, this has to work for you, too. To confirm that this is a place where you can thrive, you should ask questions about the company culture, path to growth, and career development opportunities. And don't be afraid to ask them for examples to back up what they're saying. Bottom line: the way an organization operates during the hiring process is an indicator of how things will be moving forward. If it doesn't feel good, it will probably never be good.

The more people Reece met at the company, the more she was convinced that she wanted to work there. She made multiple trips from Washington, DC, to New York, going through five rounds of interviews. In one of them, Reece was given three hours to come up with new business ideas to present to the leadership team. From her first informational interview until now, the job search had taken almost a year.

Reece felt encouraged, but also anxious. At the beginning, she had nothing to lose. Now, as much as she tried to manage her expectations, she was fully invested. She really, really wanted the job.

THE OFFER

I would be remiss if I didn't acknowledge that the job search isn't just about hard work; sometimes it just comes down to luck. If you're not hired, it doesn't necessarily mean you're not the right fit. In fact, according to Matt Youngquist, the president of Career Horizons, 70–80 percent of new jobs are never listed online but are, rather, filled internally or through networking (which is why building your network is so important!). There are a myriad of factors in play that are outside our control, such as budgeting constraints or office politics. I don't say this to discourage you, but to keep rejection in perspective.

If you don't receive an offer, you have every right to (politely) ask if they'd be willing to tell you why. It may be difficult to receive critical feedback, but it can also be liberating. Remind yourself that hearing it and acting on it is the best way to improve.

If you're not getting any interviews at all, seek feedback from someone in your network whom you trust or find a professional coach to take a look at your résumé and cover letter. If you're still not getting anything even with the updated résumé, go back to Chapter One and revisit what your strengths and values are. Perhaps it's not you who is "wrong" for the job, but rather that the job isn't right for you.

If you do get an offer, celebrate! You worked hard to both show your worth and find a good fit, two things that are not easy to do.

A few days after the last interview, Reece flew to Miami on a business trip. She'd barely landed when she got a voice mail from the hiring manager asking her to call them back. This seemed like a good sign. Once Reece got to the hotel, she Skyped the hiring manager who, smiling, said he had something that would make her very happy. She'd gotten the job of "inventor," specializing in helping companies create new products, brands, and business models. He said they were very impressed by her and saw she had the qualities to go very far. Reece was over the moon.

Her months of persistence had paid off, and the long interview process was over. But a new process was just beginning. Now Reece would have to get comfortable talking about money . . . and asking for more of it.

CHAPTER SIX

GET PAID

Whether you realize it or not, you negotiate every day. From deciding what movie to see with your friends, to getting your kids to do chores, negotiating is ultimately about finding a creative solution that satisfies everyone. You've actually been negotiating your whole life, starting as a child when you threw tantrums in an attempt to get what you wanted. (Not the best strategy now, but it may have worked then.)

Negotiating your salary feels different. Your palms are sweaty, your stomach is in knots; even just the thought of it is enough to trigger mental, emotional, and physical distress. A lot of the anxiety comes from the unknown: what to charge, if they'll say yes, or if they'll rescind the offer altogether (extremely unlikely). But it's also fears of how we'll be perceived. So many women have told me that they're afraid they'll be looked at as "combative," "money-mongering," or "biting the hand that feeds them." Many of them tell me that they'd rather not negotiate, just to avoid the terror that comes with it. I understand why.

Negotiating goes against everything we've been socialized to be. *"Be humble, be nice, don't rock the boat."* If we're expected to be accommodating, does asking for more make us look ungrateful on top of it all? To want more money is greedy and to talk about it is rude. It's easy to feel like we can't win.

SHIFT YOUR MINDSET

But negotiating is a natural, expected part of the process of getting a job. Everyone does it (or at least, everyone should). Whatever number an employer presents to you, in almost all cases they *expect* you to counter it. So, unless you respond in a rude way, simply countering their offer is not rude. Negotiating is an opportunity to showcase the value you'll bring to the company. For example, when I negotiate, I like to think of myself as a startup—the LLC of me—making the case to investors on how investing in me is actually investing in *them*. At its core, negotiating reflects an exchange of goods and services; you bring value, and the company knows they have to pay for it. In short: your salary is not a favor.

However, we may still feel guilty (or be made to feel guilty) when we ask for more. I hear this from women who work at nonprofits in particular; the rationale being that more for them means less money for others, depleting resources that could be used for those they serve. That may be true in some cases, but a savvy CEO in any kind of business knows the value of attracting and retaining good talent, and with that should come a competitive salary. If others in your same industry are making it, why shouldn't you?

Keep in mind that the most important thing is *how* you ask for it—not that you've asked for it in the first place. In fact, if you make a case that is well researched and thoughtfully presented, you'll demonstrate that you're a professional who values herself. And you'll be giving your employer exposure to you as someone who is a strong advocate, and who will bring those skills to work on behalf of the company.

If you're worried that attempting to negotiate will cost you the opportunity, remind yourself that if you've gotten this far in the process, they *want* this to work. Not only because they want you, but also because it's expensive to start over. A company can lose anywhere from 1 percent to 2.5 percent of their total revenue in the time it takes to hire and train a new employee. Think about what it would be like for the person you're negotiating with if you were to walk away. They'd have to go back to their boss and tell them they lost you. You have more leverage than you think.

UNDERSTAND YOUR MARKET VALUE

Reece had never negotiated her salary before, not because she was scared, but because she didn't know she could. It was learning about the wage gap that motivated her to start investigating how to do it. As awkward as she felt, Reece began talking about money with her friends and colleagues. She was shocked to discover that one of her male counterparts at work was making $46,000 more than her. That lit a raging fire within Reece. She swore she'd never, ever accept the first offer from now on.

Looking back at when she was first hired, Reece remembered being thrilled with what they'd offered; it was more money than she'd ever been paid before. But now, she realized that she had made a cardinal mistake. She hadn't done any market research, and instead had based her valuation on the level compared to what she had been making at her last job, which was well below market. She felt like a total idiot.

Reece isn't alone in this. I've heard from so many women that the number they come up with is based on whatever their last salary was, sometimes adding 20 percent to it. The problem with this method is that it assumes that your original salary was fair. You simply cannot take that on faith. Many states are now passing salary history bans, laws that makes it illegal to ask a prospective hire how much they currently make. The rationale is that marginalized groups make less money at the beginning of their careers and if salaries are always based on what they currently make, then any shortfall compounds over time, which in turn perpetuates the wage gap. You want to make a case based on market research for the job you're applying to, *not the job you had before.*

Do. Not. Underprice. Yourself! We pay higher prices for things—or people—we deem valuable, and if you underprice yourself, what sort of message are you sending? Plus, if you underprice yourself, there's a strong likelihood that you will become resentful, which puts you at risk of burning out at the job. And that will make you more likely to leave for a higher-paying job in the near future. Paying you less may save your new company money in the short term, but it will cost them more to search for and hire a replacement when you leave for something better. If you're the best candidate for the job, they'll either find the money or give you a combination of cash and full comp, which are other things you can and should negotiate that cost a company little to no money. We'll talk more about this later on.

Finally, underpricing yourself undercuts everyone—if each of us charges well below market rate, then guess what? Market rate drops. And it becomes a race to the bottom. Because of the gender wage gap, it's especially important not to do this—the more women stand up for their value, the more we all benefit. More money for her means more money for all of us.

When doing research on the market rate for your new job, pretend you're a detective searching for clues. The more evidence you find, the stronger your case will be, and the more money you'll get. It's important that your research be rooted in the context of your specific situation; this includes factors like location, size of the company, your skills, and years of experience.

Okay, but where do you begin? Here's the good news: there are a ton of sites out there that can help you calculate your salary. The bad news: there are a ton of sites out there that can help you calculate your salary. Searching online can be overwhelming and depending on what you do for a living, what you find may not quite be applicable.

If you have an unusual job title or do the equivalent of multiple people's jobs, it can be particularly tough to find relevant information. For example, one of my previous titles was "master of ceremonies," which was a great conversation starter at parties but made researching very difficult. Don't let this stop you from looking! You just need to get creative. For example, look at what you dedicate your time to in a given month and based on all that you do, list all the "traditional" job titles you could have. Let's say 70 percent of your month is dedicated to account management, 20 percent is being a creative director, and 10 percent is administrative. When you do your research, take a look at all those jobs so you can cobble together a salary range that takes into account all your responsibilities and gives an estimate of how much you should be compensated. It's not an exact formula but it will give you a foundation upon which you can make your case. At the very least, it will give you a rationale for how you came up with it.

While online research will allow you to see a full spectrum of possibilities and variations for a particular job, speaking to people in that industry is going to give you a much richer, and more accurate, picture of what the market is. The more sources you can find, the more confident you'll be. Talking to real people will help you validate the online research you did and help to strengthen your case.

TALK TO REAL PEOPLE

Speaking to others about salary can be uncomfortable. So, start the conversation with context; call out the elephant in the room—it's awkward to talk about money!—and express why you're asking. Mention that you've been reading about the wage gap and that you think it's important to make sure women are paid equally, and the only way to do that is to talk about it.

WHO TO TALK TO

✦ **Headhunters and staffing firms.** Given that their job is to know the market of who is hiring and how much they'll pay, recruiters are a treasure trove of information. If you can't get introduced to a headhunter, send them a note through LinkedIn. What do you have to lose? The worst thing that happens is they don't respond and the best thing that happens is that they not only give you information, they now have you on their radar for future job opportunities. (Be aware, though, that they take 10–20 percent commission on your salary, so while it's to their benefit to get you the highest salary, it's also in their interest to place as many people as possible, which means they may push you to take less to close the deal quickly.)

+ **Your alma mater.** If you went to college or participated in the Greek system, this is absolutely a resource you can and should tap into. Reach out to career services or the alumni network to ask if they have data on salaries, and if they don't, suggest that it's something they should look into. Alumni services should be particularly interested in helping you, since their main focus is to keep alumni engaged. What better way to do that than this? (And, hey, if you land a job with a great salary, you'll probably be donating more to the school down the line.)

+ **Your network.** It's crucial that you talk to real people. Make it a goal to talk to at least six people with a similar job or title, half of whom should be white men (because statistically they are likely to be making the most), about their salary range. If there isn't anyone in your immediate circle who has the information you need, go beyond those you know. As you learned in the networking chapter, the value of your network is not just who *you* know but also who *they* know. When you reach out to the Portal People, give them the information they need to easily forward you on to their friends.

Here's an email Reece sent to one of her best-networked friends (or Portal Person) when she first began looking for work:

Question about salary

ashley.t.louise@gmail.com

Question about salary

Hi Ashley,

Hope this email finds you well :)

I just sent in a job application and want to make sure I'm ready to negotiate when/if they give me an offer I was hoping either you or someone in your network could help me figure out what to charge. In my research, the range seems to be $80-110k. I'm curious if I'm off base and if so, any suggestions of where to look or people to ask. Any help is appreciated and please don't hesitate to reach out to me, if I can support you.

Here's some context that should hopefully be helpful.

About the company/position

- It's a management consulting company (recently acquired by Accenture), focused on helping companies build new products, brands, services, and business models
- Based in New York
- There are approx. 400 employees
- The position is called "Inventor" and it [FILL IN THE BLANK]

About me

- I have seven years' experience
- Got my master's degree from the London School of Economics
- Speak Farsi

Sans Serif   T   **B** *I* U A   ☰   ☷ ☰ ☰ ☲ " & ✗

Everyone has a different relationship with money. Some women have told me they know they make more than their friends so they don't want to make them feel bad by talking about it (somehow, I can't imagine a man saying that).

My response to them is: What if, by talking about how much your salary is with friends, it actually helps them make *more* money? What if, by having a few conversations, you could ultimately wind up making $20,000 more? Does that mean your silence is worth $20,000? The more information you have, the stronger your negotiation will be. Talking about money may be uncomfortable, but your livelihood depends on it. Here are a few ways to approach it, as recommended by negotiation coach Alexandra Dickinson:

HOW TO (POLITELY) INQUIRE ABOUT SOMEONE'S SALARY

1. Here's the ballpark salary I found for a position like yours; am I off base?

2. What's the ballpark salary you make?

3. Do you make more than [INSERT NUMBER]? *If they say yes, ask again but increase it by $10k. Go up or down based on their response. Even if they are hesitant to keep answering down to the nearest $10k, you'll still be able to get valuable information.*

CHOOSE YOUR NUMBERS

Salaries are calculated according to what's called a pay band, or range. The research you've done will give you a sense of what an appropriate range for this position would be. Within that range, select three numbers that will act as guardrails, giving you a framework within which to negotiate. Whatever number they begin with is just a starting point. Very rarely is it a final offer. So, having multiple numbers in your back pocket will help you know what to counter with.

THE GUARDRAILS

1. **Fuck You Money.** This is the number at the top of the pay band. If the number makes you feel uncomfortable, good. It means you're pushing yourself. Say it out loud, in the mirror, and to a friend, pushing past any discomfort. The more you repeat it, the more you will believe it. In the past, I remember quoting a high number and feeling absolutely terrified (and a bit of imposter syndrome). But now when I look back, that number seems small compared to what I make now. If you're nervous, remind yourself that in the future this number won't be so intimidating.

2. **Feelin' Good Money.** This is the number, most likely in the middle of the pay band, which you would be happy to take.

3. **No Thanks, I Respect Myself Too Much Money.** Otherwise known as your bottom line, this is the lowest you'll go before walking away. It's important to take your time to figure this out so you can feel confident to firmly stand your ground when it's

time to negotiate. It's too easy for this number to slide lower and lower as you negotiate, especially if you're afraid to lose the opportunity. Your goal here is to understand what you're willing to financially sacrifice, and why, in exchange for a job opportunity. Remember that whatever you get will most likely go up only incrementally for the duration of this job (the typical cost of living increases are usually around 1–2 percent per year), so you have to be able to live with that, or be willing to walk away; in order to be a strong negotiator, you need strong alternatives, which can come in the form of financial security like a savings account, another job offer, or a side hustle.

When you really want—or need—a job, it can be easy to find yourself agreeing to a salary below your bottom line. It's important to take an inventory of your finances to make sure you're not sacrificing what you need to live comfortably, pay off debt, and save for the future; your salary needs to be viable in the long term. However, money isn't the only factor to consider. Make a list of all the benefits the company gives you, whether the perks make your life easier (such as free meals or a short commute) or they are something you can leverage for the future (such as new skills or an impressive job title). Assessing the value this job brings to you beyond the compensation will help you make an informed decision on what financial sacrifices you're willing to make. In other words, it is a cost-benefit analysis.

Here is a three-step process for exploring your relationship with money, understanding your goals, and looking long-term.

WHAT'S YOUR BOTTOM LINE?

1. **Put together your basic budget.** To determine your bottom line, you first have to know what you're spending. When you make your budget, include all the nonnegotiable expenses (student loans, rent, food, savings, etc.) but also add in all the things that you love spending money on, like travel, a gym membership, or going out with friends. A good framework is allocating 50 percent of your income to the essential (your "needs"), 30 percent to fun stuff (your "wants"), and 20 percent to your savings or paying off debt. Remember that this should be your income *after* taxes.

2. **Make a list of the ways this job will benefit you.** I call this your list of "perks." For example, will you gain skills you can leverage for your next job? Will it look great on your résumé? Will you amass a large network? Or it could be a short commute—that's certainly a perk.

3. **Create a spreadsheet with two columns.** In one column list the job perks, and in the other, the "fun" expenses from the budget you drew up. If they offer you a salary that's below what you were expecting, what will you be willing to financially sacrifice? And are the perks of the job worth it? Weigh the perks of the job against the extras that a higher salary might have afforded you. What feels more important in the long run?

FULL COMPENSATION

The negotiation doesn't end with the salary. There are things you can and should ask for besides money. It's what's called full compensation, also known as "full comp." These are things that bring you value and that cost the company little to nothing monetarily. Examples of full compensation include things like working from home, reimbursement for school, or more vacation days. Just because a company isn't able to give you a higher salary doesn't mean they can't afford full comp. Many companies have separate budgets for these benefits, so even though they may have allocated a certain amount for your compensation, it doesn't mean there isn't more available for career development, for example. As the cliché goes, money doesn't buy happiness—sometimes it's better to take less and negotiate for something nonfinancial that is extremely valuable to you.

Before you discuss full comp with them, prioritize for yourself what things are most important to you. Since they likely won't give you everything, you need to be firm about what you value most. In the negotiation, start with the salary. Once you've gotten them to agree to the highest amount, tell them you want to discuss full comp. If you bring up full comp too soon, they might use it as leverage to give you less money. (That being said, if there's something that's a deal breaker for you, mention it earlier.)

EXAMPLES OF FULL COMPENSATION

✦ Schedule flexibility

✦ Vacation days

✦ Flexible start date

+ Moving costs

+ Tuition reimbursement

+ Executive coaching

+ Conference tickets

+ Travel costs

+ Cell phone bill

+ Title change

+ Timetable for review

+ Scope of responsibilities

+ Commission

+ Bonus structure

+ Equity

+ Expense account

Reflect on what you want and how you can present it as a benefit to the business. Anticipate any pushback so you can preemptively address it. For example, you might ask for schedule flexibility, making the case that your productivity would increase this way, as would your overall longevity in the role. (Now that nearly all companies have had the experience of an entire staff working remotely during the COVID-19 pandemic, they hopefully realize how productive we can be from home.) If they still hesitate, you could propose a check-in system, a weekly status report, or a project management tool to help you stay organized.

Another example is career development. Come with examples of classes and explain how you'll apply these new skills to your job. If there's a conference you want to attend, make the case that in addition to new skills, you'll widen your network, which could include potential clients and prospective hires.

Expect this process to take at least two rounds of back-and-forth. Each time reiterate your enthusiasm for the opportunity as well as the desire to work together to find a compromise.

Based on all of her research, Reece devised three total comp scenarios. She wrote everything down so when she got on the phone with the hiring manager, she'd have notes to refer back to. They included:

1. Tuition assistance to finish her graduate certificate in strategic management

2. Reimbursement of moving costs

3. Later start date (one week)

4. Formal end-of-year review to be considered for a promotion

As she prepared for the negotiation, Reece had a hard time committing to her Fuck You Money number. It took guts for her to even think that high. Her mom had never made even a third of her current salary and she was pretty sure her Fuck You Money number was the most her father had ever made. She started to have feelings of imposter syndrome again. "I was like, 'What do I have to offer that is worth $125,000? How dare I? I hardly have any experience; I'm a fraud if I ask for that.' My biggest fear was that I would convince them I was worth it [in negotiations] and then they would discover I was a fraud when my work was subpar."

Saying it out loud, over and over again, began to make it real. The more she said it, the more it went from "This is silly" to "Okay, one day" to "Okay, but maybe" to "Why not now?" to "Yes, WTF yes!" The number became even more real when she practiced negotiating with a few close friends. She did a good job role-playing with them; the question was, could she do it during the actual negotiation?

MAKE THE CASE

You're not going to get more money just because you deserve it (even though I know you do). You'll get it because you've convinced your prospective employer that you're a top performer who should get top dollar. Two concerns I hear all the time from women are that 1) they don't see their wins as accomplishments because in their words, they were "just doing their job"; or 2) they're afraid they won't be able to live up to their own hype. If they make themselves sound "too good," their employer will inevitably discover that they oversold themselves. (Hello, imposter syndrome!)

What I tell these women is that by talking about your work, you're showing the company what you can do for them. It doesn't matter whether it was "your job"; what's important is the impact you had. Quantify that as best as you can, phrasing it as "I did X measured by Y that resulted in Z" and tie it to the bottom line. Even though it can sometimes feel like you're a cog in a wheel at work (especially at big companies), you are part of the ecosystem. The work you do impacts someone or something else, which in turn brings in (or saves) money.

By using numbers and data, you'll be able to make the strongest case possible for either getting a raise at your current job, or the salary you want at a new one. Can you show how your work makes the company money? If you work in communications, how many stories did you get placed, and how many people read those stories? How many products did you ship this year? Another example you could give is how you saved the company money. Whether that's getting a discount from a vendor or creating a more efficient way for your team to communicate (time is money), saving money is as good as making it.

Unsure of how your work contributed to the company's bottom line? Ask! Don't be afraid to be direct with your manager since understanding how you fit into the ecosystem will help you do your job better. "What is my impact here and how does it contribute to the financial success of this company?" Be sure to keep track of your accomplishments and have ongoing conversations throughout the year with your manager to make sure you're prioritizing the right things that get rewarded. (We'll talk more about that in Chapter Eight: Get Allies.) In terms of the fear of overhyping, just ask yourself: "Would a mediocre white man feel this way?" Chances are you're actually downplaying your abilities. So, sing your praises and sing 'em loud!

CALM YOUR NERVES

Knowing what and how you're going to ask is the easier part. The harder part is handling your nerves. Asking for money can be high stakes, so it's no surprise that it makes many of us super anxious. The best remedy is to acknowledge your fears by writing them down and saying them out loud to a friend. By doing that, you're getting out of your head and into an objective place, so they stop clouding your ability to ask for what you want. Then you can start prepping for the actual process.

Prepping doesn't just mean practicing in front of a mirror. To make this as "real" as possible, find a friend and practice the scripts included at the end of this chapter. The more you practice, the more prepared—and confident—you'll feel. It's simple, it's straightforward, and it works.

Here are some exercises to help prepare for the anxiety we might feel when we negotiate:

RELAX

+ **Observe your body.** When you role-play with a friend, don't just practice your talking points. I want you to observe your body: When do you physically start to react? At what point do you feel your heart rate go up? When do your palms get sweaty? Don't fight it; rather, accept that this may—and probably will—happen during the actual negotiation. By not expecting to be perfect, you'll relieve a lot of the pressure we tend to put on ourselves. Plus, we often get triggered when emotion catches us by surprise. So, by observing beforehand what comes up, you'll find that it may dissipate more quickly when it inevitably happens during the actual negotiation.

+ **Pick a person.** Who are you negotiating for? It can be easier to advocate on behalf of someone else rather than for yourself, so thinking of a person you love or who relies on you can be helpful. This can inspire you during your preparation and become a source of strength for you during the negotiation itself.

+ **Pretend you're in a movie.** The day of the negotiation, from when you wake up in the morning through the negotiation itself, it can help to imagine you're watching yourself in a movie. You're the main character. We always root for the main character and things usually work out for them. They always go through a journey of ups and downs and as viewers, we know that whatever they're experiencing, it leads to something else. Your story doesn't end with your negotiation. This visualization can help you distance yourself from intense emotions in the moment and remain aware of the bigger picture.

THE DOUBLE BIND

Negotiating as women has an extra set of challenges that need to be factored in. And for women who are further marginalized by their race, sexual orientation, religion, or physical ability, it's even more difficult. This is what's called the Double Bind; having to consider how people react to you when you act outside of the social norms of what you're expected to be. For example, you may simply be asserting yourself or backing up your opinion in a meeting (or even out socially), but others might perceive your assertiveness negatively, as aggression or bossiness. Women of color in particular suffer from the Double Bind, because they have to combat both racism and sexism.

I've spoken to a lot of women who are aware of the Double Bind but as though they're "giving in" to it by allowing it to influence their behavior when they ask for something they want. I don't deny that it's a very complicated issue. It's my personal feeling that we can recognize that this hurdle exists and use our awareness of it to get into roles that will allow us to chip away at it, until we can finally consider it a thing of the past. You can acknowledge that the Double Bind exists without compromising or contorting yourself. Here are a few ways to do it:

OVERCOME THE DOUBLE BIND

✦ **Speak communally.** Words like "we" and "us" signify that although you're advocating for yourself, you understand that this isn't just about you and that your salary is part of a larger system. Reference the team and larger company goals; that being said, because of our tendency to downplay or discount our accomplishments, be careful about doing this too much.

✦ **Put yourself in their shoes.** What pressure is the person you're negotiating with under? How do you think they feel about this negotiation? Having empathy for the other side is crucial for a successful negotiation. Plus, you can speak to their concerns when you make your case. Acknowledging their goals will go a long way. For example, "I understand that the budget is tight this year, so what can we do to find a solution that works for both of us?"

✦ **Be aware of your body language**. Most of our communication is nonverbal. Are you smiling? Are you crossing your arms? Are you keeping eye contact? There are studies that show when humans positively interact, they mimic each other. So however the other side is holding their body, it's a good indication of how you should be. To test out this theory, next time you are in conversation, play a little game where you scratch your nose or cross your legs. It's highly likely the other person will do the same a few seconds later.

IT'S GO TIME

You're well researched, you have your three numbers, and you know your wins. But that's not enough. The key to a successful negotiation is practicing. Again. And again. On the following pages are some of the scenarios that you may encounter, and a few different ways to handle them. There isn't a one-size-fits-all approach, so you will have to evaluate and react in the moment with what feels most true to you and your situation. But having a plan is key!

✦ **Scenario #1: They ask how much you currently make or made.** Depending on where you live, this may actually be illegal. The salary history ban bars companies from using a candidate's previous pay to determine how much to offer them. This is meant to help marginalized groups who typically make less, so that their low pay isn't compounded over time. As of this writing, seventeen states have salary history bans, as do seventeen municipalities. Unfortunately, Michigan and Wisconsin have actually banned the ban; according to Salary.com, it's now illegal for local governments in those states to forbid employers from asking for your salary history.

Even if they're legally allowed to ask, it's not a relevant question, especially if you were previously underpaid. If you don't feel comfortable telling them, here are two things you can say: "My boss prefers I keep that number confidential," or "I make in the low five figures."

If they continue to press you, *don't* lie. Simply remind them that this salary was offered before you gained the skills and experience you now have and can bring to this new job. Then you can go into what those skills and experience are. By pivoting to your achievements, you're now taking back control of the conversation.

✦ **Scenario #2: They ask how much you want to make.** There's varying advice out there on whether or not you should be the first to say your number. I personally think it's easier to negotiate from your number rather than theirs (assuming they'll lowball you). If your number is rooted in the market and you can back it up with evidence, why wouldn't you aim high? You can also cite all the places you did research, so they see that it's based on market realities, and not random. If you still feel uncomfortable being the first to say it, here are some ways to respond:

+ "I'd love to give you a figure but I'm afraid I may go too high and lose the opportunity. If you can share your budget, maybe that will help us get to a figure that works for both of us."

+ "According to my research, a person with my experience typically makes between X and Y. Because I'm a top performer, I'd be looking for the higher end." Then share examples of the accomplishments that make you deserving.

+ "You have a reputation for paying a competitive salary. I expect to fit within your range. Can you tell me what it is for this position?"

If you're filling out an online application for a job and it asks for salary information, one option is to put your Feelin' Good number; sometimes companies use applicant tracking systems where applications are put through an algorithm that filters for certain keywords. Since the goal is to secure an interview, picking a salary in the middle of the band should increase your chances. Once you actually have the interview and learn more about the scope of the job, you can present your market research and make the case for a higher number. If you are a strong candidate and they want you, they shouldn't take you out of consideration for not providing a salary history or requirement. And if they do, they're probably not a good fit for you, either.

+ **Scenario #3: They lowball you.** It can be startling if they lowball you and you are not quite sure how to respond.

Tell them you were looking for [INSERT FUCK YOU MONEY], reiterating that you're a top performer, using past accomplishments as evidence. If they say that's still too high, you can counter with your [INSERT FEELIN' GOOD NUMBER]. Here are some ways to start the discussion:

✦ "[Lowball] is a good starting point, but I was thinking [INSERT FUCK YOU MONEY]. What can we figure out together to get us closer to what I'm looking for?"

✦ "I definitely understand budgeting issues, and I want to be as flexible as possible to work with your team. I'm excited about joining your company and would like to explore whether [Feelin' Good] is possible given my specific experience and skill set."

Then be quiet. Silence is supremely powerful.

✦ **Scenario #4: You lowballed yourself.** Eek! Sometimes no matter how much we prepare, our nerves get the best of us and we lose our cool. I've been there. If you've offered a lower number than you meant to, you can't go back, but you *can* remind them that you're aware it's below market and you hope that it demonstrates how much you want to work there. You could say: "I'm aware this number is below market rate for someone in this position with my years of experience. Because of that, I'd love to explore full compensation and an accelerated promotion schedule [or a signing bonus if that makes sense]."

✦ **Scenario #5: They just won't budge.** It may take a few conversations to get to a compromise. If after two rounds they still won't budge, this is the time to bring up full compensation again. You should also ask when you can have another discussion and what exactly they need to see from you in order to get closer to the number you were asking for.

SHE GOT THE NUMBER

Reece was getting out of the shower when she got the call. They were giving her her Fuck You Money! Though her impulse was to scream "YES, I'LL TAKE IT!" she knew better. In her words, "I still had the audacity to go for more." And she did. After a few deep breaths and a silent celebration, she responded, "That's a great place to start."

Reece got out the notes she'd already prepared and asked for the additional $3,000 tuition reimbursement, a later start date, and evaluation of her work to be considered for a promotion by the end of the year, all of which she had determined could move the needle for her. She also asked to be reimbursed for moving costs, received as something she could expense back to the company instead of a bonus (thus avoiding paying taxes on it). The recruiter said he would need to get back to her. It felt amazing to get a verbal offer, but she knew it wasn't done until they got her the details in writing and it was signed. Again, she would have to wait.

Fortunately, she didn't have to wait long. The next day, as she was standing in line at the grocery store, her inbox dinged. There it was. She couldn't believe what it said: *She'd gotten everything she'd asked for.* She'd barely read the offer letter when she started jumping up and down, doing a full-on dance of joy (yes, in public). Walking back home, she blasted Cardi B's "Money Bag," pausing a few times to let out a whoop.

Her bank account wasn't the only thing that changed that day. For years, Reece's friends and family had told her she was capable of accomplishing anything she put her mind to. Now she finally believed them. "I had just proven to myself that I was worth it, even if I had been at an organization that didn't value me. Yelling my Fuck You Money number out loud over and over again sunk in somewhere in my subconscious, because it worked." She also realized that more for her didn't mean it was a detriment for them. Her salary was not a favor.

Negotiating was a transformative experience because it showed Reece that she didn't have to accept everything she was given—she could ask for more. She also learned that you don't have to be born confident to be a good negotiator, making her feel even better about tackling new challenges in the future. Whatever was next, Reece thought, *bring it on.*

No matter how many times you negotiate in your life and how good you become at it, you might always get butterflies in your stomach; your palms might always turn sweaty. That's okay. It can be nerve-wracking when you want something and aren't sure if you'll get it. Don't let that deter you. Trust that if you've rooted your ask in data, demonstrated your good work, and expressed your enthusiasm, they will be open to finding a compromise. And if they aren't, maybe you don't want to work there anyway.

CHAPTER SEVEN

GET BALANCED

Amy had been in the same room for almost five hours straight. All day there were back-to-back meetings as the company was gearing up to launch a new payroll product. Everyone was there: the VP of marketing, the head of sales training, and Amy's boss, the head of product. Even though she wasn't expected to present anything, Amy thought it was important that she show her face. After five years as a teacher, Amy had recently made a pivot into the tech industry, where she'd landed a customer service job at a midsize company that provided HR solutions. She was insecure about starting behind everyone else, but was confident that if she worked hard, she would catch up quickly.

Amy looked at her watch; she hadn't had anything to eat all day except for an apple and a handful of popcorn. Things didn't look like they would let up anytime soon, so she figured she'd have to make it at least another two hours. With less and less time left in the day, Amy started to worry that she wouldn't have enough time after the meeting to get her actual work done. She resigned herself to staying at the office an extra couple of hours after this was all over.

Suddenly, Amy was jolted out of her worries. Something was dripping down her leg. To her horror, it struck her that she had just gotten her period. She froze. What should she do? If she got up and walked out, everyone would look at her. She could imagine her boss's disapproving face; no one else had gotten up to use the bathroom. If Amy wanted to show her commitment, she had to stay. She just prayed she wouldn't bleed through her pants.

BE CAREFUL

Once you land a job you care about, you'll probably want to jump in, guns blazing. Be careful. Our eagerness to please and our desire to prove ourselves mean that we often invest so much energy into the day-to-day that we lose sight of ourselves and what we really want. As you saw in Chapter One: Get Aligned, without pause and self-reflection, it's difficult to know if we're headed in the direction we want.

It's not as easy as simply saying no or refusing to work. As women, we are expected to be accommodating, and so negotiating our boundaries, as much as we might want to, often doesn't seem to be an option; we don't want to jeopardize our relationships or our jobs. We're afraid that if we push back against our bosses it might make us look unwilling, incapable, or worse, as if we're complaining.

The result? A combustible combination of internal voices and external pressures that can result in resentment, anxiety, burnout, and depression, all playing out within an environment where working 24/7 is looked at as a badge of honor. Because of technology, which makes it possible to work from anywhere at any time, on-demand availability becomes the expectation. If we do any less, will we look like slackers? Will we be sidelined, or even fired?

Millennials have been dubbed the "burnout generation," suffering from it more than any other cohort. We're crippled by student debt (women hold the majority of it) and graduating into the financial crisis of 2008 has left an indelible, collective trauma where job prospects feel fleeting and we feel dispensable. COVID-19 and its aftermath have only made it worse. There is no real safety net to lessen the load, and the lack of affordable childcare and paid family leave, plus entrenched gender norms mean women carry the biggest burden out of everyone.

In this chapter, you'll follow Amy as she struggles to learn—and implement—boundaries and self-care. For as long as she can remember, Amy has measured her worth by how hard she could push herself, and burning out was a sign that she was doing her best. To embrace a new way of operating, she needs to understand the deep damage she was in-flicting upon herself. Eventually this allows her to give it her all, though within the boundaries she set.

You will also meet Giselle, who as a Black woman carries an even bigger burden. Women of color are often looked at as simultaneously threatening and less competent. That, coupled with both overt and in-sidious racism, has devastating consequences for Giselle emotionally, physically, and financially.

Our well-intentioned attempt to serve our jobs and others cannot come at the expense of our health and well-being. When our energy be-gins to be pulled away—whether by our own impossible standards or the invisible emotional labor we're expected to perform—having the tools to replenish ourselves is essential.

One of the things I hope you gain from reading this book is the abil-ity to step back and look holistically at your life and what place your work has in it. Ideally, you can use that knowledge to be intentional about the choices you make and then make educated decisions about what is best not just for your career but for your life as a whole. Ultimately, the goal is to find balance, whatever that looks and feels like to you.

I'm not talking about not working hard or not paying your dues. What I am talking about is working at such a blistering and relentless pace that we cannot see where we're headed or if we can sustain ourselves long enough to get there. Building a successful career requires endurance, and to do that, we must learn good habits from the beginning that keep us from going overboard. We have to learn how to identify the warning signs of burnout and how to rejuvenate ourselves. We need to know when to say no and then have the courage to actually do it.

PAY ATTENTION TO THE WARNING SIGNS

Almost immediately after she started her new job, Amy's manager quit. With no real guidance, Amy tried to keep her head above water, unsure of whom to go to when she needed support. So she did the best she could, staying quiet, and hoping that she was doing what was expected of her. Things seemed to pay off when, six months later, Amy was asked to work on a special new initiative, run by a team that brought together people from various departments. This would be a chance to get some real experience under her belt and show that she was capable of taking on more complex work. However, it quickly became apparent that she was expected to continue her current role with no accommodations made for the additional work she was taking on. Amy started coming in two hours early and staying later than most of her peers. Her days were now consumed by meetings for this new role, with little time for her to do the work she was actually hired to do. She was now effectively working two full-time jobs with no additional pay, no title change, and no end in sight.

Time away from the office provided no reprieve; when she wasn't working, she was still *thinking* about working. On top of the pressure from her superiors, Amy also felt a personal responsibility to the 70,000 people her company provided healthcare coverage for. If she made even a minor mistake, it could cause serious negative consequences in someone's life. She began to experience insomnia, lying in bed, going over and over all the things she needed to get done at work the next day. When she finally did fall asleep, she'd wake up a few hours later, her mind racing.

Working on two teams, Amy constantly felt pulled in different directions. She knew that confirming priorities with the project lead would probably help, but she was concerned that in bringing up her workload, she might be looked at as if she weren't up for the challenge, or worse, incompetent. So she pushed through, rationalizing that if she just kept working hard she would eventually be rewarded. She calculated that exhausting herself in the short term was a small price to pay in service of what would hopefully be long-term payoff.

BURNOUT BEGINS

Amy was accustomed to moving so fast that she didn't diagnose or take seriously the warning signs that were leading her down the path to burnout. Amy was losing weight and her chronic neck pain was worsening, but she didn't have time to deal with them. To Amy, this was par for the course. In fact, it was an indication to her that she was pushing herself to do and be the best she could: "I exercise all the time until I'm injured. I train for half marathons and there's always supposed to be a rest day. I'll just go, 'I don't believe in the rest day,' because why would you rest?"

One of Amy's favorite compliments was being told how much self-control she had. But these days, it seemed that the more Amy pushed herself, the more out of control she felt. It wasn't unusual for her to feel so stressed and overwhelmed that she'd break down in tears when she got home at the end of a long day.

When her friends started to disappear, Amy didn't view that as a warning sign, either. She didn't have much time to see them anyway, she rationalized. On the rare occasion she did, she was like a zombie, completely checked out, barely able to engage. Though her friends were understanding at first, eventually they stopped calling her back.

Amy began to spiral. She knew she was being a bad friend, but was she a bad person? Amy realized she didn't have much of a life outside of work. Even worse than that, she didn't even love her job. Now she was starting to numbly move through her days in a fog. Amy needed to make a change, but she had no clue what to do, or how.

The goal is to catch the warning signs before you get burned out. The Mayo Clinic recommends asking yourself the following key questions to determine if you have burnout symptoms:

CATCH THE WARNING SIGNS

+ Have you become cynical or critical at work?

+ Do you drag yourself to work and have trouble getting started?

+ Have you become irritable or impatient with coworkers, customers or clients?

+ Do you lack the energy to be consistently productive?

+ Do you find it hard to concentrate?

+ Do you lack satisfaction from your achievements?

+ Do you feel disillusioned about your job?

+ Are you using food, drugs, or alcohol to feel better, or to simply not feel?

◆ Have your sleep habits changed?

◆ Are you troubled by unexplained headaches, stomach or bowel problems, or other physical complaints?

THE BREAKING POINT

One night, Amy came home from work and collapsed. She began to hysterically and uncontrollably cry; it was as if a dam had broken. She couldn't stop. Pretty soon she started hyperventilating and felt a tightness in her chest that made her wonder whether she was having a heart attack. (She was, in fact, having a panic attack.) Nothing happened that day that would've elicited this kind of heightened reaction—things were actually going pretty well. "I didn't have the words to describe where all this was coming from. I was suddenly so aware of how sad and scared I was. I'd spent months feeling all this anxiety, stress, and pressure, and I had definitely reached the point where I didn't feel like a whole person. I didn't even feel like half of one. I had this moment of, *'I don't know why I'm doing this anymore. And I don't know how to get out of this hole.'"*

For the next few weeks, Amy felt like she was constantly holding back tears; it was as if she'd lost all control and her emotions had taken over. While Amy may not have been intellectually conscious of what all this pressure had been doing to her, her body knew. It had stored everything up until it no longer could handle the stress. She needed professional help.

But Amy felt guilty for even feeling this way. In her mind, her problems were insignificant; after all, she was just trying to cope with work—everyone was stressed about their job. The thought of telling someone about her situation made her feel embarrassed. Still, desperate to feel calmer, Amy started googling self-care, but then that, too, made her feel guilty, even silly. Facials, spa visits . . . it all felt so self-indulgent. Amy's resistance to self-care came from a lack of understanding of it, its origins, and all the different ways it can be implemented.

Prior to the 1960s, self-care was a medical concept, usually used in reference to mentally ill and elderly patients. Academics also used the term to define coping mechanisms for those working in high-stakes and emotionally intense lines of work (for example, firefighters and EMTs). During the civil rights era, self-care became a means of survival. Shut out of the mainstream medical establishment, people of color needed to take their care into their own hands. Led by the Black Panthers—and in particular, Black women—free medical clinics were opened up as a way of bringing justice and services to communities that were not just left behind by the healthcare system but actively excluded from it.

Like many other movements initiated and led by Black women, self-care was then co-opted: first in the 70s by those touting wellness (think granola and Birkenstocks), then morphing into a fitness-focused movement in the 80s (Jane Fonda's workout tapes), and finally becoming codified in the 90s with an explosion of gyms. Self-care had officially gone mainstream and business was booming.

Today, there is a billion-dollar industry of wellness influencers who tout the importance of clean eating, positive thinking, and probiotics. Similar to Jane Fonda, whole exercise methods have developed around cult personalities (think Tracy Anderson or Taryn Toomey), with individual classes priced at no less than $35. While the commitment to health is of course a good thing, self-care has become synonymous with wealth, whiteness, and time. If you work at a demanding job (or have multiple jobs), there seems to be little room in your schedule—and bank account—for self-care.

But it doesn't have to be this way. Self-care is about taking care of oneself, and that can come in many different forms (free of charge). It turns out you don't have to buy a $5,700 ticket to the GOOP Wellness Summit to feel good about yourself.

In order for Amy to be willing to explore self-care, she needed to shift her mindset and get over her preconceived notions about it. She had to learn to practice self-care in her own way.

IT GETS WORSE BEFORE IT GETS BETTER

In the weeks after her panic attack, Amy began to see a therapist. She discovered that her drive to push herself to the limit was a way of distracting herself from deeper, painful truths in her life that she needed to confront in order to move past them. For example, her father rarely praised her growing up, focusing instead on her flaws or fumbles. Amy has memories of him videotaping her sports games and then making her watch them afterward so he could point out all the mistakes she made. It was no wonder Amy worked herself into the ground.

She realized that while she'd intellectually distanced herself from those memories, her body still carried them. It was only now that Amy identified it as the source of her chronic neck pain.

Though she resisted it at first (it felt too "woo-woo"), Amy adopted a meditation practice. She started small—five minutes in the morning—and when she became more comfortable sitting still, she added another five minutes until she was doing twenty minutes daily. Meditating and doing breathwork helped her slow down and get in touch with her body.

If meditation and breathwork doesn't feel right to you, find an activity that will have the same effect of pulling you off your usual frantic path and getting you attuned to your body. For many people it's doing something physical, which is good for your health, but be careful: Are you going overboard? Do you need movement or stillness? The goal here is to really listen to your body and what it needs. Working out, at least for Amy, was a way to blow off steam (which is great), but she often pushed herself too far. Until you can learn your limits, try an activity where you get quiet with yourself.

FOCUS ON WELLNESS

Before you set boundaries, you have to see where you need to set them in the first place. It begins with taking an inventory of where you are spending the majority of your time and energy. How available are you making yourself logistically and emotionally? Are you spending your energy in a sustainable way?

Once you do that, you can decide where and how to make adjustments. For example, when Amy analyzed what she was spending most of her time on at work, she realized that there were a number of tasks that could be delegated to someone else (in fact, she was probably not the right person to do them in the first place). She also saw where she needed support, which got her thinking about the best way to make the case that she should have a direct report.

In addition to tracking your time, it's good to conduct a more holistic assessment of your general wellness. When, where, and why do you feel your energy start to deplete? The only way to know that is to examine your schedule in detail over the course of at least two weeks.

WELLNESS ASSESSMENT

✦ **Where are you spending your energy?** Track what you do, hour by hour, for two weeks. You can do this using a tool like Brendon Burchard's High Performance Planner, or by creating your own spreadsheet. By tracking and analyzing your time, you'll be able to see where your energy is being drained and what tasks can be redirected or removed entirely. For example, are there things you can automate? Delegate? How often are you checking social media or being distracted by non-work-related things? In short, the goal is to work "smarter" and not harder.

✦ **Note when you feel particularly anxious or agitated.** For the same period that you track your energy, also note when you start to feel any kind of negativity, whether it's anxiety or agitation. For example, maybe it's the constant pings of a new email, or maybe it's an overwhelming workload. Getting in the habit of checking in with yourself and your whole range of feelings will help you prevent the emotional buildup that can lead to burnout, as we saw in Amy's case.

After analyzing where your time and energy are going, see where and how you can make adjustments. It's important to be proactive in establishing good habits, but you also want to have a plan for what to do when you start to feel anxious or overwhelmed. Here are Amy's three major energy drainers, and some solutions she could enact:

✦ Overflowing inbox

✦ Long commute to work

✦ Overwhelming workload (including endless meetings and calls)

CONQUER YOUR INBOX

✦ **Create labels and filters to easily find what you're looking for.** As a way to prioritize, group emails by urgency; for example, Today, This Week, This Month.

✦ **Create an email ritual.** Limit how many times you check it (it can help to use a plug-in like Inbox Zero to "hide" it). Decide when and where you're going to check your inbox. If it tends to be a stressful experience for you, can you make your environment make you feel better? For example, light a candle and play nice music.

✦ **Start from the end of the chain.** It will have the most information—things may have already been resolved and don't need a response (i.e., don't waste your time).

✦ **Stop playing tag.** How many times do you go back and forth with someone, trying to schedule a call or a meeting? Sometimes that can take more time than the meeting itself! Avoid the back-and-forth by using a scheduling app like Calendly.

✦ **Put up an away message.** Doing that sets the expectation of when the sender may get a response, plus it provides a person to contact if it's urgent. Then don't check your email. Seriously! The world isn't ending without you (probably).

◆ **Don't be afraid to delete.** If you've gone through your inbox and responded to urgent or important emails, don't feel obligated to respond to everyone. Your time is more valuable than anything else and you have to protect it. Trust that if it's really important, that person will follow up with you. As soon as you read and respond to an email, delete or archive it. Having an empty inbox is heaven.

Amy could try to negotiate for work-from-home days to minimize her overall time spent commuting, or she can find ways to make it more enjoyable. If you also have a long commute, use the time to focus on things you enjoy (such as podcasts or catching up on sleep), rather than work in the form of calls or emails; you might find that you actually start thinking of it as "me time."

If you're generally feeling overwhelmed, you'll most likely need to talk to your manager about setting some boundaries. However, there are also good habits you can establish that will help prevent you from getting overwhelmed in the first place.

LIGHTEN THE LOAD

◆ **Stop multitasking.** First of all, there's no such thing. It's really just changing quickly between tasks. While this may make you feel like you're getting a lot done, it's actually hurting your ability to stay focused. Plus, when you multitask, you're setting yourself up to feel guilty since you're never really giving enough attention to any one thing. It's better to do a great job on fewer things than a half-assed job on many.

+ **Schedule your day and week accordingly.** This is unique to the individual. You know your work style, your energy and concentration levels (throughout the day and the week), and what is actually possible given your workload and how your company operates. If possible, pick set days that are dedicated to calls and meetings, for example, and others that are mostly for longer blocks of uninterrupted concentration.

+ **Prioritize.** The best way to safeguard against feeling overwhelmed or scattered is to prioritize. Spend time at the end of each day arranging your tasks for tomorrow according to what's urgent, important, and nonessential. Oftentimes we categorize things as urgent when they're not and can actually be delegated to someone else. (If you need help figuring out how to do this, revisit Chapter Three.) We can also overestimate how quickly we're able to get things done, so select your top priorities carefully. Sometimes you'll need to rearrange priorities throughout the week, or even throughout the day, so be flexible. But rest assured that if you've accomplished the things you prioritized, you are doing a good job. It's better to spend more time upfront planning and optimizing so you don't constantly feel like you're playing catch-up.

+ **Take breaks.** Too often we dismiss taking breaks as something that will take time away from getting things done, when in fact it helps us do our jobs better. Our brains need it. To make it more likely you'll actually take a break, plan something you'll do during it. Even if it's sitting still with your eyes closed for five minutes, having something tangible and specific to look forward to will make it feel purposeful while also giving your brain a break.

To make sure she had time to adequately recharge, Amy blocked off an hour in the middle of the day, whether it was to go for a walk or eat her lunch in a common space rather than in front of her computer. Amy also began limiting her hours in the office, coming to work at 9:00 a.m. and leaving at 5:00 p.m., moving any unfinished tasks to the next morning. One key piece for Amy was putting these recharge times on the calendar to signal to everyone else that this was her time. She also started speaking up about how she best received information; instead of having hundreds of Slack messages constantly pinging her, she asked her team to consolidate and send information by email, only reaching out via Slack if it was a true emergency.

While setting these boundaries worked for a few weeks, they weren't as sustainable as Amy had hoped. Sometimes there were meetings she couldn't get out of, and so taking an hour of lunch simply wasn't possible. The solution was to reclaim her time in other ways. That might mean a thirty-minute lunch one day and leaving fifteen minutes early other days that week. Or if thirty minutes at one time wasn't feasible, she could take three ten-minute breaks throughout the day, going outside where no one could stop by her desk to ask her something. She also started bringing in her own food so she wouldn't be held hostage by whatever sugary snacks were in the office. (Sugar is the first thing you should cut if you don't want to crash.)

REPLENISH YOURSELF

If you work somewhere where you can't reduce the workload, it's important to find ways to balance and refuel. The goal is to be both aware of and proactive about where we dedicate our time and energy, and to understand how you can fill yourself back up when you get depleted. What are things you can do for yourself right now and on an ongoing basis that replenish you? The following chart has examples that can help identify what will recharge your batteries. As you identify the activities that will fill your own chart, make sure there are enough activities that are low cost and low time commitments, so you'll increase the chance you'll stick to them.

If you've been operating at breakneck speed for a long time, it's unrealistic to assume you can just snap your fingers and change your life. Here's the good news: none of this requires tectonic shifts, but rather tweaks in perspective and behaviors. The best way to introduce a new behavior is by integrating it into a current habit.

For example, the beginning of my day used to be a time of anxiety—my mind would instantly race to my current to-do list, reminding me of all the things I needed to get done. I decided to work on short-circuiting this response. When I wake up in the morning, I usually feel like I'm running behind. Now when I put on a cup of coffee, instead of waiting impatiently for it to brew, I use this time to activate all my senses with a mini meditation. I smell the fragrance, I feel the warmth of the cup, I taste the bitterness. It takes less than a few minutes, a reminder that it doesn't require much to slow down and shift your focus to being in the moment rather than in your head. The key is to be *consistent*, otherwise any new behavior or even a changed mindset won't take root and create lasting change.

GIVES ME ENERGY	(REALISTIC) COMMITMENT
Take a walk	Once a day, at 4:00 p.m. (afternoon slump)
Get a massage	Every 6 weeks
Reduce screen time	Don't look at my phone past 8:00 p.m. (or if you struggle with willpower, use your phone's built-in screen time alerts)
Exercise	Do a 20-minute home workout twice per week and attend weekly spin class (have a friend hold you accountable)

SET BOUNDARIES

Therapist and writer Lia Avellino believes that the difficulty in setting a boundary comes from the misconception that it will be seen as alienating to the people around you when, in fact, boundaries are a way of bringing people closer. It takes vulnerability to express a need, and it signals to the other person that you want to do your best work—and that together, you will figure it out.

Setting boundaries can cause discomfort for those who fear being seen as selfish. In her book *Rising Strong*, Brené Brown writes that "Compassionate people ask for what they need. They say no when they need to, and when they say yes, they mean it. They're compassionate because their boundaries keep them out of resentment." Setting boundaries isn't about helping yourself at the detriment of others; it's about finding balance and making sure that your needs are factored into the equation alongside the needs of those around you. Maybe you can't lessen your load at work, but you can make a change that makes it easier to carry.

Establishing boundaries is a negotiation. Just like discussing salary, bringing up what isn't working can feel uncomfortable. So when you talk to your manager, focus on contextualizing your needs and providing a solution that works for everyone. For example, one way Amy could cut down her commute would be to adjust what time she arrived and left as to avoid rush hour. Or when there was a project that required more hours than usual, she might ask for a three-day weekend when things died down. The key is to present the boundary as something that will help you do better work.

Here are some sample scripts for what to say when someone wants to pull you away from what you're doing.

HOW TO SET BOUNDARIES

+ **Your colleague asks you to help them with something:**

  + "Thanks for thinking of me! Unfortunately, I have a lot on my plate right now, so I don't think I'm the best person to help. Let me know if I can be of help later down the road."

+ **Your boss asks you to take on something new or outside your scope:**

+ "I'm concerned that if I take X on, it will distract from Y. Should I be prioritizing things differently?"

+ **Multiple coworkers have been asking you for help, so you decide to talk to your boss:**

  + "A lot of people have been approaching me to help with X. In theory, I'd love to help, but in reality, I don't have much time given the other things I'm working on. I wanted to flag it for you in case there are additional resources or support they can get. Or maybe there's someone else I should be directing them to?"

EMOTIONAL LABOR: MEET GISELLE

Unfortunately, if you're in a toxic environment, sometimes no amount of boundaries you set or adjustments you make will work. Depending on how damaging your situation is, the best solution might be to find another job. But for Giselle it seemed that every job was varying degrees of toxic.

As a Black woman, Giselle had experienced insidious and overt discrimination throughout her career. Her last job was particularly bad; it had a culture where people were territorial with their work and she felt repeatedly undermined by her boss.

Fortunately, she recently finished her doctorate in leadership and organizational behavior and now, with a degree in hand, landed a job at a prominent health system. As an executive coach, she would support leaders and design an organizational system to help improve the workplace culture. It was her dream job.

Stepping out onto the top floor of her new office building, as she surveyed the magnificent view, Giselle felt she'd made it (with the six-figure salary to match). On her first day, her boss (we'll call him "Bob"), an older white man, gave her a big binder with an overview of the department and her responsibilities as well as a list of the qualities he valued most. His number one request? That she be willing to push back if she had an idea or opinion different than his. This was a welcome surprise; in previous jobs, Giselle had learned that disagreeing could come at a cost and that her superiors weren't always happy when she voiced her opinions. Bob's desire to be challenged reassured Giselle that she had made the right decision in taking this job.

Right before Giselle started, a performance evaluation had been administered to 5,000 of the administrative staff. After she had been at the job for a short time, Bob called a team meeting to discuss the results. It didn't look good. In fact, it was really bad. Almost 70 percent of those reviewed received poor marks on their communication and managerial skills, including basic things like giving feedback or facilitating teamwork. As they discussed how to best address this, Bob declared, "In our department, we're like Stanford graduates. This health system? They're aboriginals. No matter what you do, they're just not going to get it." Giselle was stunned by the comment and had no idea how to respond. She debated speaking up at all, but then remembered the binder; he wanted her to push back. No one else looked like they were going to, so she did: "What you just said was really inappropriate." Bob protested, "No, you don't understand. Stanford graduates are really smart."

Bob's bigotry wasn't a one-time thing. Once when Giselle complimented his suspenders, he responded, "These aren't suspenders, suspenders are for poor people." (He preferred the term "braces.") When they were encouraged by the CEO to hire more people from the surrounding urban area, which was predominantly people of color, he joked that

Giselle would have to "figure out how to hire felons." Comments like these made her feel constantly on edge. She knew that speaking up could mean rocking the boat but staying silent made her feel sick. Every time Bob said something offensive, Giselle would question him, hoping that she could get him to realize his insensitivities. It was exhausting. At least Giselle felt reassured that she was doing the right thing; after all, he'd told her to push back.

It wasn't easy to do. Because she'd experienced negative consequences at other jobs when she'd voiced her opinions, she'd learned to keep quiet, often numbing herself to just make it through the day. She worked hard to counter the stereotype of the "angry Black woman," always going above and beyond to make others (mostly white men) comfortable. And she did all this while enduring insidious—sometimes imperceptible— acts of discrimination, which were felt but hard to define: these micro- aggressions were things like being singled out to take notes in a meeting, or when people were surprised to learn that she had a doctorate in health science.

What Giselle was experiencing was emotional labor. Coined by American sociologist Arlie Hochschild in her book *The Managed Heart: Commercialization of Human Feeling*, emotional labor is described as "in- ducing or suppressing feeling in order to sustain the outward counte- nance that produces the proper state of mind in others." In short, it's pri- oritizing the comfort of others, even at the expense of our well-being.

Emotional labor requires us to monitor ourselves and/or take on extra considerations in order to placate those around us. For example, listening to personal issues (being the "work wife"), smiling even when we don't feel like it, policing what we wear (it can't be too sexy, too loud, too fun, too cheap), or changing how we speak, whether it's uptalk or code switching.

Emotional labor is something all women experience, regardless of race. However, for women of color, it's compounded by the additional energy they spend trying to counter assumptions that they're not as smart or as hardworking as their white counterparts, as well as tempering their assertiveness in order to avoid being stereotyped—just as Giselle did to not be seen as the "angry Black woman."

Another phenomenon, no less prevalent, is what's termed "invisible labor." It's the work done (mostly by women) that makes life easier for everyone else. Invisible labor is usually used in reference to the lopsided division of responsibilities performed in a household (such as coordinating schedules or packing lunches), though it also extends to office life. For example, organizing going-away parties (and cleaning up afterward), remembering birthdays (and getting everyone to sign a card), or making coffee for a meeting (and then taking notes during it).

Sometimes we're asked to do these things, and sometimes we volunteer ourselves. Maybe we do it because we've always done it; or maybe we do it because we want to be recognized for going above and beyond. Ironically, performing invisible labor can have the opposite effect; a study by New York University psychologist Madeline Heilman found that women who stay late to help a coworker are ranked 14 percent less favorably than men who did the same thing. Invisible labor such as taking notes during a meeting can also undermine our authority. And as is so often the case, it's even worse for women of color. Not only do they tend to carry the most invisible labor, according to a UC Hastings College of Law study, Black and Latinx women in the workplace "report being regularly mistaken for cleaning ladies and janitors."

Sometimes we perform invisible labor because we're afraid there will be repercussions if we don't. This calculus is not entirely wrong. The same study that showed that women rank less favorably than men when they help coworkers also showed that if the women declined to help, they were rated 12 percent lower than a male peer who did the same. This kind of behavior circles back to the double bind we discussed in Chapter Six: Get Paid. We're constrained by gender norms and we can easily feel like we're left with no real option other than to be the good girls we were raised to be.

Despite the effort Giselle put into performing this balancing act, Bob nicknamed her AK-47. (So much for wanting to be challenged.) Still, she tried to make it work. She did some fact-finding, going to other people on the team to understand how to work with him better. They concurred that they, too, found him inappropriate and warned her to be careful. Alarmed, Giselle reached out to the person whom she had replaced, a woman named Morgan. She'd been there for six years and no doubt would have good advice; plus, she was also a Black woman, and would know the additional considerations that came with that.

Morgan told Giselle that to be successful in this job, it was best to laugh at Bob's jokes and ignore his offhand comments. She told Giselle about the ways she'd tried to manage the situation. When he'd ask Morgan to do nonsensical things, she did them anyway. She'd silenced herself in service of keeping the peace, which, in a sense, enabled him. Morgan carried the emotional labor that so many women do because for her, it was better to not rock the boat.

Giselle now understood that's what the problem was. She was hired with the expectation that she would be a "yes woman," just as her predecessor was. But now that Bob realized she wasn't, her assertiveness was grating to him. Maybe it was partially a mismatch of personality, but maybe it was the color of her skin. Did he assume that because she was Black, that she would be passive? It was impossible to know.

Two months later, during one of their weekly meetings, Bob offhandedly quipped, "I didn't think you were that smart when I interviewed you, but you are smart." Giselle was stunned.

All weekend, Giselle stewed, unable to forget his comment. Why would he say that to her? Why was she hired in the first place? Did it mean that all her experience and accolades and accomplishments were insignificant to him? "I think the important thing that a lot of people don't realize is that me showing up as a Black woman is radically threatening to anyone. The way we have to navigate as Black women is incredibly stressful because you have to think about other people's feelings, on top of your feelings of 'Am I good enough for this job?'" In other words, damned if you do, damned if you don't.

GISELLE TAKES A CHANCE

As scared as she was of the potential repercussions that came with pushing back, continuing to carry the load was crushing her. So, the following Friday, Giselle asked for a meeting.

"I just keep thinking about why you told me you didn't think I was smart initially; that statement was hurtful," she said. "Why would you say that?" Bob leaned back in his chair, as if trying to figure out if what he had said was offensive. He decided that yes, it probably was. "Yes, I guess it could be offensive. I'm sorry." Giselle was instantly flooded with relief. She felt proud that despite the potential consequences, she had prioritized her mental and emotional health. Because she brought up her concern, they could now rebuild a relationship based on mutual respect and trust.

Unfortunately, that never happened. The next week, Bob called Giselle into his office. "This isn't working," he said, handing her an envelope. She'd been fired.

This had never happened to Giselle before. She always left her previous jobs on her own terms for better opportunities. Faced with something new to her, she had to wonder, was it her? If she was fired for performance, that would be one thing, but she did what was asked—actually, *encouraged*—of her; it said so right in the binder. This *was* personal. She was let go for seemingly no other reason other than that Bob didn't like her. Maybe it was because she was Black. Giselle would never know.

But what she did know was that she had to do something about it. Reflecting on her career, Giselle concluded that the emotional burden she carried from previous toxic workplaces and the discrimination she endured was not because she was simply unlucky to have had bad bosses. It was the result of a system and institutions that not only tolerated this behavior but also enabled it. Giselle decided she needed to forge a new path.

Since earning her doctorate, she'd dabbled in consulting for companies on the side. Now, what was once a side hustle became a full-time job. Giselle founded her own consulting firm, with a purpose to help organizations strengthen their diversity, equity, inclusion, and belonging practices so that no woman, person of color, or marginalized employee has to go through what she did. Knowing firsthand the kind of mental and emotional fallout that can come from being in toxic work dynamics, she now gives presentations on the importance of mental health and support for women of color in the workplace. It turns out that being fired was the spark she needed to reclaim the effort of all that emotional labor and use it for good.

IDENTIFY INEQUITIES

If you've never experienced discrimination before, Bob's behavior might appear extreme. Sadly, for women of color, this might be a familiar experience. As awful as it is to be treated this way, at least the behavior is identifiably inappropriate, and would be more likely to be recognized as such by HR. The more universal but no less demeaning experience many women have is a message of inferiority largely communicated by three factors: the wage gap (particularly for mothers), the kind of work that we're assigned, and a general feeling that we don't belong.

If you're on a team or in a department where you're in the minority, you're not the status quo. This can be painfully obvious if your company doesn't make efforts to foster an inclusive culture. For example, in 2015 a team at Twitter hosted a "frat party," complete with Solo cups and kegs. To make things worse, this happened at the same time a lawsuit was filed by a former engineer who claimed that the process for promotion was not transparent and was biased in favor of men. But inclusivity doesn't just mean a lack of discrimination or tone-deafness. It requires efforts that are goal-oriented and done with purpose, and people who are held accountable. This could include diverse planning committees, thoughtful wording around what "culture fit" means, and support for employee resource groups (which we'll talk more about in Chapter Ten).

The kind of work that we're assigned can also signal a sense of inferiority. In an article in the *Harvard Business Review* by Joan Williams and Marina Multhaup, women, and women of color in particular, describe being asked to do more supportive tasks while men are given the plum, high-level projects that give them exposure to senior leadership, as well as face time with clients (something Alisha experienced when at the last minute her new colleague Paul was asked to deliver her presentation). In the same article, it refers to the difference between these tasks as "glamour work" and "office housework." It's difficult to position yourself for a promotion if the kind of work you're doing doesn't appear worthy of it.

Many of the behaviors that contribute to an inequitable environment for women are unconscious, because they are so deeply entrenched as "the way things are." Workplaces have operated like this for so long that until we speak up (and by "we" I mean more than just women) and demand change, they will continue to do so. Fortunately, recent trends have shown that companies are becoming more and more committed to protecting the well-being of their employees. And even more importantly, we're ready to make more noise about it.

THRIVING IN THE LONG TERM

Just like grappling with imposter syndrome and perfectionism, learning to protect your energy is a lifelong journey. Part of what Amy discovered is that learning how to prevent burnout has helped her become a better manager. When a new hire was added to Amy's team, she proudly told Amy that she never takes time off and always brings her computer home to do work. (She also admitted that she feels guilty if she doesn't.) Amy told her that she could relate, but that her mindset was unsustainable and would eventually make her miserable. There will always be a deadline, but never a "right" time to go on vacation. Going forward, Amy hopes she can pass on to her what she's learned about a healthy work-life balance: "I'm hoping that since she sits next to me, I can tell her all the things I wish I'd known."

Even when there is a lot to get done, managers can take specific and deliberate measures to help their direct reports avoid long-term burnout. If you have people reporting to you, be aware that you set the tone for the team and so you should model behavior you want to see from them. (And if you don't have direct reports, keep this in mind for when you do!)

Rebecca Weaver is the founder of HRuprise, a consulting firm that helps individual employees and companies work through cultural challenges and other concerns that would otherwise be handled by an HR department. As someone with twenty years of experience with companies such as Target and the Home Depot, she's seen her share of burnout and breakdowns, some that led to taking medical leave. She has advice for how managers can encourage their direct reports to work hard and be productive, but not at the expense of their well-being:

SUPPORT YOUR REPORTS

✦ **Trust employees without making them "earn it."** Treat people as the adults they are, and deal with the one-offs as necessary. Far too often, company culture and policies are written with the lowest common denominator in mind. Company policies are often formulated to prevent people from taking advantage of the system, rather than trusting people to do the right thing and trusting people to be able to function as adults.

✦ **Model the behavior, don't just talk about it.** Take time off to take care of personal issues (doctors' appointments, mental health days, take care of kids, etc.) and be loud about what and why you're doing it. People will pay much more attention to what you do than what you say. You'll give them permission to take time for themselves only if you model it.

✦ **Set clear and realistic expectations and be explicit about them.** Technology is a double-edged sword. Just because you have the capability to work whenever and wherever doesn't mean you should. Make it clear that flexibility does not equal on-demand all the time. For example: as a manager, I always tell my direct reports that I sometimes keep strange hours, either because I have kids who don't sleep and/or because of my husband's work schedule. I tell them explicitly that if something happens in the evening or over the weekend that is truly urgent (very rare), I will call them directly and say that. Otherwise, they should know that if they get an email from me during off hours, it is just because that is when I happened to get to it, and I do not expect a response outside of work hours, however they define those for themselves.

✦ **Focus on the final output.** This is putting the concepts of flexible work arrangements to the real test. The idea that face time equals productivity is a long-held and unbelievably difficult concept to break. But there is no evidence that it is true. In fact, there's a lot of evidence that the opposite is true. So focus on coaching your team through what they will deliver and when they will check in and provide updates, and trust them to figure out how to get it done. Tell them that this is what you're doing. If you start from a place of trust and communicate it, I've found that most people will rise to the occasion.

✦ **Speak up.** If you see women, people of color, or any other marginalized group being treated unfairly, say something. Your voice, role, and/or race can have a huge impact.

Everything I've said so far in this chapter was with a salaried worker in mind. If you are an hourly worker, live paycheck to paycheck, or your income is predicated on working as much as possible, I understand that your ability to stand up for yourself may feel limited by what's in your bank account. For anyone, no matter where they work, it can be difficult to butt up against the culture and still hope to get ahead. However, I believe that everyone, no matter who they are or what they do, can find pockets of pause and self-advocacy.

While you should work hard and strive for excellence, you cannot sacrifice yourself along the way. Otherwise you run the risk of setting yourself back and erasing the progress you've worked so hard for. As we'll talk about in the next two chapters, what you do today gets you ready for tomorrow. You need to be cognizant of the sustainability of your present work so that you have enough energy and far-reaching perspective to keep heading in the direction you want.

When you draw a boundary or take time for yourself, it is a declaration of your worth. By prioritizing your well-being, you are telling the world that your energy is deserving of protection, that you are the most important person in your life, and that it's not selfish to say so.

PART THREE

LEVEL UP

*There's nothing wrong with being driven. And there's nothing
wrong with putting yourself first to reach your goals.*
Shonda Rhimes

If you've gotten to this part of the book, that means you've built a strong foundation of self-belief, networked your way into a job that's aligned with your values, and negotiated a big salary that's worthy of your work. You've also learned good habits to protect your energy and ensure that you can do your work in a sustainable way. You're playing the long game now.

Part Three is about making moves toward that long game. What does making progress in your career look like to you? How do you define power and what it feels like to have it? As you saw in Chapter One: Get Aligned, there is no one model of success. It's different for everyone. Is it getting a promotion for you? Having a direct report? A more manageable workload? Maybe it's an office instead of a cubicle, or maybe it's just being excited to come to work every day. Don't let your current circumstances dictate it to you. What you want should not be limited by what you think is or is not possible. This is the time to think big; in order to get there, you have to start by imagining that you can.

Promotions don't just happen because of luck and hard work (though the second element is necessary, and the first one doesn't hurt); they happen because you've established a reputation of excellence, amplified by others. But in order to have done that, you need to build relationships with key people, and then leverage them to take advantage of opportunities that help you achieve your goals.

Taking advantage of opportunities doesn't mean taking advantage of people. And leveraging relationships doesn't make them any less genuine. But the narrative around who gets promoted and who is looked at as leadership material has historically felt very "male": competitive, cutthroat, brash (think about how women in the 1980s masculinized their shape by wearing power suits with giant shoulder pads). Does that mean the only way to get ahead is to act like someone we're not?

It's a mistake to do that. As you learned in Chapter Six: Get Paid, the double bind can have real consequences for acting outside the social norm of femininity. So the question is: How do we navigate internal dynamics like office politics without sacrificing our integrity or changing who we are? How can we push ourselves to grow and seek recognition when we do?

Part Three will help you do just that.

CHAPTER EIGHT

GET ALLIES

In this chapter, you'll follow Shelmina's journey as she goes from being a young girl in Tanzania to a high-ranking executive at IBM. While she didn't set out with the explicit goal of becoming an executive, she was always driven by a desire to learn and to challenge herself, choosing roles and role models that helped catapult her forward.

What Shelmina discovers is that hard work is just one factor of achieving what you want. It's also understanding how your organization operates and how to navigate it to your advantage. It's finding ways to make yourself visible and be unafraid to sing your own praises. It's building relationships purposefully and getting people to buy in and to believe in you not just for what you've done but also for what you're capable of doing. (This is especially important for women, since men are more likely to be promoted based on potential, whereas for women, promotions are based on past performance.)

The odds are stacked against us. Despite holding almost 52 percent of all professional-level jobs, women represent a mere 25 percent of executive- and senior-level positions. (To be clear, ambition is not the issue; according to a Nielsen survey, 64 percent of Black women say that their goal is to make it to the top of their profession.) So, what's happening? We have too many obstacles in our way. As you've seen, some of those roadblocks are internal: the inner critic tells us that the penalty is too high to take big risks, but more often there are systemic barriers like entrenched sexism in who is assigned highly coveted tasks and then how they are evaluated. This might intimidate you, but don't let it stop you. Use it as *fuel.*

AIMING FOR SOMETHING MORE

Growing up in Tanzania in the 70s, Shelmina knew only three kinds of women: homemakers, hairdressers, and secretaries. She wasn't sure what she wanted to be when she grew up, but she knew it wasn't any of those. Most girls dropped out of high school by tenth grade, but Shelmina wouldn't let herself be one of them. She resolved to graduate and get herself to college.

Her parents put together what little money they had and sent her to India, where there were more educational opportunities. As Shelmina struggled to find her place in a foreign country where she didn't speak the language, her initial excitement began to fade. Self-doubt set in, and she began to experience self-limiting thoughts that she wasn't going to be able to do this and that she'd be better off if she just quit and returned home.

But leaving would mean giving up on her dream of attending college. Disappointing her family would have been bad enough but disappointing herself would be worse. She'd already come so far. She'd had the courage to leave home, the ability to learn a new language, and the grit to keep going; Shelmina had already demonstrated she had what it took. She could—and would—go even further. Shelmina set her sights on attending college in the United States, and three years later she was accepted into the computer science program at the University of Wisconsin–La Crosse.

Soon she was braving Midwestern winters, improving her English, and wondering what was next. Fortunately, Shelmina got recruited right out of college to work at a company that built supercomputers. When the company shut down four years later, she was able to land a job at IBM. She was one of the few women (and the only woman of color) in the systems engineering department. She quickly established herself as a hard worker and less than a year later, she won the Systems Engineer Rookie of the Year award. As part of her reward, she was invited to participate in a closed-door meeting with high-ranking women at IBM as they discussed how to better support female talent.

At the meeting, there was one woman who stood out from the rest. Her name was Susan Whitney and she ran marketing and sales across the entire Midwest region. Shelmina was struck by the way she carried herself and how she communicated, looking every person in the eye, making each person feel as though she was speaking directly to them.

Before the meeting, Shelmina's manager had encouraged her to personally introduce herself, and so Shelmina went up to Susan and offered to walk her back to her office. As they made their way down the hall, Susan congratulated her on winning the Rookie award. "Where do you see yourself in five years?" she asked. Shelmina didn't quite know how to respond. She'd worked hard to get to this point, and now she was working hard to stay afloat. The future seemed very far away. When Shelmina said as much, Susan looked thoughtful. "It's important to do your current job well, but it's also very important to always be learning new skills and new competencies that help you think about what you're going to do next . . . and then next."

The idea of doing your job while also positioning yourself for the future wasn't something Shelmina had ever considered. She'd always just put her head down, worked as hard as she could, and then taken whatever next step presented itself. But here was someone important with the assumption—and expectation—that Shelmina could rise even higher, and not only that, go in whatever direction *she* desired. Maybe she could; she'd just need to figure out how.

ALLY #1

Two years after she joined IBM, Shelmina had her first baby. The salary that had once seemed generous now barely covered her expenses. She was the primary breadwinner, so she started to look within IBM for positions where she could translate her skill set and make more money. Her technical background and people skills made her a good candidate for the sales department. That said, she'd never worked in sales before and knew very little. So when Shelmina got transferred, she knew she had a lot to prove.

She threw herself into work, putting in long hours, chasing down every opportunity she could. Her manager, Keith, who was only a few years older than her but well established at IBM, gave her game-changing feedback: instead of focusing on just any lead that might lead to a sale, it was wiser to spend the most energy on those that she had the best chance to close. He pointed out how much time she could lose on every small potential deal and explained that it was more efficient to work on those that could have a much larger impact. At first, Shelmina was slightly embarrassed and worried that she looked as though she didn't know what she was doing. But she took his feedback seriously and was soon closing deals left and right. What Shelmina learned was how crucial it is to take in feedback because if she hadn't, she would still be going after dead-end deals, most likely missing her quota.

Not everyone is as lucky as Shelmina to have as good a manager as Keith, who recognized that her success was his success. Therefore, it's on you to establish a good relationship with your manager starting from day one, as it's the most important relationship you'll have at work. Your manager has a front-row seat to what you do and what you're capable of, and they have the power to give you opportunities, promotions, and connections, helping to shape the trajectory of your entire career.

Instead of waiting for your supervisor to manage you, learn what their expectations, priorities, and goals are. How do they define success? How do they measure it? Be proactive in gleaning information from them that can help you do your job better. Knowing exactly what you need to do to succeed can help you make a strong case when you have your annual review.

Think of the relationship you have with your manager as a relay race in which they hand off tasks and you run with them. Good communication is what makes the handoff seamless, and like any relationship, that takes work. It's important to understand their capacity to manage you and the way they prefer to stay in touch, including how they want to receive updates and information from you.

The following are some useful questions to ask your manager about how to best work with them. Ideally, you'd have this conversation when you first start working together, but don't worry if you didn't. Asking for a time to confirm priorities will always be looked at positively. The goal is to avoid any future misunderstandings, and the way to do that is by level-setting now.

MANAGER GROUNDWORK

✦ What are your expectations of me?

✦ What are your goals for this year? This quarter?

✦ What things should I prioritize?

✦ How do you define success, and how do you measure it?

✦ What's your preferred mode of communication?

✦ What's your bandwidth for communication? For example, do you prefer a daily check-in by email or a biweekly lunch?

✦ How would you like me to bring up any potential issues or challenges I'm experiencing?

Be sure to have periodic check-ins and when you do, create an agenda for yourself (feel free to share it with them ahead of time) to make sure you cover everything you want to discuss, including anything you might need from them (approval, information, help, etc.). Even a simple "How can I make your job easier?" goes a long way. This is also a good opportunity to talk about your wins (which you should be tracking, as you saw in Chapter Six: Get Paid), bringing with you any positive feedback you received, such as complimentary emails from clients. It's not bragging if you're just assuring them that you're doing a good job. Remember, your success is their success.

SOLICITING FEEDBACK

As Shelmina learned, thanks to Keith, feedback from your supervisor is crucial to doing your job well. If you're not receiving any, you *must* solicit it. According to research by the *Harvard Business Review*, women tend to receive less concrete feedback than men, which in turn hurts their ability to do their best work, and in the long run can negatively impact their chances of being promoted. (And when they do get feedback, it's more focused on personality criticism and communication style, such as "You come across as abrasive," whereas feedback for men tends to be about meeting their business goals.)

Remind yourself that without feedback, you won't grow. This may be a moment when you need to keep a tight rein on feelings of insecurity and vulnerability, so you don't get derailed by legitimate feedback, even if it's delivered in a less-than-ideal way. Always search for the nugget of actionable information, even if you have to sift through less-than-helpful muck surrounding it. This might be a good time to revisit Chapters One and Two to prepare yourself to see progress and potential, not just criticism.

It can be as hard to give feedback as it is to get it, so you may need to guide your manager to be as specific as possible. You want feedback you can act on so that you're confident about the steps you can take to improve.

HELP YOUR MANAGER HELP YOU

✦ **Get them to be as specific as possible.** In a study done by Shelley Correll and Caroline Simard of the VMware Women's Leadership Innovation Lab at Stanford University, they found that women consistently received less feedback tied to business outcomes. In other words, they were told generalities about their performance, but not specifics about what they did well or poorly. It's difficult to know how to improve if you're unsure of what you need to be improving in the first place! One way to do this is to ask your manager how she would have done things differently. Emphasize that clarity and context will help you do your job better.

✦ **Don't act defensive.** It may be tempting to want to defend whatever you did. Instead, if you want to provide context, walk them through your decision-making process. Perhaps they're not fully informed on the work you've been doing. That being said, it's a fine line between explaining yourself and acting defensive. Depending on what happened, it may be better to swallow your pride and simply thank them for the feedback.

✦ **Work together to find a solution.** In order to know how best to remedy the situation, solicit their ideas for how they suggest moving forward. It will also turn the conversation from a potentially negative one into an actionable, future-forward one where you work together.

DEALING WITH DIFFICULT MANAGERS

It's not uncommon to find yourself in a difficult situation with a superior at some point during your career. Maybe you have a micromanager for a boss; maybe they're never around; or maybe they're not clear about what they want. When you notice a pattern of behavior that is making it difficult for you to do your work, you might want to discuss it with your manager.

Given the power dynamic, it can feel scary to have this conversation. Approach it with the assumption that your manager is probably unaware of what's going on. The best way to aim for a positive outcome is to address the situation with as much constructive energy as possible. You never know what battles people are fighting in their own lives or what pressure they're under, so better to go in with empathy rather than anger.

CREATE A PATH FORWARD

+ **Don't make assumptions.** Separate the behavior from the assumption that you're making about that behavior. For example, if your manager yelled at you, you might assume that it was because they were angry at you. Maybe they were or maybe they were just having a bad day (either way, it's not acceptable). When you bring this subject up with them, concentrate on the behavior itself and the impact it had on you. Focusing on that, rather than why you think they did it, will keep the conversation more productive.

+ **Focus on the impact.** To prevent them from getting defensive, Rebecca Weaver (of HRuprise) suggests using the framework of "Situation, behavior, impact." For example, you were in a meeting (situation), your manager yelled at you and pounded their fist on the table (behavior), and it made you question your ability to do your job (impact). Put it in the construct of "when you do this, this is how it affects me." Some of the impacts can be "I didn't understand where you were coming from," or "I didn't fully understand the point you were trying to drive home." It doesn't necessarily have to be how it made you feel since that may put you in a more vulnerable position than a lot of people are willing to go, especially in a situation like this.

✦ **Bring solutions.** Move the conversation in a positive direction by bringing suggestions of how to remedy the situation. By doing that, you won't be looked at as complaining but rather problem solving. It also demonstrates that you respect their time since they probably have limited bandwidth to address this. Plus, it improves the chances that you get what you want!

✦ **Confirm.** A way to wrap up the conversation is to repeat the main points and confirm you've correctly understood them. This will help determine any next steps and prevent miscommunication moving forward.

✦ **Send a recap.** Immediately follow up with an email, recapping the conversation and thanking them for taking the time to connect. It's important to put this in writing so you have a paper trail in case you need to refer back to it (or get HR to step in).

✦ **Document everything.** Whatever the situation is (a difficult manager or a catty colleague), you should be documenting it. Things such as "this was the date it happened, here's what was said, here's how I responded" will be helpful for HR to review if you need them to get involved. If possible, include copies of any relevant communications between you as well as testimonials from colleagues who may have witnessed the behavior. Rebecca suggests doing this on a personal computer or phone, rather than on your company computer.

If you find yourself in a situation where you feel unsafe, skip what I just told you and go directly to HR. Alternatively, you could go to someone you trust, though be aware that most companies would require this person to report to HR if the behavior went against policy. If you're unsure whether a certain behavior constitutes harassment, consult your company handbook or a lawyer. Another time to go directly to HR is if you're experiencing an issue with a high-level person who ranks above your manager in the chain of command.

One reason to go to HR is that there may have been other complaints about this person, and your voice is the one that determines how the company will act. This is important information that should be recorded.

If you're reporting harassment or feel unsafe, in order for HR to understand the severity of the situation, make it extremely clear. It helps if you can make suggestions of how you might want them to respond. Do be aware that it's often easier to move a subordinate to a new team than it is to move a manager. If this is something you experience, it might feel like you're being penalized. You're not. It's likely strictly organizational.

Sometimes you've done all that you can, and the only thing left is to walk away. If the management issues have crossed the line and you are truly being mistreated *and* the company doesn't offer any viable solution, finding another job may be the best way forward. This is why it is *so important* that you have money saved up—i.e., a financial cushion—so you can get out of there. You don't deserve to be treated poorly, and if that's the case and your company won't protect you, they certainly don't deserve to have you.

You should never be stuck because of your financial situation; for far too long women have relied on others to provide for them. The best way to be independent is to have savings. While you should continuously be putting money away, here are some ways to quickly save up cash.

TIPS TO SAVE

1. **Write down your money goals.** A study by Dr. Gail Matthews, a psychology professor at Dominican University of California, showed that writing down your goals makes it 42 percent more likely you'll actually achieve them. But you'll be even more likely to achieve them if you break things down into smaller, more bite-sized goals. Be realistic about it—you don't want to set yourself up for failure. When you reach those mini goals, be proud of yourself. What you're doing is hard, especially if you've never been much of a saver before.

2. **Make a budget.** This is something I talked about in Chapter Six: Get Paid, but it bears repeating. The best way to budget is to take your post-tax income and divide it into three parts. At least 50 percent of it should go toward your "needs," such as rent, food, and utilities. Thirty percent should go toward your "wants," which could include things like going to the movies, taking a vacation, or having drinks with friends. The final 20 percent should go toward paying off debt or saving for the future. You should be tracking your spending throughout

the year (there are apps like Mint that can make it easy). If you need to save more, just adjust your percentages.

3. **Cancel subscriptions.** If you're tracking all the money coming in and out, you'll be able to see where you can save. For many people, they're paying for subscriptions that they either weren't aware of or forgot about. Unless you're still using them, cancel them. It's the quickest way to start saving.

4. **Set up automation.** You don't need willpower to save if you automate it. There are a number of tools (such as Digit) that will automatically transfer small amounts of money from your checking account to savings. You can just set it and forget it.

5. **Negotiate with vendors.** Did you know you can negotiate your utilities? Things like your cell phone, cable, even electricity can all be negotiated down. Jim Wang, the founder of Wallet Hacks, says, "If something has a contract, you can negotiate, and if you don't, you're subsidizing the people who do." Here are four ways to do it:

    a. Research their competitors.

    b. Know what you want and prepare your ask.

    c. Decline whatever first offer they suggest. (*"I was hoping for something closer to x . . ."*)

    d. Be polite. Stand up for what you want but don't do it in an antagonistic way. Make them *want* to help you.

FIND A SPONSOR

After she met Susan Whitney, Keith urged Shelmina to stay in touch with her. Keith explained that although they didn't work out of the same office or even in the same city, that shouldn't stop Shelmina from maintaining a relationship with someone who had demonstrated a genuine interest in her. Susan could be someone very valuable in her career.

Over the course of eight years, Shelmina would periodically send Susan emails about everything from personal news (babies being born) to professional progress (getting a promotion). These were short emails that didn't require a response, so they weren't a drain on Susan's time. Staying in touch kept Susan invested in Shelmina's progress, and whenever she traveled from her office to IBM's Seattle headquarters, she would take Shelmina out to lunch.

Though they never formally talked about it, Susan became Shelmina's sponsor: a person of influence within the company who could wield that influence to advocate for Shelmina's advancement. A sponsor is different from a mentor, who provides advice and counsel and is often outside your organization; it is also different from a coach, who helps more with short-term skill development.

As you navigate upward, a sponsor can be a critical resource. Research by the Center for Talent Innovation finds that men and women with sponsors are more likely to ask for pay raises (and get them), be invited to join a high-visibility team, and experience greater career satisfaction.

Unfortunately, not enough women have a Susan Whitney in their lives. Research published in the *Harvard Business Review* shows that women have an overabundance of mentors but not enough people who can use their clout to help them level up, putting them at a serious disadvantage. Men are three to four times more likely to have a sponsor than women. Without sponsors, we are less likely to discover and secure plum assignments, get promoted, and get higher pay.

Why is this? It could be that high level men sponsor other men not because they're sexist but simply because they remind them of themselves. This is known as affinity bias; you're more likely to bond with a person who is similar to you, and since a disproportionate number of positions of power are held by men, it perpetuates a cycle where women have to advocate and fend for themselves without an internal support framework. There is also the issue of optics: career development site Fairygodboss suggests that "older men don't want to sponsor younger women because they don't want people thinking they are having an affair. And on the flipside, younger women don't want to be sponsored by older men because they don't want people thinking they've slept their way to the top."

Essentially, we're between a rock and a hard place. We're at a disadvantage in securing a sponsor, but we're also at a disadvantage in not having one. Something has to give. (In Chapter Ten, we'll talk about how you can pitch a sponsorship program to your company.) In the meantime, we need to be proactive. Our career advancement depends on it.

Here are some guidelines on how to find and develop a relationship with a sponsor.

HOW TO GET A SPONSOR

1. **Identify them.** To know who a good sponsor for you might be, you first need to think about what you're trying to accomplish. What parts of the business are you interested in learning about? What projects do you want to work on? What skills do you want to gain? Where do you want to go in your career and

at the company? Potential sponsors don't necessarily have to be in your department, nor do they necessarily have to have a senior title. However, they do need to have access to rooms where the gatekeepers are and enough clout so that when they go to bat for you, people will listen. Don't feel as if you can only have one sponsor; in fact, the more people who are aware of and invested in you, the better.

2. **Reach out.** As you learned in Chapter Four, you have to shoot your shot, no matter if you think you'll get a yes. If you're able to make yourself visible first, that would be ideal. When you do reach out to a potential sponsor, be specific about why you're emailing (mention details, including anything you may have in common) and be clear about what you hope to learn from them. Give them the option of connecting over the phone so they don't feel pressure to spend time they may not have meeting in person.

3. **Talk about your aspirations.** The clearer you can be about your goals and aspirations, the more helpful your sponsor can be. Get them invested in you by talking about work you've done and success you've had. They'll feel more confident in developing you as a leader if they know that you have the potential to become one.

4. **Be patient.** Developing a relationship takes time. Unless your company has a sponsorship program, this does not have to be official; no need to get down on bended knee and ask someone to be your sponsor. Keep them abreast of your progress and how their advice has helped you. If there's an opportunity

where their support could make a big difference (for example, a new position opened up or you have an idea for an initiative), you could go to them. Just be aware that this kind of "ask" should be used sparingly. And always express gratitude when they help you.

5. **Remember, it's not a favor.** This doesn't have to be a one-sided relationship. Even though they hold the power, you can be valuable to them, too. It's helpful for them to be aware of what's going on in the company at a ground level. Plus, one day you may work for them, so building a relationship now could benefit you both.

PEERS

Your colleagues are also key to moving ahead. (As you saw in Chapter Four: Get Connected, your peers can be the ones who help you get your next job.) Building strong relationships with them will make it easier to collaborate, but they can also be your co-advocates if you want to pitch a new initiative, whether it's a project or an employee resource group, which we'll go over in Chapter Ten.

Don't rely on the company to help you bond. Seek out people you work with and get to know them one-on-one. Not everyone has to become your best friend, but everyone benefits from having a rapport in which you work well together and can sidestep whatever office politics might be happening around you.

Here's how networking internally fits into the larger picture of navigating upward.

MAKE CONNECTIONS WITH PURPOSE

✦ **Find common ground.** Everyone has goals they're trying to achieve; some might be personal (getting a promotion), some might be organizational (getting a project funded), or some might be simply because of a shared life experience (women of color seeking other women of color). Ask your colleague what they want to accomplish and how you can support them. That way when you need their help, they'll be much more inclined to support you.

✦ **Practice Shine Theory.** Coined by Ann Friedman and Aminatou Sow, the coauthors of *Big Friendship* and the cohosts of the podcast *Call Your Girlfriend*, Shine Theory is a "practice of mutual investment with the simple premise that 'I don't shine if you don't shine.'" One way to do this is by publicly acknowledging each other's contributions. For example, during a meeting, reference what your colleague said earlier, even throwing in a compliment if that feels genuine, e.g., "As Ruth said . . ." or "I thought Ruth had a good idea." Not only will this help you build goodwill with others, it will also set the tone that this should be a positive and collaborative culture. (You can also do this privately by telling someone's manager that you were impressed by something they did or said.)

✦ **Amplify each other.** In the Obama White House, the women adopted a strategy they called "amplification" as a way of ensuring men didn't take credit for their ideas. When a woman in their group made a key point, another woman in the room would repeat it, giving credit to its author. This simple tactic forced the men in the room to acknowledge the first woman's contribution—and denied them the chance to co-opt the idea and claim it as their own.

✦ **Get involved.** If there are preexisting groups and activities at your company, join them! You can also organize your own; for example, suggest bringing in a speaker for a "Lunch and Learn." However, whatever you plan, be aware that after-work hours can be difficult for those with families.

PLAY THE GAME

Office politics. The draining, annoying, and inevitable part of every organization. Whether it's a miscommunication, competing agendas, or a mismatch of personalities, sometimes there's no amount of goodwill and collaboration that can help prevent it. There are company cultures that encourage it (as in Alisha's and Reece's cases), and other times they're oblivious to it. Either way, it's up to you to learn how to navigate it and maybe even use it to your advantage.

Men have been comfortable playing office politics for years. They use it as an opportunity to gain visibility, form allies, and increase influence. Women, on the other hand, "regard office politics as something to avoid at all costs," according to a study by the *Harvard Business Review*. Those in power (men) set the tone for how politics are played (competitively and often aggressively). In a study by Gerald Ferris, Dwight Frink, and Maria Carmen Galang, they describe office politics as a "white man's game."

Does this mean we have to act like men to play the game? No. In fact, that can backfire. If women—and particularly women of color—play the game the way men do, they're at risk of facing the double bind: we're penalized if we don't engage and when we do, we have to be careful in how we do it. As we do in so much of our career, we have to walk that tightrope.

"Playing politics" isn't just about dealing with conflict when it arises; it's really about being aware of dynamics between people and proactively building relationships. Shelmina credits Keith's advice about office politics as game changing. One day after a team meeting, he pulled her aside and said, "I admire the fact that you are a straight shooter. I'm not asking you to change any of that. I'm asking you to understand who the audience is. Every single person: know their agenda, what motivates them, and where their allegiances are." For Shelmina, this was eye-opening. Understanding where people were coming from would allow her to communicate in a way that would get the most buy-ins possible.

Ultimately, playing office politics is about seeking an agreement of mutual respect where you can do your best work. Here are some ways to achieve that.

NAVIGATE OFFICE POLITICS

✦ **Shift your mindset.** Instead of looking at office politics as a necessary evil, think of it as an opportunity to demonstrate leadership potential. According to a research report published by the Center for Work-Life Policy, "To their detriment, women perceive cultivating relationships and mobilizing them on their behalf as, at best, an occasional necessity rather than the key exercise of leadership. They fail to see that the practice of seeking out powerful people, cultivating favor and cashing in those chips is itself a demonstration of leadership potential." It's simply about figuring out who you connect with and learning the most effective communication strategies with those around you.

✦ **Keep your ear to the ground.** You know that assistant who has been at the company forever? Or the IT guy who has fixed pretty much everyone's computer? These kinds of people are the veterans of the office and a treasure trove of information. They're tapped into everything that's going on behind the scenes; they can be your window into how the business operates. To successfully navigate the workplace, you have to know its culture—and they can help you learn it. Be nice to these folks, ask how they're doing, take them out for coffee. As always, be authentic in developing relationships here. No one wants to feel used.

✦ **Be direct.** If you need help, don't be afraid to ask for it, as long as it's appropriate. It doesn't have to feel compromising or emotionally draining. And besides, it can make people feel good to feel needed.

Another aspect of office politics that Shelmina struggled with was her desire to be liked. Just as Shelmina had chased after every opportunity as a new sales manager, she also spent a lot of energy seeking others' approval. "Keith pointed out, 'You're not here to win a popularity contest. You're here to earn their respect. When you become a leader, this skill will serve you well. There will always be people who don't like you, but they [will] respect you. At all times, you must do the right thing and not be concerned about whether people like you or not.'"

Trying to get everyone to always agree will not only waste your energy, it may actually limit your influence. Leadership often requires making the right decision even when not everybody agrees. Shelmina learned, "We must be able to make a decision and say, 'Here is why X person and Y person disagree with me, but this is what we need to do anyway.' We need to quit relying solely on agreement and consensus and instead show we have a point of view and can stand by our decisions." Shifting your focus to being respected rather than liked can help you take things less personally. Trying to make everyone your friend is a waste of energy.

There are inevitably going to be times when communication breaks down, personalities don't jive, or people just suck. When that happens, you have three choices: tackle it directly, adjust your approach, and if all else fails, involve HR to help resolve it. Sometimes it's difficult to know which course of action is the correct one until you've already gone down one of them. But like so much else in your career, the more times you navigate these scenarios, the better you will get at listening to your gut and knowing what response is right. Even when you find yourself in a difficult situation and realize you could have handled it better, you will learn from that experience and be able to avoid similar missteps in the future.

Let's take a look at a case study where Molly, a senior vice president at one of the world's largest media companies, finds herself during the prime of her career—unprepared to handle office politics. She prided herself on the relationships she built and was loath to play office politics. She'd gotten pretty far without them. We'll examine what she did, how she could have handled her dilemma better, and how we can pick ourselves up when we inevitably make the wrong choice (it happens to everyone, and is a very effective way to learn—you will not want to make the same mistake twice).

CASE STUDY

CIRCLE YOUR WAGONS

W HEN DANIEL GOT FIRED, the company was in chaos. He was the chairman of a large media company and Molly was his second-in-command. When he was let go, they'd been working on some considerable deals, all of which were now a question mark. A few days after Daniel's departure, Molly got the opportunity of a lifetime. She was named the president of her entire division. She picked up where her predecessor left off, green-lighting a number of projects that would ultimately bring in millions of dollars to the company.

Less than a year later, the rumors started. Molly had heard whisperings that some people were gunning for her job. Her suspicions were confirmed when a colleague gave her the details: for some time, two men had been scheming to make the case to the higher-ups that Molly should go and that they were the ones who should take over. Her colleague gave her a grave warning: "You need to circle your wagons."

Molly wasn't totally shocked; she'd always had somewhat of a rocky relationship with those two men. But the thought of going to her colleagues to make the case why they should align themselves with her . . . that left a bad taste in her mouth. Molly had been excelling at her job, and surely her boss would see that. Plus, the idea of playing office politics felt totally out of character. She was above that.

It was only a matter of weeks before Molly was summoned to her boss's office. She had just sat down when he said, "This is a really hard meeting for me, but we're going to go another way."

Molly sat there, stunned. The rest was a blur. He said something about needing to restructure, that things would be clearer for everyone. Then he dropped the bomb. One of the men who'd been plotting the coup was getting her job; the other one was becoming his number two.

"But don't worry," he assured her. "We'll find something else for you."

Molly felt her blood begin to rise. As calmly as she could muster, she looked him right in the eye. "Let's call it what it is. You're taking my job away. I'm fired." And she walked out.

Looking back, Molly recognizes that experience as a huge wake-up call. Just because you know you're good at what you do (and are told as much), that doesn't mean office politics can't get in the way. As much as we might like to think that everything works out the way it's supposed to, that's not the world we live in. If you believe in what you do, you have to fight for it.

Molly admits her colleague was right: she should have circled her wagons.

If she could do it over, Molly would've sought out her allies for more intel and to ask them to support her if things got ugly. She also would have gone directly to her boss the minute she heard the rumblings, acknowledge that there was politicking going on, and ask if she needed to strengthen her case to him about why she was right for the job. She's not certain that this would've prevented her from being fired, but it would've made it much more difficult for things to come down the way they did.

She also would have asked for a meeting with the men angling for her job and called them out, telling them that she was going to fight—and win.

But Molly, of course, couldn't go back. What was done was

done. And so as painful a lesson as it was, Molly emerged stronger, ready for whatever was next.

However big you think your life can be, think bigger. Even if you don't have the experience, skills, or access (yet!), these are all things that are attainable. As you saw with Shelmina, her willingness to be a sponge, to absorb and implement what others taught her, was the key to propelling her forward. It was precisely her willingness to learn (and to follow through) that made people like her manager want to help her.

Don't be afraid to do hard things. Things like addressing office politics or difficult managers, shooting your shot with the executives, or asking for help when you need it. No matter how it may appear on the outside, we're all doing our damnedest to make things work. For some, it may be harder than others. But if we collaborate, if we support one another, everyone can rise.

CHAPTER NINE

GET PROMOTED

Whether or not you want to become an executive, if you've done good work and proven your capacity for excellence, you should get at least a promotion (and a raise!). But how do you make that happen? You approach it from all angles. Positioning yourself for a promotion begins with surrounding yourself with allies, but in order to secure it, you need to leverage those relationships. You also should be strategic about the opportunities you take, and when there are none, be audacious enough to make your own. In order to grow, you have to be willing to challenge yourself, which, as you've learned in Chapters One and Two, means making mistakes. Hopefully by now, you've built a strong enough foundation to not only keep moving past the obstacles but also to use what you've learned from them to keep propelling you forward.

In this chapter, we'll catch up with Shelmina, who says yes to things that she's never done before, things that scare her. She's brave enough to try but also humble enough to know when she needs help. She also has the resilience to pick herself back up and try again. Part of her success might be luck, but most of it comes from her own sheer will. While Shelmina may have had the odds stacked against her and her path has strayed from the traditional, her story demonstrates the possibility of upward momentum. That possibility exists for you, too.

SPEAK UP IN MEETINGS

The first step in positioning yourself for advancement comes long before advancing is even a possibility. It means making yourself visible. At Shelmina's first job out of college, at a company that built supercomputers, she had been on a student visa; she was insecure, inexperienced, and totally intimidated. Everyone there was older than her and had PhDs from places like MIT; to say that she experienced imposter syndrome was an understatement. During meetings, she felt obligated to keep quiet, assuming that there was nothing she could ever add to the conversation.

As the company geared up for a major launch, Shelmina sat through a number of brainstorming sessions while her team worked through a few issues they'd run into. Then she had an idea. A really good idea. But like so many other women, she stayed silent. She knew that her solution had value, but that critical voice inside her (the one that almost convinced her to go home to Tanzania years earlier) now told her there was no way someone of her age and status could possibly contribute value.

Then someone else spoke up, offering their solution. It was the same solution Shelmina had come up with. Not only did the issue get solved, but that person received a huge bonus, a promotion, and recognition in front of the entire company of 500 employees. That marked a realization for Shelmina; that could've been her. It *should've* been her. It became a turning point: she resolved to never let that happen again.

When Shelmina first started to speak up in meetings, she was really nervous, and it affected her delivery. She would ramble or talk really fast. She used weak language, such as "I just" or "I'm sorry," which detracted from the credibility of what she was trying to say. Often someone would speak over her and she'd let them. Clearly it wasn't just about having confidence, it was also learning to communicate in a way that made others *want* to listen. Shelmina also began observing who was spoken over and who wasn't. "Taking notes, [I realized that it's all about] the choice of words, pace, energy, how you project belief in your own idea. I had to visualize myself speaking powerfully and confidently until I mastered it."

Shelmina's struggle to speak up isn't unique. In a 2012 study, researchers at Brigham Young University found that in a room full of men, women speak less than 25 percent of the time and when they do, they're more than 50 percent more likely to be interrupted (by both men and women). That's why as Shelmina gained confidence, she still had to fight to be heard. When people interjected, she learned to calmly say, "Let me finish." She deliberately wouldn't use the word "please," because in her words, "They weren't doing me a favor by listening."

Eventually, Shelmina got so good at public speaking that she became known for it. When her student visa was set to expire, the company hired an attorney and sponsored her to stay. Shelmina credits her ability to communicate her value as the reason she was able to stay in the United States and eventually make her way to IBM.

In order to be recognized at work, people need to know who you are. You need to establish your reputation beyond the people you work with directly. Meetings are a great place to do that. As you saw with Shelmina, having confidence is key to speaking up, but it isn't the only factor. She also needed to be strategic in how she spoke up. In addition to the strategies Shelmina used—observing the culture of communication, having a clearly articulated agenda, and practicing speaking calmly and fluently—

it can also be helpful to seek out key players and have a conversation before a meeting. That way you can be more prepared and at ease, and you approach the meeting as a continuation of that conversation.

COMMUNICATE EFFECTIVELY

+ **Take up space.** When you take up space, people notice. To make sure you're being seen, station yourself in the middle of the table. That way you'll be in everyone's eye line during the meeting. Simple things like leaning forward and gesticulating will also make your presence known.

+ **Don't wait too long.** Take time to absorb what's being discussed and what the dynamics are, but don't put off speaking up for too long, otherwise you'll psych yourself out (or as we saw happen to Shelmina, someone else could get your idea out first).

+ **Introduce yourself.** If you're in a meeting with people you don't know, state your name and title when you speak up.

+ **Involve the room.** Reference others by building on their ideas or asking targeted questions. This will help you stay active in the conversation, making you more memorable.

+ **Stand your ground.** Because women are more likely to be interrupted, be ready to stand your ground if and when someone butts in. Tania Luna, a partner at LifeLabs Learning, suggests interjecting with "Before we move on, I'd love to wrap my thought," or "I'm seventy-five percent done with my thought." People will be interested in what the other 25 percent is.

GO WHERE YOU CAN GROW

Four years after joining IBM, Shelmina had become one of the company's best salespeople, making her way up to lead a team of 120 people, with a $880 million target.

This was a critical time in Shelmina's career. She'd proven her worth enough to make a compelling case to be promoted within her department. When Susan Whitney came to town, Shelmina couldn't wait to catch up and tell her how well she was doing.

Susan didn't quite have the reaction Shelmina was expecting. She was impressed by how Shelmina had grown but warned Shelmina that she was potentially reaching a cap for how much further she could go. Rather than setting her sights on the next promotion within her department, Susan argued that having exposure to other areas of the business and learning additional skills would make Shelmina even more valuable. Susan urged her to think strategically about where the business and the industry were going and find a way to go with it. In this case, it was away from hardware sales and into the business and technology services department. "If you want to get a more meaningful promotion, you need to position yourself in an organization where IBM is investing because if they're investing, it's an area of growth, and in turn, that's where the executive positions will open up."

Susan was pointing out an important consideration for Shelmina's next move and possible promotion. The question was, where did she want to be promoted to? It could be a linear move: there were senior sales positions she could take. But Susan saw her potential to go even further. By venturing into a new area and learning new proficiencies, Shelmina would become like a Swiss Army knife, making her a unique asset to the company.

This is where thinking strategically becomes crucial. When it's time to take the next steps in your career, you want to carefully consider what will expand your world (not just your paycheck), and what the opportunities will be at the *next* stage. Will a different job significantly increase your network? Will you be learning new skills, will you have access to avenues of development unavailable to you in your current environment?

Something else to consider is the earning potential. A major contributor to the wage gap is something called "occupational segregation," which occurs when one demographic group is overrepresented or underrepresented in a certain kind of job or industry (e.g., men are 53 percent of the US labor force, yet they hold 98 percent of construction jobs).

Occupational segregation can have a damaging effect on career growth and therefore earning potential. Women tend to be clustered in roles and departments that are more "supportive," whereas men hold positions that directly generate income, which translates to larger paychecks and more authority. For example, sales and software engineering departments (which bring in more money because they are directly tied to making and selling the product) are dominated by men, whereas marketing and human resources are overwhelmingly female.

Another example of occupational segregation is in education. While the majority of teachers are women (70 percent), three-quarters of school district superintendents are men. Can you guess which group gets paid more?

Does that mean you need to change what you do for a living? No. It is beneficial, however, to be aware of how pay is structured at your company, and to know where there is the most opportunity to advance and earn more. And it is crucial information to have when trying to understand—and solve—the wage gap.

If you're unsure of where you want to go, talk to people in other departments; inquire about the problems they're solving, the skills they're using, and what it takes to be successful in their area of expertise. Make sure to also ask them about their day-to-day, as you may discover deal breakers about their lifestyle, such as how much of a work-life balance they have. That way you can you can be confident you're making the right move for *you*.

When contemplating Susan's advice to consider a move away from hardware, Shelmina sought out Carolyn Maher, someone she'd worked with in a previous position at IBM. Carolyn was familiar with business and technology services and was able to give her valuable insight. Shelmina decided to apply for an open position in that department, and with Carolyn's help, she secured the role. She was ready to embark on a new chapter.

But with growth can come growing pains. If you want to challenge yourself, be ready to make mistakes. As you move up, the stakes will be higher, the learning curve steep, and any stumbles that much scarier. For those of us who struggle with perfectionism, this can be particularly tough.

KEEP GROWING

Shelmina learned the hard way. Almost immediately after accepting the new position, she regretted it. She remembers being on a conference call, in her first week, sweating bullets and furiously taking notes, trying to keep up as everyone spoke quickly in an unfamiliar shorthand. At the time, Shelmina kicked herself for leaving a role that she was good at and known for; now it seemed she had to start over. In addition, there were some underlying politics at play: her job had been promised to another man who was now—along with three other men—reporting to her. So not only did Shelmina have to deal with a steep learning curve, she also had to battle the insecurity of knowing that her reports might think she got the job not because of her top-of-the-line qualifications but because she was a woman of color.

For the first time in Shelmina's career, she didn't make her quota. She could feel herself returning to self-limiting thoughts she hadn't experienced in years. But fortunately, she was able to marshal a second wave of thoughts. There had been a time when she wasn't good at sales. She'd learned. There had been a time when she didn't know how to effectively communicate her ideas. She'd learned. And there had been a time when she didn't know how to sing her own praises. She'd learned. It wasn't going to be easy, but Shelmina was determined to not only learn this new business but *master* it.

In order to understand how to improve in this new position, Shelmina needed to ask for feedback from the people who had turned down the services she'd pitched them. She started by calling them. It was humbling but also enlightening; even though it was sometimes tough to get the feedback, Shelmina's genuine desire to learn not only helped her adjust her strategy, it also helped earn the trust and confidence of these clients. Her team went from being one of the worst performing in the company to the best.

It was this experience that showed Shelmina what made her truly valuable. Yes, she was great at sales; but most importantly, she was resilient and learned quickly, two qualities of a leader. The higher-ups at IBM took note.

GET YOURSELF THE PROMOTION

If you wait until annual review time to advocate for yourself or position yourself for advancement, it's too late. Not only do you want to be taking up space and making yourself visible long before any conversation about a promotion, as you saw in the last chapter, it's also crucial that all throughout the year you communicate your value to your manager. This way, you're ahead of the curve, staying in sync with what he needs to see from you in order to eventually get promoted. Hopefully you've already had explicit conversations about his priorities and measures of success, so that you can use this information as you prepare your case. If you can integrate his own language into the eventual case you make, that's even better.

Your review is a good time to shine a light on any of your achievements that might've gone unnoticed or forgotten. Managers are busy and you cannot expect them to remember all your accomplishments, especially if they happened months ago. Ground your achievements in facts and data, demonstrating how your actions have impacted the bottom line.

If you didn't perform well that year, be upfront. Talk openly about why your performance was lacking, things you would've done differently, and what you learned from it. The key is to show growth, transparency, personal responsibility, and accountability. That being said, stop and question whether you're being too hard on yourself. According to a study by Harvard Business School and the Wharton School at the University of Pennsylvania, "women systematically provide less favorable assessments of their own past performance and potential future ability than equally performing men."

When it comes to asking for a raise, the same principles apply as when you're negotiating your salary at a new job. (This would be a good time to revisit Chapter Six.) The additional benefit to negotiating at a current job is that you can speak to specific ways you helped make, or save, the company money. You can—and should—also bring in ideas for the future. Speak to the next job you want and use what you've already done to demonstrate that you have what it takes. This might mean going to someone who has held the role before to better understand their challenges and what it entails to do a good job. Negotiating a raise at your current job is less a reward for the past and more of a vote of confidence for the future. If they give you a title change without a pay bump, you should still try to negotiate for more money. If they won't budge, bring up full compensation and get a time on the calendar in the next three to six months to revisit your salary.

This is also an opportune moment to ask for funds for career development. Whether it's taking classes or attending a conference, it doesn't have to be specifically related to your job function, but you do need to make the case for how it will help you do your job better. In other words, you need to show how it benefits the business.

Here's one way you can structure a professional development request to make sure you're addressing everything they need to see in order to say yes.

SAMPLE LETTER TO SUPERVISOR

Dear [INSERT NAME]

I recently came across [INSERT CONFERENCE], which is dedicated to leadership and networking within our industry, and I'd love to attend. It's being held on Saturday, November 2, in Brooklyn.

I think this will be a great opportunity to learn leadership skills and network with over 1,000 other industry professionals from around the country. In addition to leadership training, other themes include how to build an inclusive company culture, financial literacy, and how to be an effective communicator.

Speakers include [INSERT SPEAKER NAME AND TITLE] and [INSERT SPEAKER NAME AND TITLE]

I'm excited to bring what I learn back to [THE COMPANY], and I'd be happy to give a presentation to the team on any of the material.

Here's a breakdown of the costs to attend:

✦ Conference fee: [INSERT NUMBER]

✦ Airfare: [INSERT NUMBER]

✦ Travel to and from the airport: [INSERT NUMBER]

✦ Transportation to and from the hotel via shuttle: [INSERT NUMBER]

✦ Hotel: [INSERT NUMBER]

In addition to learning valuable skills, this is a good opportunity to meet potential clients and even candidates for this company. Who knows, maybe we'll end up hiring someone from this conference!

Thank you for your consideration, and I hope we can discuss more this week.

Respectfully,
[INSERT NAME]

CREATE YOUR OWN OPPORTUNITIES

If you're not feeling challenged at work or that you haven't been able to demonstrate your full potential, see if you can create your own opportunities. For example, is there a gap in the business that you could fill? Do you have an idea that could improve the way things are done? A new way to make money or generate buzz? Be proactive in finding or creating initiatives where you can shine. That doesn't mean going rogue or shirking your current responsibilities. You need to galvanize support before you add anything else. Otherwise you run the risk of alienating your manager, which is the exact opposite of what you're intending to do. Still, looking for your own areas of growth is a huge part of building a path toward advancement.

PITCH YOUR IDEA

1. **Get buy-in.** Before you bring your idea to management, you need to get buy-in from anyone who might be impacted by it. Understand how this fits into their preexisting priorities and what their capacity is for working on this. Get them invested by seeking their feedback and brainstorming ideas. Build momentum by asking them who else they recommend you speak with.

2. **Work backward.** Anticipate all the reasons management might say no so you can be proactive in addressing them. The three major concerns will most likely be how much money this will cost, how it fits in with your current responsibilities, and how you'll measure success.

3. **Prepare a beta.** If you're proposing something that's never been done and/or requires a budget, have an alternative idea in your back pocket. Something that's low resource but can be a proof of concept. For example, if you're pitching a video series, you might want to use Instagram Stories as a way of "testing" it out first.

4. **Don't give up.** If they say no, ask them why. Get as specific feedback as possible so you understand what you need next to get them to say yes. Schedule a time in the next few months when you can present again. If nothing else, pitching your idea will have at least demonstrated to them that you think big and are self-motivated.

IT PAYS OFF

Eighteen months into her new role in the business and technology services department, Shelmina received an invitation to shadow Rodney Adkins, a senior vice president at IBM, for a year. This was a big deal. Shelmina's stellar performance, diversity of skills, and sponsors she'd cultivated had all led her here. Now she would have access to one of the most powerful people in the industry and get an insider's look at how the company ran at its highest level.

Shelmina was flattered but also concerned. Her kids were two and four years old at the time, and she was worried that this job would require her to constantly travel, which would be a problem for her as a single mom. She reached back out to Carolyn Maher (who had helped her change departments) to seek her counsel. Shelmina wanted to know if declining the job would lower her chances of eventually becoming an executive. Carolyn assured her that it wouldn't. However, she told Shelmina if she did take this position, it would pretty much guarantee her an executive role.

Before formally accepting, Shelmina decided to take a chance and discuss her concerns with Rodney. He answered her that yes, there would be travel, but also assured her that given that this was a temporary position, she could always go back to her current position, leading business development and sales. This solidified her decision; Shelmina knew the importance of having a good manager, and the way he responded made it easy for her to say yes. She came away with the realization that she should never be the one to say no to herself; in other words, she shouldn't let assumptions prevent her from moving forward.

Working for Rodney catapulted Shelmina into a new stratosphere. Around three and a half months into her tenure with Rodney, she got an opportunity to step out of his shadow. They'd been working closely together on a five-year strategy that Rod was going to present to their top twenty clients in a meeting overseas. This was incredibly important; these were clients that could make or break their business.

The night before they were set to leave, Rodney sent Shelmina and a group of other executives involved in the project an email marked "urgent." His wife had just gone to the ER and he didn't think he'd be able to make the trip. The team (which included the VP of sales, the VP of strategy, and the VP of operations), went into a frenzy. What were they going to do? Who was going to present? Then it became obvious: Shelmina would do it. She was the only one besides Rod who knew the ins and outs of the strategy. Shelmina was overwhelmed by the magnitude of this assignment, but she knew this was her chance to really step up. She spent the entire flight to Italy preparing when it dawned on her: She could do this. She'd helped come up with the material and she'd observed Rodney long enough to feel confident about how to best communicate it.

She arrived at the airport and managed to decompress a bit before the meeting. And when it came time for her presentation to the clients, she hit it out of the park.

Soon enough, Shelmina started getting inquiries from other departments at IBM that had open roles. She'd built such an impressive reputation that she was now in the position of getting her pick of opportunities. This wasn't luck—Shelmina had worked hard for this. Given how critical relationships had been in her career, she evaluated her offers by how much she could expand her network, as well as the skills she would gain.

Shelmina ended up taking a position where she could work with IBM's global business, eventually running a portfolio of $1.25 billion. She ended up staying at IBM for more than ten years, going from being afraid to speak up in meetings to eventually speaking in front of the CEO (who told her she'd conducted one of the best strategy sessions she'd ever been a part of).

In some ways, Shelmina's story is full of contradictions. She stayed focused on moving up but was flexible on where that took her. She leaned into her strengths but also sought new ones. She let her work speak for itself but also knew when she needed to be her own advocate. Shelmina understood the importance of letting things unfold organically, but she also acted strategically. It was she who drove her success, but it was her relationships that pushed her even further.

If there is one thing you learn from this book it is that you cannot go it alone. From getting a job to getting ahead, the relationships you build are the key. Don't let your current lack of network, a language barrier, or a marginalized status keep you from achieving. You have every right to take up space, to grow and succeed, and your company should feel lucky to have you.

PART FOUR

MAKE A DIFFERENCE

*[Women's lack of progress is] seen as a personal
failing when in fact, it's a systemic failing.*
—Kristin Rowe-Finkbeiner, cofounder and CEO of MomsRising.org

By this point in the book, you've learned how to take control of your career and find opportunities to advocate for what you want. But trying to succeed within a system that's stacked against you can feel like trying to swim against the current. Even if you make it, you still feel as if you're gasping for air. This is the experience for many working women, especially women of color, in this country. The norms and structures of our workplaces were not built with us in mind, and there continue to be policies and practices that actively make it harder for us to succeed.

Until this section, the book has covered how you can move through self-doubt toward getting ahead and getting paid. But to only focus on how each of us can better ourselves is a disservice to all of us. Systemic change won't happen unless we actively work to change the system. If we don't, our growth will be capped, making it that much harder to achieve upward mobility.

It's easy to feel helpless with the depressing statistics and countless workplace horror stories. I felt this way for a year after my experience at the advertising festival. But we don't have to let our feelings have the last word. When you begin to feel overwhelmed, you can choose to recenter yourself. Ask yourself: What is within my control? When I go to work on Monday, what is one small thing I can do? Then that action can grow larger: How do I galvanize my colleagues to join me? How can we influence our boss to buy in? (If you're in a position of power, how will you make change?) And ask yourself the biggest question of all: How can we advocate for better laws?

In the next two chapters, you will hear the stories of Sarah and Madeline, two women who encounter injustices at work and put their desire to make change above the fear of retaliation. Sarah struggles with being a new mom and the lack of support (and sometimes blatant discrimination) that working parents can face. Madeline tries to hold on to her dignity in an environment where women are routinely objectified, passed over for promotions, and severely underpaid.

Their situations may strike you as extreme. Or maybe they'll feel familiar. Whatever your current situation, Sarah and Madeline are all of us. The issues contained within their stories—lack of paid family leave, gender discrimination, and pay inequity—have *the* biggest, most far-reaching impact on the wage gap and how quickly we can close it. Our companies and governments should be enacting policies to address these problems and bring about the structural change we need. But most are taking too long to do so.

And so, it falls to us to carry the burden. But here's the beautiful thing: if we do it together, it won't feel as heavy. And together, we can achieve great, big things.

CHAPTER TEN

GET YOUR COMPANY ON BOARD

Sarah had been at her company, a music streaming platform, for almost seven years when she got pregnant. She was working toward a big promotion at the time and was concerned about what an upcoming maternity leave would mean. She had a frank conversation with her manager, who told her not to worry, the promotion would be waiting for her when she returned to work. Sarah knew how lucky she was to be able to combine her company's paid leave policy and her vacation time, which gave her five months of leave in total. It was way above the norm at the time in her state, where six weeks of paid leave was standard.

During her whole pregnancy and subsequent leave, Sarah found herself worrying about how motherhood might affect her. She was career-driven and had always prided herself on working hard and being ambitious. Would having a child affect her identity? Would she be treated differently? Ultimately, despite her natural feelings of anxiety, Sarah felt confident that her hard work combined with her clear commitment meant that she would be fine. Plus, before she left for maternity leave, she had the assurance from her boss that she'd get the promotion she'd worked for.

But one week before she was set to return, Sarah got an email. The promotion that she'd been promised was given to someone else—someone she'd trained two years ago! Not only that, the person who had been reporting to her was being removed, so now Sarah didn't even have a manager title. She was shocked. There were no indications at work that this might happen; her performance reviews had always been stellar. Sarah spent her final week of leave in a panic.

There was tension from the day Sarah returned. She was being micromanaged in a way she'd never been before, was asked to do unnecessary travel, and got her performance review rescheduled multiple times. The head of Sarah's department had been known to say "I don't do favors for working parents"; it felt pretty clear to Sarah that she was being pushed out, or at least sidelined. Her suspicions were confirmed when she asked her manager (the one she'd trained, who had been promoted above her) if this was happening because she became a parent. The woman nodded.

Sarah couldn't imagine that she was the only one who was feeling frustrated, marginalized, or demoralized. When she talked to her colleagues with children about her experience, they, too, shared her concerns, and many of them had been looking to leave for months. Childless colleagues who had contemplated starting a family but had witnessed what happened to Sarah were now having second thoughts. Sarah wasn't the kind of person to just sit there and do nothing. But the question was, what could she do? Sue them? Even if she did try to effect change, she was concerned that the leadership was too checked out, the toxicity too entrenched, and that no matter what she did, she wouldn't even make a dent.

THE BROKEN RUNG

Sadly, Sarah's experience is not isolated. The promotion that evaporated, and the culture that enabled it, is part of what the consulting firm McKinsey calls the Broken Rung. In their 2019 report on women in the workplace, conducted in partnership with the Lean In Foundation, they found that one of the biggest barriers to women's professional advancement is their difficulty in getting past middle management. In fact, the report defines the broken rung as a more serious problem than even the glass ceiling. For 78 percent of women, bottlenecking at entry-level jobs (where we make less money) means always lagging behind our male counterparts in terms of both promotion and pay.

When women don't make it into management, it means that there are fewer women to begin with for companies to promote into leadership positions. So senior leadership continues to be primarily composed of (white) men, and as a result, corporate culture continues to reflect their unconscious biases—which is bad for everyone, not just the people who get shut out of opportunities. A limited range of perspectives can hurt both the company's culture and its bottom line. A study by the Boston Consulting Group showed that companies that have more diverse management teams have 19 percent higher revenue due to the greater innovation that comes from different points of view.

An entrenched problem like the broken rung requires a holistic solution. You can't just pull a lever and promote more women; you have to gain an understanding of the life cycle of an employee, from how they are recruited, to the work they are assigned, to how they are evaluated. It's also about the work culture: Is this an environment that is inclusive, where everyone can thrive? Sometimes the problems simmer under the surface, but other times, they're out in the open and undeniable. In Sarah's case, it was the latter.

SARAH MAKES A MOVE

As Sarah tried to figure out her next moves, a recruiter from another company reached out to her. Their culture was known for its inclusivity, and the pay was better. Sarah decided to go for it. She was relieved to get out of her toxic situation, though this company also had areas to improve when it came to working parents. For example, the all-hands meeting was held every week at 5:30 p.m., a time when parents need to be home with their kids. And while there were a number of employee resource groups (ERGs), none were specifically dedicated to parents and other caregivers.

Employee resource groups started in the 1960s as networking and social groups for women and people of color within companies. Now they've expanded to provide a way for employees to come together to spread awareness of issues that are facing a certain demographic, whether it's veterans, parents of children with special needs, or the LGBTQIA+ community. Given all the contorting we as women often do to accommodate others, it's important to have a space where we can release that burden and just be ourselves. In addition, ERGs enable employees who may feel marginalized to come together to discuss ways the company can address their needs and make the culture more inclusive.

Sarah decided that unlike before, she wasn't going to minimize the fact that she was a parent. She would wear her identity as a mother proudly, and she would make sure everyone else felt comfortable to do so, too. But how? It seemed that the best place to start was by creating her own ERG.

Sarah's first step was to reach out to the leaders of the other ERGs at her company and ask how they got started, what their challenges were, and the things they'd learned. Her next step was to look at what her company's competitors were doing about diversity and inclusion. All the tech companies in Silicon Valley were fiercely competing for talent and

Sarah knew that having ERGs was a great way for them to signal their support for their employees and dedication to creating a positive workplace. By having an ERG for parents, they could market themselves as a family-friendly company.

Sarah knew that in order to make a strong case for the ERG, she needed to demonstrate that there were other people who wanted it, too. After speaking to some colleagues who agreed to support her, she posted her idea on an internal platform the company used to help employees communicate with one another. Coincidentally, the two cofounders of the company had just become parents themselves, so she tagged them in her post, along with all the executives she could find who were also parents. It was a bold action, but Sarah figured a little public pressure wouldn't hurt.

Around the same time, a new chief diversity officer joined the company. Sarah pitched the idea of a Take Your Kids to Work Day to him as a way to gauge interest in creating an official ERG dedicated to parents. She was able to strengthen her case by collecting pledges from colleagues who wanted to join. It worked; Sarah got approval. Now she was off to the races.

Whatever ERG you want to start, the best case you can make is how it will help the company retain and attract talent. For example, engaging your employees fosters an environment where people feel supported and enthusiastic about coming to work every day. Keeping morale high is good for productivity, and it signals to potential candidates that this is a company with a positive culture.

Here are steps you can take to get your ERG the green light:

HOW TO START
AN EMPLOYEE RESOURCE GROUP

1. **Do your research.** Look at other ERGs at your company (and competitor companies) to learn their best practices. If it makes sense to partner with any of them, that might be a good way to get started. In addition, try to find out if your ERG has been proposed before and if so, what happened.

2. **Rally support.** The more interest you can show for the ERG, the stronger your case will be. Find one to two other people who will come on board as co-organizers, as well as others who express interest in attending. Rebecca Weaver, founder of HRuprise, recommends gathering people across different parts of the organization since that demonstrates a larger, company-wide need.

3. **Create a proposal.** Whether it's a PowerPoint or a Word doc, lay out the plan for how the ERG will operate. It can be organized in the following way:

   a. State your mission and overall goal.

   b. Examples of programming. Include a range of ideas but be aware that you'll need to start small before you can show traction.

   c. How you'll spread the word. As great as your programming ideas are, you need to have a plan to market them.

   d. Ways to measure success. What are the metrics you'll use to determine the success of your ERG? Is it the number of event attendees? Positive feedback you receive after the event?

e. Resources you'll need. Whether it's conference room space, food and beverages, or compensation for a speaker, include a ballpark budget. Be prepared with low-cost or no-cost ideas in case they don't have enough money to give you.

4. **Find an executive sponsor.** You can start with your boss, but look for one to two people in senior positions who can help provide guidance, advocate for a budget, and be the liaison to the company's leadership. They don't have to share the same diversity identity as the ERG's members; they just need to be willing to be a champion for them. Their association with your ERG will highly increase the likelihood of its approval, sustainability, and overall success.

SHE HAD BIGGER PLANS

When researching employee resource groups, Sarah realized bringing people together was only a first step toward making change. She thought about her last job and how her growth had been stymied, from the off-hand comments to the denied promotion, and wondered if she'd just had bad luck or if there was something that could have been done on a company-wide level. Real inclusivity had to come from the top and it needed to be codified into policy.

In her research, Sarah was shocked to discover the systematic deduction in pay that mothers suffer. It even had a name: the Motherhood Penalty. For every child a woman has, her pay goes down by 4 percent (whereas for every child a man has, his pay increases by 6 percent). The cumulative effect of the motherhood penalty is, in fact, one of the largest contributors to the wage gap.

For Sarah, researching was like pulling on a thread. The more she tugged, the more she unraveled. Digging deeper into workplace discrimination against mothers, Sarah homed in on the lack of paid family leave (as well as the lack of universal pre-K and subsidized childcare) as a major inhibitor to women's progress, in terms of both promotions and pay.

There's an abundance of research that shows that mothers across all education levels drop out of the workforce at a disproportionately higher rate than fathers. Part of this is because of how we're socialized (women are expected to be caretakers), part of it is financial (childcare is expensive), and part of it is the fact that very few companies offer paid family leave longer than three weeks if they offer it at all.

The United States is the only industrial country in the world without universal paid family leave. Not only is there no federally mandated family leave, only 12 percent of employees in the United States have access to any paid family leave at all. Currently the only legally required support for leave is the Family Medical Leave Act (FMLA), which protects your job until you come back, but is unpaid.

According to the Pew Research Center, women provide twice as much caregiving as men, so they often find themselves struggling with where to allocate their time. Between the inflexible structure of work and the exorbitant expense of childcare, staying home or cutting back hours is often a financial necessity. Sure, they might have the power to "choose"; but when the choice is between leaving a job and saving money or going back to work and increasing expenses, it's not really a fair choice.

It turns out that being paid less and promoted less often than men aren't just blips on a résumé but rather an entrenched and perpetuated practice with long-term effects, not just for women but for everyone. Perhaps it's no surprise that mothers are twice as likely as fathers to say that being a working parent has made it harder for them to advance in their jobs or careers (and COVID-19 has only made it harder).

This is precisely why paid leave needs to be understood as family leave, and not maternity leave. If it's only defined as maternity leave (which it traditionally has been), it perpetuates the stereotype that women are the default caretakers and that men don't need to bond with their newborns (which is a loss for everyone). Another reason to think bigger than "maternity" leave is the benefit it has on closing the wage gap. The World Economic Forum has found that countries that offer paternity leave have been the most successful in closing the wage gap between men and women.

The truth is time away from the office can limit opportunities for exposure, and in turn recognition. But women shouldn't be the ones to suffer this. It's important that companies not only institute a gender-neutral policy but that they actively encourage their male employees to actually take their allotted time.

For single mothers, of course, paid leave is even more important. They don't have the option of staying home without pay. As both the sole caretakers and breadwinners, they are caught in a precarious situation; in most single-mother households, one salary (already limited by the wage gap) barely covers regular expenses, let alone childcare. Single mothers of color suffer the brunt of the wage gap and the motherhood penalty. Many are concentrated (i.e., occupationally segregated) in jobs and industries that are hourly, which means lower wages, are less secure, and offer no form of leave. According to a 2015 report by the Center for American Progress, approximately 40.2 percent of Black workers have zero access to paid family leave or medical leave.

Because African American and Hispanic women are more likely to be raising children in single-parent homes, the consequences are dire. Nearly two in five families headed by Black and Hispanic women live in poverty. Single-mother households of other races don't fare much better, with more than one in three in poverty, according to research done in 2018 by the National Women's Law Center.

Being realistic about her bandwidth, Sarah decided to focus her time and energy on trying to improve her company's paid family leave. Given that she worked for a prominent tech firm that would make the news if they adopted a new policy, Sarah now saw the creation of her ERG as her first step to generate enthusiasm around supporting parents. The next step would be leveraging that enthusiasm to show that a benefit to employees was a benefit to the company and its bottom line.

TIMING IS EVERYTHING

After speaking to a few of her colleagues, Sarah learned that budgets were going to be decided in three months, and so she worked backward from that date, doing research and finding other employees who would support her. She was introduced to the leaders of a parental ERG at another major tech company who had just started a new initiative aimed at bringing together the leaders of parental ERGs across the tech industry, helping them to share ideas and support one another. They compared one another's policies, what family-friendly perks their respective companies were providing, and any anecdotal data that could help bolster all of their cases. It was through working with this group that Sarah met Orli Cotel from Paid Leave for the United States (PL+US), an organization committed to winning federal paid family and medical leave by 2022. When Orli heard Sarah was gearing up for her pitch, she offered help, and in Sarah's words, became her "partner in crime."

KEEP IT MOVING

Sarah had great success with her Take Your Kids to Work Day; in the aftermath one of the company's cofounders wrote an email letting her know how fantastic it was. She used that momentum to secure a meeting with the director of benefits in the HR department, and she invited the chief diversity officer, who had become the executive sponsor of her ERG, to join. Though they weren't parents themselves, they understood that an improved policy would have a large impact on anyone who might be considering having a family. It was the right thing to do, but it was also a strategic way to build a stronger company.

Sarah positioned her pitch just as she'd done for her ERG: as a benefit to retaining and attracting talent, which is a money-saver for the company. For example, when a skilled salaried employee leaves a company, it costs about twice the annual salary of that person to replace them, between recruitment costs, training and onboarding costs, and time.

Below is a pitch template put together by Paid Leave for the United States. It originated as a way to provide a structure and inform best practices in lobbying for improved leave policy, but it can be adapted to whatever policy change you want to see happen.

POLICY PITCH TEMPLATE

1. **A Strong Opening and Ask on Page 1.** Busy CEOs want to know immediately on page 1 why you're meeting and what you're asking for.
2. **Why Statement.** Introduce paid family leave and why a good policy matters to your company's interests and values.

3. **Employee Testimonials.** People are often moved to action because personal stories are more powerful than just facts and figures alone.

4. **Current Policy.** Include your company's current paid family leave policy.

5. **Benchmarking Competitor Policies.** Provide a comparison of competitors' policies from within your industry or geographic region. Find competitor policies that demonstrate that your company needs to catch up. Be cognizant of context; for example, a small company doesn't necessarily have the resources of a large one.

6. **Proposed Policy.** State the current policy (if there is one) and the specific changes you're proposing.

SHE MAKES HER CASE

The director of benefits took Sarah's materials and presented them at the annual benefits meeting with the company's executives. She told her it went well but that it was probably going to take a few months to know whether it had been approved. Sarah felt optimistic but tried to temper her excitement in case it was a no.

Six months later Sarah got an email from the chief diversity officer and the director of benefits, who were asking to meet with her. She walked into the conference room, where she was greeted with big smiles. They told her that the company's cofounders wanted to extend a personal thank-you to her for bringing the issue forward. Not only were they extending paid family leave from twelve weeks to eighteen weeks for primary caregivers and from four to six weeks for secondary caregivers, they also made it retroactive from the previous year so that anyone who had had a baby then and needed that time could use it moving forward. In addition, they were extending bereavement leave from three days to three weeks. The updated policy was to be enacted immediately.

After thanking them, Sarah ran to a phone room. Big fat happy tears rolled down her cheeks. She'd done it. She gathered her emotions and called her husband to let him know the good news.

When the news was announced at her company, Sarah was overwhelmed by all the emails she received from her coworkers. "It was so profoundly moving. People were in tears saying, 'I get to have my child visit their grandmother on the other side of the world because we now have this time.' There were way too many stories to even recount."

And Sarah was right that improving paid family leave would help the company attract talent. Less than a year later, an article by Fatherly ranked her company as one of the best places for dads to work. And a few months after that, one of their main competitors increased *their* paid leave policy. To Sarah, this was evidence of the change that can come from one person speaking up and the domino effect it can have. It also reminded her of her own grit and capacity for courage. "I didn't realize how resilient I was, going through something that painful and being able to turn my pain into progress. I may never need paid leave again in my lifetime, but I still want to do as much as I can to make sure this generation, tomorrow's generation, my daughter's kids one day, don't have to go through these workforce issues in the future. I still want to make sure every single person has an opportunity to be with their family when it matters most."

GET RECOGNIZED

After her victory, reflecting on the skills she learned and the leadership she'd demonstrated, Sarah felt emboldened to ask her bosses for two things: that her efforts be included in her quarterly performance reviews, and that she could shift a percentage of her overall responsibilities to explicitly work on this. Sarah made the argument that this work benefited the business (it impacted hiring and retention) and had measurable goals and milestones of success. Somewhat to her surprise, her bosses said yes! A week later she received a little gift from both of them; it was a charm necklace with an engraving on the back: NEVERTHELESS, SHE PERSISTED.

Sarah's story is a happy one. She took her toxic experience and stood by her values, knowing that she deserved better. She didn't deny her identity as a parent and held on to the belief that it's possible to be in a workplace where you don't have to change who you are to fit in. Sarah also understood the importance of bringing people along with you. Her willingness to learn and seek support—just like Shelmina—was what helped her achieve her goals. Also, her foresight to do things like work backward from the budget cycle helped her make the most compelling case: to get the executives to say yes, they had to see their way to a solution that would not only work for them but benefit them in the long run.

If you are someone without a great deal of influence at work (i.e., more junior or middle management), don't let that stop you from going to those that have more. We spend most of our waking hours at work (over 90,000 hours over a lifetime!), so being miserable is simply unsustainable (and unhealthy). Fortunately, there is a growing trend of companies making policy changes because of demand from their employees, as well as their customers. For example, in 2017 thousands of Walmart's employees signed a petition for better paid leave, garnering lots of press, as well as the support of one of their board members. Soon after, Walmart changed its policy.

If you are someone with influence at your organization, please use it for good. If you can make your voice heard, please speak up. The change you make goes beyond the people you employ; it affects their families and their communities. It sets an example for other companies and makes positive policies the norm. Take solace in Sarah's story and have the confidence that you, too, can make the change you want to see.

CHAPTER ELEVEN

CASE STUDY: GET EQUAL

The last woman we'll meet, Madeline, experienced workplace discrimination on multiple levels. While her situation might seem extreme, and her response drastic, I view her story as one that brings together many of the other experiences and issues faced by the other women featured in this book. From questioning herself to activating her allies, the core of Madeline's struggle is how to best advocate for her value—and that of the women around her. In structure and story, this chapter includes less direct advice prescribed throughout it. Madeline's story speaks for itself. Her decisions are personal, and her particular experience may not translate to universal lessons so much as act as an inspiration. I trust you will take what resonates and actualize it in a way that makes sense for you. And maybe it will be a catalyst that moves you to fight for justice for yourself and other women.

WELCOME TO THE CLUB

Pancola Partners was a prestigious boutique investment bank with a boisterous frat boy founder who turned his inherited millions into billions by leveraging his community of wealthy family friends to invest in his deals.

Madeline was a forty-year-old partner at another highly regarded bank when Pancola Partners recruited her. They were looking for someone to be their head of talent analytics and her experience in organizational management made her an ideal candidate. She was hesitant at first. In her research about the company she had found that out of the seventy-five investment professionals there at the time, only one was a woman. Same for the twelve managing directors—there was also just one woman.

Madeline had been on Wall Street long enough to know what kind of boys' club she might be getting herself into, but after considering the opportunity, she felt optimistic enough to believe she could effect positive change. She pitched the company on building a diversity and inclusion program to help recruit beyond their typical hire, which tended to be a Harvard or Wharton graduate hailing from Connecticut, and almost always male. She was there to be part of the solution.

After a lengthy negotiation, Madeline was in. She started almost immediately.

The first sign that something was seriously wrong came about a month after Madeline joined, when a female senior executive on her team took her to lunch. They hadn't even ordered their food when the woman burst into tears. Over the course of the meal she opened up to Madeline about how she was making about a third of her male counterparts' salaries, and when she went to HR to report and try to remedy the discrepancy, they told her they didn't have the budget to do anything about it. Not only that, they would be cutting salaries—hers included—

to make up for this shortfall in their budget. However, not too long after, a wave of new men were hired at paychecks three to four times the size of hers.

Things got even worse, she said, when she went on maternity leave. Less than a week after she gave birth, one of the executives tasked her with putting together a report. Though she'd just barely left the hospital, she didn't feel pushing back was an option, and so for fear of being fired, she put her head down and did it. She was still traumatized.

Madeline had dealt with chauvinism before, but this lunch signaled to her that this was different. She'd noticed some concerning signs herself, like witnessing an executive ask a female manager to clean up garbage after a meeting. Madeline was beginning to question if this kind of toxic culture might be too much, too entrenched for even her (and her diversity and inclusion program) to improve. The next troubling experience happened a few months later. She was at a fundraising event, in conversation with two male executives. Another woman joined their conversation for a bit, and when she left one of the men turned to the other and asked, "Do you want to fuck her? You can. She works for me."

But just as that female senior executive had done before her, Madeline put her head down and kept pushing forward. She continued to focus on the platform she was building, trying to assure herself that she was doing her part to improve the company culture.

THE DISCOVERY

A few months after the fundraiser, Madeline was going through the hiring budget when she was stopped in her tracks. There was a stark difference between the compensation that was being offered to men and the compensation offered to their female counterparts. It didn't matter their level, background, or skills, the men were categorically paid more. One new hire stood out in particular; he was coming from a firm that was being shut down, and although he was partly responsible for their revenue loss, his salary was still three times higher than the female hires on the same level. Madeline couldn't understand why that was, so she took it to the head of recruitment. His response? "The boss likes him."

Madeline went digging for her own salary. Sadly, she wasn't an outlier: the men on her level were making more than *double* what she was. She was instantly filled with shame and humiliation. She'd been so proud of how hard she'd negotiated when she got the job. Now she realized how little they valued her. And she'd had no idea.

Madeline couldn't sleep that night. Or the next night, or the one after that. She spent hours poring over everyone's résumé, trying to find what the men had that she didn't. If the wage difference was this wide, there must be an explanation. Maybe they had more advanced degrees, or maybe they managed more people. Maybe they were just better than she was. But the more Madeline tried to justify it, the more frustrated she got. She couldn't rationalize herself out of this one; the discrepancy was too large.

The guidelines for approaching a difficult conversation about your salary are similar to how you might address a challenging manager (as is laid out in Chapter 8: Get Allies). The best thing you can do is stay calm, give your manager the benefit of the doubt, and make the case for why you deserve more.

YOU JUST FOUND OUT YOUR COWORKER MAKES MORE—NOW WHAT?

1. **Separate your emotions.** Most likely this is an intensely emotional experience for you, but you have to do your best to isolate how you feel from what you're going to do. Letting your emotions overwhelm you will make it harder to be as objective and as analytical as possible. Plus, the more emotional you seem, the easier it is for you to be dismissed.

2. **Seek guidance.** Is there someone at the company who might have advice on how best to handle this? Choose this person carefully so as to be as discreet as possible.

3. **Get information.** Don't assume that the pay discrepancy is due to sexism. There are multiple factors that go into determining compensation, so in order to better understand the situation, inquire about what the pay structure is and where your salary falls in relation to others. Perhaps they prioritize master's degrees, or your colleague has a unique background or skill set.

4. **Ask what you can do.** Assuming that the purpose of bringing this issue up is to get a raise, have them tell you what you need to do to get one. Maybe you're already on track, or maybe they will suggest you take on a stretch assignment; e.g., a new project, role, or task that helps you develop skills. If your annual review isn't coming up within the next six months, request to have another meeting in three months in order to make sure you're doing the work they need to see to increase your compensation.

Going into work after the discovery was difficult for Madeline. It was as if all her colleagues had numbers floating above their heads, the men's salaries dwarfing the women's, and all the women were seemingly unaware, just as Madeline had been. She debated whether she should tell them. But given that she was still trying to process it herself, Madeline decided to keep it to herself for the time being and push the women around her—especially the more junior women—to ask for raises. That included her; if she couldn't close the wage gap for everyone, the least she could do was make more money herself.

Madeline spent time meticulously preparing her case for a raise. Knowing how much other people were making encouraged her to swing big and to her relief, her manager agreed, in theory. He wasn't the final decision maker, but he promised that he'd strongly advocate for her to the higher-ups.

Madeline eventually got a raise, though it wasn't what she wanted. It was a 20 percent bump, which, under any other circumstance, would've been great. However, it was still almost 300 percent less than what her male counterparts were making. To say it was a slap in the face was to put it lightly. It wasn't just unfair, Madeline thought, it was outrageous. She'd gotten a perfect performance review and her newly built strategy team was considered a huge success. It made no sense. For about five minutes, Madeline contemplated quitting. But that would mean they'd won. She couldn't let that happen. She had to do something. But what?

Speaking out against inequity comes with the risk of you being perceived as an agitator. That's why it's extremely important to take the utmost care in preparing your case. Be methodical in mapping out your options and who will stand with you. Take your time.

Madeline turned her dining room into a war room. She laid out large pieces of paper and mapped out all the possible next steps she could take and what the various outcomes might be. A friend suggested she leak these huge pay gaps to the press and then put pressure on the company to do an official pay audit. That didn't feel ethical to Madeline. She thought about who her allies were at the firm and who could help her make the case for pay parity. But she knew that even those she thought might be sympathetic would be worried about what it might do to their reputation. Relationships are everything in the finance industry, and no one wanted to do anything that might potentially rock the boat.

To test the waters, Madeline reached out to some senior men she knew at other firms to get their input. They warned her in no uncertain terms that if she spoke up, there would be repercussions.

All the while, the workplace consciousness was rapidly shifting. Brave women were beginning to speak up about sexual harassment and pay inequity, powerful men were starting to get pushed out, and entire industries were in the process of being upended. But the finance industry had been left untouched. Despite its boys' club reputation, no one had publicly spoken up about her industry. So who, then, would be the first? Who would hold them accountable?

Madeline knew the risks—she'd mapped them on her dining room table—but she also knew her privilege. She had savings. She was senior enough and had a long enough track record that if she needed to get a new job, she'd probably be able to find one. If not her, who? If not now, when?

As she reflected on her options, Madeline figured that the best course of action was to hire an employment lawyer. Together they decided to sue Pancola Partners for discrimination. They filed on a Friday at noon, and by the end of the business day word was out in the industry. There was no turning back now.

Madeline went to work the following Monday. She walked through the doors with her head held high; it was actually the best she'd felt in a very long time. She'd carried the shame silently for months, but by bringing it out into the open, she would no longer have to shoulder the burden alone.

Most of her colleagues didn't know how to react. During a meeting, a bunch of men giggled nervously. No one could look her in the eye.

Pancola Partners denied her claim and the lawsuit dragged on for the next four years. For some months after filing, Madeline continued to go into the office. Her colleagues treated her with resentment and anger, but she was left alone to do her work. It was hard to pretend that things were normal, but she tried. Eventually, she was placed on administrative leave.

No matter how hard it got (and it did), nothing compared to that initial painful discovery of how little they had valued her—and so many other women. Whether she'd win or lose the lawsuit wasn't really the point. Madeline was proud of herself for being courageous and for the example she was setting for everyone else. They were Goliath and she was David. Madeline considers the day she filed the suit one of the best days of her life.

Madeline eventually left the firm but refuses to leave the industry. She strongly believes that working in finance is the most direct way to generate wealth, and so it's imperative that women—and in particular, women of color—stay. Otherwise, they will never be able to reach the highest levels of power and influence that men have always held. Social movements may start from the bottom, but Madeline sure as hell wasn't going to cede her place at the top.

Madeline's experience and the steps she took, while heightened, contain within them much of the DNA of this book. She questions her worth (*"there must be a reason they're paying me less"*), she lobbies for a raise, and activates (or at least tries to) the allies she's made both inside and outside the company. She recognizes the importance of strategy and she takes her time considering her options and making her case. Madeline knows that to get what she wants, she needs to tread carefully. But she also knows when she's had enough. It took enormous bravery to not only sue her company but to continue to come in to work there every day. Madeline stood by her convictions and wouldn't let her corporation bully her.

That's not to say her path is the only one. Madeline acknowledges it was her privilege that enabled her to take such risks. Her refusal to cede her place at the top demonstrates her awareness that this is bigger than any one of us as an individual, a message I hope you will take away from this book. The best thing about Madeline is she never lost the belief that she could make change. I wish this for you, too, that you can nurture this belief about your power—and let nothing take it away.

CHAPTER TWELVE

CONCLUSION

I wish I didn't have to write this book. If women were paid equally to men, if half of companies were run by us, if we owned half the wealth of the world, I might be resting instead of writing. You'd be leading instead of reading.

But we know that's not how things are. You saw that in the stories of Alisha, Reece, Kate, Phoebe, Amy, Giselle, Shelmina, Sarah, and Madeline. While their circumstances may not have been the same, at some point each one of them felt—or were made to feel—as if they were less than.

Then each one of them, in her own way, did something about it. They identified what was standing between them and what they wanted, and they learned how to go above it, around it, or through it. Each of them had an *aha* moment that changed the course of their careers.

For Shelmina, it was first refraining from sharing her ideas and then learning to lobby for them. For Alisha and Giselle, it was their toxic bosses who lit the fire to find their purpose. For Reece, it was standing up for her Fuck You Money number, and for Madeline, it was standing up for herself—and for all the women at her company. For Phoebe, it was opening her own doors, and for Sarah it was making sure they were open for everyone. For Kate, and for Amy, it was learning to trust herself.

But for an *aha* moment to happen, you have to be open to seeing it. And for that moment to mean anything, you have to decide to do something about it. And before *all* of that, you first have to believe you can. There are so many women who haven't yet realized that things can be better than they are. That they don't have to accept what they've been given. Maybe they don't think that it's possible, or they believe that their circumstances won't allow it. Yes, it will be more difficult for some than for others. It always is.

But if you're in a position to ask for more, ask for it. If you can make change, make it. The path will be challenging; as you saw in these stories, progress isn't linear, and asking for more requires vigilance but also patience. People will tell you "no," "not now," or "wait your turn." Don't let that deter you; use it as fuel. Setbacks don't have to set you back; in fact, they often illuminate the path forward. This is when you must ask yourself, without judgment: "What has this taught me? What wisdom can I take with me?"

Nothing will change if you don't fight for it. I know it's easy to feel alone or like you don't matter. This could not be further from the truth. There are so many women who, in so many different ways, are standing up and saying to the system: We want better. We *deserve* better. Being asked to take notes in a meeting may seem small, but it takes guts to be the woman who says no. Getting a $2,000 raise might not seem like much to some, but for the woman who negotiates, it can be life-changing. Remember, individual action begets collective change. You saw it in AOC's decision to run for office and in Sarah's push for paid family leave. If you're willing to try, and have the resilience to try again, you will see it in yourself. Remember, we're all in this together.

Now go get paid.

ACKNOWLEDGMENTS

First and foremost, thank you to all the women who've shared their stories with me over the past two years. You're my inspiration and I hope I've done you justice.

Of course, to my family: Mom and Dad; Paul, Isaac, Mira, Mr. Paul, Jodi, and Anna; my grandparents, Corinne and Bill, Al and Ann. And I can't forget Whoopsie, Jackson, Phoebe, Wee Gillus, and Angus. Also, to Ashley's family: Roger, Lydia, and Lindsay, who cheered me on from afar (and let me take over their printer, numerous times).

To Ashley, my partner-partner and so much more. I love you.

To everyone at Gallery Books, with a special thank-you to Jennifer Bergstrom and Aimee Bell for giving this book the green light and for being my champion as it came to life.

To my editor, Karyn Marcus, who deserves all the credit in the world for her persistence (and patience!) in pushing me out of my comfort zone and really bringing the book to the next level.

Thank you to Rebecca Strobel for getting this over the finish line, and to Carla Benton for making sure I didn't make any embarrassing grammar mistakes!

So much gratitude goes to the marketing, PR, and design teams for their enthusiasm for this book (and for putting up with all my ideas and all my emails), especially Sally Marvin, Lauren Truskowski, Sammi Sontag, Bianca Salvant, Lisa Litwack, John Vairo, Sarah Wright, and Davina Mock. And to my Orion team in the UK, Anna Valentine and Cathryn Summer-Hayes.

To my agent, Alexandra Machinist, for being the first to believe in me and for showing me what a badass negotiator can do. Shout-out to Hannah Linkenhofer for telling me I had a book within me, and to Deborah Ross, who is the reason all of this happened in the first place.

An enormous thank-you to Alessandra Lusardi, my book doctor, hand holder, and just an overall wonderful person. Words cannot express how grateful I am to you.

I'm also indebted to Akilah Cadet, who opened my eyes and held me to task.

A shout-out to Senator Alessandra Biaggi, who contributed to the appendix and whose energy and determination continue to inspire me.

I'd be remiss not to thank Justin Gignac and Adam Tompkins for being the first sponsors of Ladies Get Paid and to Leta Sobierajski, who motivated me to start in the first place (and who designed the Ladies Get Paid iconic money scrunchie!).

To Eric Holstein and his family for being there in the early days and especially to his mother, Carol Booth, for her love and support as I figured out what the heck all of this was.

To the Ladies Get Paid community and those who have helped along the way, in particular: Molly Small, Allie Mullen, Maria Pahuja, Sage Quiamno, Danielle Vogl, Stella Gold, Kelsey Woodworth, Jen Mussari, Jess Hooper, Kathleen Trainor, Austen Zoutewelle, Shenae Simmons, Shalia Skjong, Claire Bernhard, Arielle Patrick, Claire Lorenzo, Aaron Rasmussen, David Buckmaster, Alex Center, Jackie De Jesu Center, Alex Daly, Lydia Fenet, Lauren McGoodwin, Sabrina Orlins, Beth Comstock, Susan Lyne, David Cohen, Stephane Bibeau, Stephanie Louis, Megan Cesare-Eastman, Mark Conrad, Warren Metlitzky, Patricia Parker, Dan Bauman, Aditi Fruitwala, Karen Cahn, everyone who contributed to our crowdfunding campaign, and to anyone I forgot.

A special thank-you to the Ladies Get Paid ambassadors, past and present. You helped build this movement.

And finally, to the men who sued me for gender discrimination because, without your venom, I wouldn't be as strong as I am today.

APPENDIX

HOW TO EFFECT POLICY CHANGE

From the French Revolution to #TimesUp, change always starts with the people. First comes the rumbling of dissatisfaction. Brave souls stand up and speak out, often putting their livelihoods and their bodies on the line. Over time, the rumbling becomes a collective roar so loud that those in power no longer have the luxury of looking away or covering their ears. Pressure may come from the outside, but for wide-ranging and long-lasting change, we need the laws to change.

Just as you are strategic in getting ahead at work, so must you be in navigating policy change. It begins with familiarizing yourself with which policies help close the wage and leadership gap; the next step involves understanding the system and how it operates, and finally, it requires identifying the best ways to make your voice heard. Remember, laws change when people demand it. Your representatives work for YOU and it's their job to listen. You have the power (and a responsibility) to vote them in and out of office. Wield that power well.

POLICIES THAT MAKE CHANGE FOR WORKING WOMEN

As of 2020, the following are a number of policies (in different stages of progress) that seek to rectify the wage gap. They don't just benefit women, however; more money in the pockets of women means more money for the economy. Closing the wage gap in general doesn't just benefit women; the Institute for Women's Policy Research estimates that if you pay women more, $512 billion could be added to the GDP.

POLICY
Minimum Wage
WHAT IT IS
The federal minimum-wage provisions are contained in the Fair Labor Standards Act (FLSA). The federal minimum wage is $7.25 per hour effective July 24, 2009. Many states also have minimum wage laws. Some state laws provide greater employee protections; employers must comply with both.
HOW IT HELPS
Two-thirds of minimum-wage workers are women. They are also often the breadwinners (81 percent of Black women are), and so raising the minimum wage will help lift more families out of poverty.

RESOURCES

+ National Employment Law Project (nelp.org)
+ Economic Policy Institute (epi.org)

POLICY

Salary History Ban

WHAT IT IS

Prohibits employers from asking applicants about their current or past salaries or benefits.

HOW IT HELPS

The rationale is that if you're paid unfairly at your first job and all future jobs are based on that salary, the wage gap will only get wider with time. The salary history ban seeks to stop that.

RESOURCES

+ Society for Human Resource Management (shrm.org)
+ HR Dive (hrdive.com)

POLICY
Paycheck Fairness Act

WHAT IT IS

According to the ACLU:

The bill would update the Equal Pay Act of 1963, a law that has not been able to achieve its promise of closing the wage gap because of limited enforcement tools and inadequate remedies. The Paycheck Fairness Act would make critical changes to the law, including:

+ Requiring employers to demonstrate that wage differentials are based on factors other than sex;

+ Prohibiting retaliation against workers who inquire about their employers' wage practices or disclose their own wages;

+ Permitting reasonable comparisons between employees within clearly defined geographical areas to determine fair wages;

+ Strengthening penalties for equal pay violations;

+ Directing the Department of Labor to assist employers and collect wage-related data; and

+ Authorizing additional training for Equal Employment Opportunity Commission staff to better identify and handle wage disputes.

HOW IT HELPS

The name says it all!

RESOURCES

+ National Partnership for Women & Families (nationalpartnership.org)

+ Center for American Progress (americanprogress.org)

POLICY

Paid Family Leave

WHAT IT IS

Paid family leave (PFL) refers to partially or fully compensated time away from work for specific and generally significant family caregiving needs, such as the arrival of a new child or serious illness of a close family member.

HOW IT HELPS

Given that women are the majority of caregivers, paid family and medical leave would help them remain in the workforce throughout their careers.

RESOURCES

+ Paid Leave for the United States (paidleave.us)

+ A Better Balance (abetterbalance.org)

POLICY
The Healthy Families Act

WHAT IT IS
The United States has zero mandated paid sick days, except for sickness due to COVID-19 (it only applies to companies with less than 500 employees and does not cover hourly workers). The Healthy Families Act would set a national paid sick days standard.

HOW IT HELPS
Instituting federally mandated paid sick days will help close the wage gap, given that it's often women who forgo pay because they are the ones who end up staying home with a sick family member.

RESOURCES
✦   Paid Sick Days, a project of the National Partnership for Women & Families (paidsickdays.org)   ✦   Family Values @ Work (familyvaluesatwork.org)

POLICY
Universal Child Care and Early Learning Act

WHAT IT IS

Ensures that every family has access to high-quality, affordable childcare and early learning opportunities by establishing a network of federally supported childcare.

HOW IT HELPS

The Universal Child Care and Early Learning Act helps women in two major ways. Ninety-seven percent of childcare workers are women, the majority of whom are single mothers. This act will pay them a living wage, which in turn helps to close the wage gap and lift them out of poverty. The other benefit is keeping working mothers who often quit or reduce their hours because they can't find affordable childcare.

RESOURCES

+ Child Care Aware of America (childcareaware.org)
+ National Child Care Association (nccanet.org)

POLICY

Fair Workweek

WHAT IT IS

Laws that require employers to provide at least two weeks' advance notice of schedules.

HOW IT HELPS

Millions of people—mostly women—work in industries like restaurants, retail, and hospitality that have low wages and lack benefits. According to the National Women's Law Center, "Unstable and unpredictable work hours yield unstable and unpredictable incomes and make it extremely challenging for working people to manage responsibilities like caregiving [the majority of whom are women.]" The following benefits help keep women in the workforce, putting more money into their pockets.

✦ Opportunity to work enough hours for a living wage

✦ Ensures 10–11 hours of rest between shifts

✦ Allows flexibility without fear of termination, reduction in hours, or other retaliation.

RESOURCES

✦ The Fair Workweek Initiative (fairworkweek.org)

✦ National Child Care Association (nccanet.org)

MAKE SURE YOUR VOICE IS HEARD

If you're able to, showing up in person is the most effective way you can get your representative to listen to you. Look at their website and social media to find out what events they may be attending; you can also simply call their office to find out.

IN-PERSON ADVOCACY

✦ **Town halls.** Elected officials regularly hold public in-district events to show that they are listening to constituents. Interacting with the community in this format is becoming more and more popular, which means that holding them any less often than quarterly may cost them reelection. If your district doesn't have one scheduled, determine when the last town hall was held, and if it's been more than a month, file a request for one to be held.

✦ **Non-town hall events.** Politicians love cutting ribbons and kissing babies back home. This isn't just a time for photo ops; use it as an opportunity to bring up issues and hold them accountable.

✦ **District office sit-ins/meetings.** Every elected official has one or several district offices. You are within bounds to visit these offices, request a meeting, and if the officials are difficult to get ahold of, go to the press.

Calls require minimal effort but can have a big impact. The goal of calling is to generate a high volume of calls that require staffers to record them. The best way to do that is by organizing a group of people to barrage your representatives at an opportune moment and on a specific issue. The most effective calls will be to your district representatives; however, if there's a pressing national issue that you're passionate about, you should also call your congressional representative.

It can be nerve-wracking to make a call, but don't worry about being asked about the issue. All you need to do is state where you're from and why you're calling. When calling an elected official, be prepared to say the following:

PHONE CALL TEMPLATE

✦ Give your name and your location

✦ Why you are calling: oppose/support legislation, issue, etc.

✦ Leave a voice mail if they're not there. If voice mail is full, press "0." This will typically connect you to a receptionist who may be able to take your message or transfer you to a voicemail box that isn't full.

If you choose to write an email or a letter, think of it as a persuasive essay. To make it as powerful as possible, it should be personal, short, and to the point. Be upfront about your goals; for example, "I need X," "I want you to sign on to Y," "I'm inviting you to speak." Here's an example from the AccessLex Institute:

The Honorable
Office Address
United States House of Representatives/United States Senate
Washington, DC (20515—House / 20510—Senate)

Date:

Dear Representative/Senator_____:

As a constituent and a graduate, I urge you to support
_____.

This issue is important because _____.

The federal government's role in _____will ensure that
America as a nation continues to prosper. Continued investment in
_____ensures that we can continue to make strides in this
sector and to lead the way in innovation. If not for _____,
we will surely lose our competitive advantage.

Here are some specific facts to help illustrate my point.

+ Fact 1

+ Fact 2

+ Fact 3

+ Fact 4

Your support for _____is critical because I have
benefited from the program. *(Your story _____.)*

More to the point, the people I serve have benefited from it.
There are several constituents in *(state/district)* _____that are
benefiting from *(program)* _____.

Please ensure that you support and remain committed to
_____, benefiting all of American society. Thank you for
your consideration and please feel free to contact me if you would
like to discuss this issue further.

Sincerely,

Your Name

Your Title (if applicable)

Optional: Your Address, Your City, State, Zip, Your Phone Number

SOCIAL MEDIA

Posting on social media is a great way to publicly hold your elected official accountable. It also helps garner attention and get other people to amplify your message. Twitter is the best platform to use; a tweet that will cut through the noise will tag the people who can influence the elected official (such as other elected officials or people who run large organizations related to the issue you're tweeting about), along with messaging it in a way that will motivate them. The following tweet is a great example:

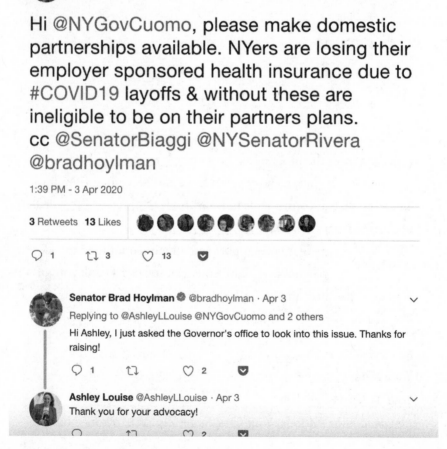

In response to this tweet, Governor Cuomo made it possible for people to get domestic partnerships and marriage licenses online. It goes to show that you don't need money, just access to the internet, in order to drum up attention and galvanize others.

DONATE

Money is power and those who donate the most get prioritized by elected officials. Don't worry, you don't need to be the Koch brothers (who spent almost $1 billion on the 2016 presidential election alone), to effect change. As Barack Obama's and Bernie Sanders's campaigns demonstrated, grassroots giving can shift the cultural conversation; $1, $5, $10, taken collectively, is all that it takes. However, research shows that women don't donate to politics as much as men. We need to change this. Money talks and you should make sure you're heard.

RUN FOR OFFICE

When Hillary Clinton lost the 2016 presidential election, her national operations director, Alessandra Biaggi, was not deterred. After mourning the loss and reflecting on what happened, she made the bold decision to run for the New York State Senate. To say she was a long shot is an understatement. Her opponent, Jeff Klein, had been in office for thirteen years and had millions of dollars in the bank, and the support of every powerful Democrat in the state. Similar to the story of Alexandria Ocasio-Cortez, Alessandra, against all odds, won. At age thirty-two, she became one of the youngest women ever elected to the New York State Senate.

If you're considering entering politics, Alessandra put together the

---

following guide for She Should Run, a nonprofit that helps to increase the number of women running for public office.

10 STEPS TO RUNNING FOR OFFICE

1. **Know your why.** What are your reasons for running? Lay out your vision and platform:

   a. Identify the problems in the district and the solutions you would propose

   b. Identify what works and how you would be a good vehicle to move progress forward

   c. Identify how your experience and skills can address these local issues

2. **Identify the political landscape**

   a. Community + Special District Boards

   b. City Council

   c. Assembly + Senate

   d. US Congress + Senate

3. **Create your political map**

   a. Where do you live? Who is in office in each elected role?

   b. Identify battleground districts

    c. Identify the demographic of your district

    d. Identify seats with term limits. Will a seat be opening up soon?

4. **Select the level of office and district to run in**

    a. Define the qualifications to run and visit the websites of the County or State Board of Elections or of the Secretary of State for specific rules

    b. Age + Residency requirements; for example: For US Congress you must be a resident in the state you are running in and at least twenty-five years old. For the New York Assembly, you must be a resident of the state for five years and resident of your district for twelve months immediately preceding election (in a redistricting year, you may be a resident of county for twelve months immediately); you must also be at least eighteen years old

    c. Ballot + Signature requirements

5. **Opponent/Incumbency**

    a. Familiarize yourself with their platform and identify ways for you to contrast (in a positive way) their experience and positions

    b. Opposition Research: voting record, allies, committees served on

6. **Write a campaign plan**

   a. Timeline: for example, petitioning and filing deadlines; voter registration deadlines; primary and general election dates, holidays, etc.

   b. Know what number you need to win; for example: How many people are in the district? How many people vote? How many people voted in the last two elections for this seat? How many people registered?

   c. Field plan for reaching voters. This includes door knocking, phone banking, sending mailers, paid and earned media, and social media.

7. **Fundraising plan**

   a. Create a budget

   b. Identify donation contribution limits for your race

   c. Fundraising goal (including small/large donors and PACs)

8. **Hire a campaign team**

   a. Campaign manager

   b. Fundraiser

   c. Scheduler

   d. Field coordinator

    e. Digital director

    f. Communication lead

    g. Researcher

9. **Identify important allies**

    a. Identify organizations and community leaders that would support your campaign

    b. Identify elected officials that would endorse your campaign and offer introductions to other organizations

10. **RUN!** Stay grounded. Stay close to your why. Trust your team; trust yourself. Be your authentic self. Remember: Running for office is not about *you*. It is about service to your community. There is much to learn even when you lose. People identify with those who struggle yet have grit and enough tenacity to get back in when it doesn't go their way. Now go out there and run!

Whether or not you want to run yourself, here's a list of organizations that support those who do.

TRAINING PROGRAMS

✦ New Leaders Council (gender neutral)

✦ Arena (gender neutral)

✦ Run for Something (gender neutral)

✦ She Should Run

✦ VoteRunLead

✦ Eleanor's Legacy

✦ Emerge America

✦ Center for American Women in Politics at Rutgers University

✦ Women's Campaign School at Yale

REFERENCES

Abed, Robbie. *How to Build Relationships and Get Job Offers Using LinkedIn.* Fire Me I Beg You, 2017.

Advisory Board. "How Often Are Women Interrupted by Men? Here's What the Research Says," *Today's Daily Briefing,* July 7, 2017. https://www.advisory.com/daily-briefing/2017/07/07/men-interrupting-women.

Akerlof, George A. *Explorations in Pragmatic Economics: Selected Papers of George A. Akerlof (and co-authors).* New York: Oxford University Press, 2005.

Akerlof, George A., and Rachel E. Kranton. "Economics and Identity," *The Quarterly Journal of Economics* vol. CXV, August 2000. https://public.econ.duke.edu/~rek8/economicsandidentity.pdf.

———. *Identity Economics: How Our Identities Shape Our Work, Wages, and Well-Being.* Princeton, NJ: Princeton University Press, 2010.

Allen, David. *Getting Things Done.* New York: Penguin Books, 2001.

Alonso-Villar, Olga, and Coral del Rio Otero. "The Occupational Segregation of Black Women in the United States: A Look at Its Evolution from 1940 to 2010," Society for the Study of Economic Inequality, September 2013. https://econpapers.repec.org/paper/inqinqwps/ecineq2013-304.htm.

American Association of University Women (AAUW). "The Simple Truth About the Gender Pay Gap," https://www.aauw.org/research/the-simple-truth-about-the-gender-pay-gap/.

American Civil Liberties Union. "Equal Pay For Equal Work: Pass the Paycheck Fairness Act," https://www.aclu.org/other/equal-pay-equal-work-pass-paycheck-fairness-act.

Artz, Benjamin, Amanda Goodall, and Andrew J. Oswald. "Research: Women Ask for Raises as Often as Men, But Are Less Likely to Get Them," *Harvard Business Review*, June 25, 2018. https://hbr.org/2018/06/research-women-ask-for-raises-as-often-as-men-but-are-less-likely-to-get-them.

Barada Associates, Inc. "Salary History Bans: What Employers Need to Know." https://baradainc.com/salary-history-bans/.

Barrica, Andrea. "Diversity Debt: How Much Does Your Startup Have?," *Medium*, July 27, 2015. https://medium.com/@abarrica/startups-diversity-debt-and-what-to-do-about-it-cd385364506#.epwzwpm5k.

Baxter, Judith. *The Language of Female Leadership*. New York: Palgrave Macmillan, 2009.

Bazelon, Emily. "A Seat at the Head of the Table," *New York Times Magazine*, February 21, 2019. https://www.nytimes.com/interactive/2019/02/21/magazine/women-corporate-america.html.

Beard, Mary. *Women and Power*. London: Profile Books, 2017.

Beauboeuf-Lafontant, Tamara. *Behind the Mask of the Strong Black Woman: Voice and the Embodiment of a Costly Performance*. Philadelphia: Temple University Press, 2009.

Benioff, Marc, and Monica Langley. *Trailblazer: The Power of Business as the Greatest Platform for Change*. New York: Currency, 2019.

Bennett, Jessica. *Feminist Fight Club*. New York: HarperCollins, 2016.

Berkner Boyt, Maureen. "3 Reasons Women Have Fewer Sponsors Than Men," *Fairygodboss*. https://fairygodboss.com/articles/women-fewer-sponsors-than-men.

Berry, William. "The Relationship Double Bind: From Frustration to Enlightenment," *Psychology Today*, August 3, 2011. https://www.psychologytoday.com/us/blog/the-second-noble-truth/201108/the-relationship-double-bind-frustration-enlightenment.

Berwick, Carly. "Keeping Girls in STEM: 3 Barriers, 3 Solutions," *Edutopia*, March 12, 2019. https://www.edutopia.org/article/keeping-girls-stem-3-barriers-3-solutions.

Bethell, Katie. "Paid Leave for All—Katie Bethell Is Seizing the Moment to Fight for Radical Policy Change," *Inflection Point with Lauren Schiller*, June 5, 2019. https://www.inflectionpointradio.org/episodes/tag/family+leave.

Beyer, Sylvia. "Gender Differences in the Accuracy of Self-Evaluations of Performance," *ResearchGate GmbH*, November 1990. https://www.researchgate.net/profile/Sylvia_Beyer/publication/232546479_Gender_Differences_in_the_Accuracy_of_Self-Evaluations_of_Performance/

links/55e0c63008ae2fac471cb8fe/Gender-Differences-in-the-Accuracy-of
-Self-Evaluations-of-Performance.pdf.

Bivens, Josh. "What Should We Know About the Next Recession?," *Economic Policy Institute*, April 18, 2019. https://www.epi.org/publication/next
-recession-bivens/.

Blanchard, Ken. *One Minute Mentoring*. New York: HarperAudio, 2017.

Bracken, Becky. "Eye-Opening Study Shows Women Receive Harsher Performance Reviews," *SheKnows*, September 6, 2014. https://www
.sheknows.com/living/articles/1049241/study-bosses-give-women
-harsher-performance-reviews/.

Brown, Brené. *The Gifts of Imperfection*. Center City, MN: Hazelden Publishing, 2010,

———. *Daring Greatly*. New York: Avery Publishing, 2012.

———. *Dare to Lead*. New York: Random House, 2018.

———. *Rising Strong*. New York: Random House, 2016.

———. *Braving the Wilderness*. New York: Random House, 2017.

Brown, Jennifer. *How to Be an Inclusive Leader*. Oakland, CA: Berrett-Koehler Publishers, 2019.

Brown, Josh. "Male Teachers Provide Important Role Models," *EdSource*, December 21, 2017. https://edsource.org/2017/male-teachers-provide
-important-role-models/591879.

Budig, Michelle J. "The Fatherhood Bonus and the Motherhood Penalty: Parenthood and the Gender Gap in Pay," *Third Way*, September 2, 2014. https://
www.thirdway.org/report/the-fatherhood-bonus-and-the-motherhood
-penalty-parenthood-and-the-gender-gap-in-pay.

Burnett, Bill, and Dave Evans. *Designing Your Life*. New York: Alfred A. Knopf, 2016.

Cain Miller, Claire. "As Women Take Over a Male-Dominated Field, the Pay Drops," *New York Times*, March 18, 2016. https://www.nytimes
.com/2016/03/20/upshot/as-women-take-over-a-male-dominated-field
-the-pay-drops.html.

———. "Pay Gap Is Because of Gender, Not Jobs," *New York Times*, April 23, 2014. https://www.nytimes.com/2014/04/24/upshot/the-pay-gap-is-because-of
-gender-not-jobs.html?smid=nytcore-ios-share.

———. "The Motherhood Penalty vs. the Fatherhood Bonus," *New York Times*, September 6, 2014. https://www.nytimes.com/2014/09/07/upshot/
a-child-helps-your-career-if-youre-a-man.html?smid=nytcore-ios-share.

———. "Why the U.S. Has Long Resisted Universal Child Care," *New York Times*, August 15, 2019. https://www.nytimes.com/2019/08/15/upshot/
why-americans-resist-child-care.html.

———. "Why Mothers' Choices About Work and Family Often Feel Like No

Choice at All," *New York Times*, January 17, 2020. https://www.nytimes ,com/2020/01/17/upshot/mothers-choices-work-family.html.

Cain Miller, Claire, and Quoctrung Bui. "Equality in Marriages Grows, and So Does Class Divide," *New York Times*, February 27, 2016. https://www .nytimes.com/2016/02/23/upshot/rise-in-marriages-of-equals-and-in -division-by-class.html?_r=0.

Cecchi-Dimeglio, Paola. "How Gender Bias Corrupts Performance Reviews, and What to Do About It," *Harvard Business Review*, April 12, 2017. https://hbr.org/2017/04/how-gender-bias-corrupts-performance-reviews -and-what-to-do-about-it.

Center for Women and Business at Bentley University. "Men as Allies: Engaging Men to Advance Women in the Workplace," Spring 2017. https://www.ceoaction .com/media/1434/bentley-cwb-men-as-allies-research-report-spring-2017. pdf.

Chamberlain, Andrew. "Is Salary Transparency More Than a Trend?," *Glassdoor*, April 2015. https://glassdoor.app.box.com/s/j0ntaw9w0hib3mrcvxky5xjw zvgfb16y.

Chemaly, Soraya. "At Work as at Home, Men Reap the Benefits of Women's 'Invisible Labor,'" *Quartz*, January 22, 2016. https://qz.com/599999/at -work-as-at-home-men-reap-the-benefits-of-womens-invisible-labor/.

Cherry, Kendra. "Why the Halo Effect Influences How We Perceive Others," *Verywell Mind*, February 9, 2020. https://www.verywellmind.com/what-is -the-halo-effect-2795906.

Clausen, Lily B. "How to Get More Women on Corporate Boards," *Insights*, Stanford Graduate School of Business, April 24, 2017. https://www.gsb .stanford.edu/insights/how-get-more-women-corporate-boards.

Cloud, Henry, and John Townsend. *Boundaries*. Grand Rapids, MI: Zondervan, 1992.

Coburn, Derek. *Networking Is Not Working*. Influential Marketing Group, 2014.

Collins, Caitlyn. *Making Motherhood Work: How Women Manage Careers and Caregiving*. Princeton, NJ: Princeton University Press, 2019.

Collins, Cory. "What Is White Privilege, Really?," *Teaching Tolerance*, Southern Poverty Law Center, Fall 2018. https://www.tolerance.org/magazine/fall -2018/what-is-white-privilege-really.

Cooper, Belle Beth. "Pros and Cons of Salary Transparency," *Culture Amp* (blog). https://www.cultureamp.com/blog/pros-and-cons-of-salary-transparency.

Cornett, Larry. "How to Handle a Boss Who Gives You Vague Feedback," *Fast Company*, August 6, 2019. https://www.fastcompany.com/90384884/how -to-handle-a-boss-who-gives-you-vague-feedback.

Correll, Shelley J., and Caroline Simard. "Research: Vague Feedback Is Hold-

ing Women Back," *Harvard Business Review*, April 29, 2016. https://hbr
.org/2016/04/research-vague-feedback-is-holding-women-back.

Correll, Shelley, Stephan Benard, and In Paik. "Getting a Job: Is There a Motherhood Penalty?," *American Journal of Sociology*, March 2007. https://gap.hks
.harvard.edu/getting-job-there-motherhood-penalty.

Cotter, David, Joan M. Hermsen, and Reeve Vanneman. "The End of the
Gender Revolution? Gender Role Attitudes from 1977 to 2008," *American Journal of Sociology* vol. 117(1), July 2011. https://www.jstor.org/
stable/10.1086/658853?seq=1#metadata_info_tab_contents.

Covert, Bryce. "How Raising the Minimum Wage Would Help Close the Gender Wage Gap," *ThinkProgress*, Center for American Progress, June 5, 2013.
https://thinkprogress.org/how-raising-the-minimum-wage-would-help
-close-the-gender-wage-gap-6bcb95cc2e30/.

Diversity Best Practices. "Best Practices in Corporate Sponsorship Programs,"
June 2011. https://www.diversitybestpractices.com/sites/diversitybestprac
tices.com/files/import/embedded/anchors/files/_attachments_articles/
rr-sponsorshipjune2011.pdf.

Donahoe, Sean. *Management Mentor*. Independently published, 2017.

Donghi, Davide. "How Learning to Say No at Work Saved My Life," *Thrive
Global*, January 13, 2019. https://thriveglobal.com/stories/saying-no-at
-work-can-save-your-life/.

Donovan, Sarah A. "Paid Family Leave in the United States," *Congressional
Research Service*, May 29, 2019. https://fas.org/sgp/crs/misc/R44835.pdf.

Doyle, Glennon. *Untamed*. New York: The Dial Press, 2020.

Draznin, Haley. "Rent the Runway CEO: Giving All Employees the Same
Benefits Is the 'Right Thing to Do,'" *CNN Business*, CNN, Inc., July 3, 2018.
https://www.cnncom/2018/10/01/success/rent-the-runway-ceo-interview/
index.html.

Education and Labor Committee. "Raise the Wage Fact Sheet," https://edlabor
.house.gov/imo/media/doc/RAISE%20THE%20WAGE%20ACT%20
-%20Women%20Fact%20Sheet.pdf.

Ellevate Network. "Moms, Beware: The Gender Pay Gap Hits You Hard-
est," *Huffington Post*, June 13, 2017. https://www.huffpost.com/entry/
moms-beware-the-gender-pay-gap-hits-you-hardest_b_59403045e4b0d
99b4c920f34.

Eltahawy, Mona. *The Seven Necessary Sins for Women and Girls*. Boston: Beacon
Press, 2019.

England, Paula. "The Gender Revolution: Uneven and Stalled," *Gender &
Society*, vol. 24(2), March 19, 2010. https://journals.sagepub.com/doi/
abs/10.1177/0891243210361475.

Evans, Dayna. "A Labor Lawyer Explains What to Do If You Suspect You're Getting Unequal Pay at Work," *The Cut*, April 4, 2017. https://www.the cut.com/2017/04/equal-pay-day-2017-dealing-with-unequal-pay-at-work .html.

———. "1 in 5 Americans Say Their Workplace Has a Hostile or Threatening Social Environment," *The Cut*, April 14, 2017. https://www.thecut .com/2017/08/rand-corp-survey-workplace-hostility.html.

Fenet, Lydia. *The Most Powerful Woman In the Room Is You*. New York: Gallery Books, 2019.

Ferrante, Mary Beth. "7 Steps to Fight for Better Paid Leave in Your Workplace, From the Mom Who Expanded Leave at Lyft," *Forbes*, March 15, 2019. https://www.forbes.com/sites/marybethferrante/2019/03/15/7-steps-to -fight-for-better-paid-leave-in-your-workplace-from-the-mom-who -expanded-leave-at-lyft/.

Ferris, Gerald R., Dwight D. Frink, and Carmen M. Galang. "Diversity in the Workplace: The Human Resources Management Challenges," *Human Resource Planning* vol. 16(1), 1993. https://web.b.ebscohost.com/abstract? direct=true&profile=ehost&scope=site&authtype=crawler&jrnl=0199 8986&AN=9503103275&h=KCRbWtQSG7Xch8mcwk9hpFO %2f3rgZq%2f%2fc60WSPso2EORHnlDW5YSiFC3h52LgJs N%2bTqyjui7iugjPyTmw4Op%2fuw%3d%3d&crl=c&resultNs=Admin Web.

Fins, Amanda. "National Snapshot: Poverty Among Women & Families, 2019," National Women's Law Center, October 2019. https://nwlc-ciw49tix gw5lbab.stackpathdns.com/wp-content/uploads/2019/10/PovertySnap shot2019-2.pdf.

Fisher, Milia. "Women of Color and the Gender Wage Gap," Center for American Progress, April 14, 2015. https://www.americanprogress.org/issues/ women/reports/2015/04/14/110962/women-of-color-and-the-gender -wage-gap/.

Flynn, Jill, Kathryn Heath, and Mary Davis Holt. "Three Ways Women Can Make Office Politics Work for Them," *Harvard Business Review*, March 8, 2012. https://hbr.org/2012/03/three-ways-women-can-make-offi.

Frank, Lydia. "How to Use Employee Referrals Without Giving Up Workplace Diversity," *Harvard Business Review*, March 15, 2018. https://hbr .org/2018/03/how-to-use-employee-referrals-without-giving-up-work place-diversity.

Freifeld, Lorri. "How-To: Start a Corporate Mentoring Program," *Training*, Lakewood Media Group, November 23, 2011. https://trainingmag.com/ content/how-start-corporate-mentoring-program/.

Garcia, Cardiff, and Stacey Vanek Smith. "Gender Segregation in the Workplace," *Planet Money*, NPR, March 8, 2019. https://www.npr.org/sections/money/2019/03/08/701713656/gender-segregation-in-the-workplace.

Gassam, Janice. "Your Unconscious Bias Trainings Keep Failing Because You're Not Addressing Systemic Bias," *Forbes*, December 29, 2019. https://www.forbes.com/sites/janicegassam/2020/12/29/your-unconscious-bias-trainings-keep-failing-because-youre-not-addressing-systemic-bias/#1d5e744e1e9d.

———. "How to Be Better Allies to Women of Color at Work," *Fast Company*, September 2, 2019. https://www.fastcompany.com/90397620/how-to-be-better-allies-to-women-of-color-at-work.

Gladwell, Malcolm. *David and Goliath: Underdogs, Misfits, and the Art of Battling Giants*. Boston: Little, Brown and Company, 2013.

Glei, Jocelyn K., Fred Stella, and Laural Merlington. *Manage Your Day-to-Day*. Amazon Publishing, 2013.

Glynn, Sarah Jane, Heather Boushey, and Peter Berg. "Who Gets Time Off?" Center for American Progress, April 26, 2016. https://www.americanprogress.org/issues/economy/reports/2016/04/26/134824/who-gets-time-off/.

Goldin, Claudia. *A Pollution Theory of Discrimination: Male and Female Differences in Occupations and Earnings, in Human Capital in History: The American Record*, eds. Leah Platt Boustan, Carola Frydman, and Robert A. Margo. Chicago: University of Chicago Press, 2014.

Gould, Elise, Jessica Schieder, and Kathleen Geier. "What Is the Gender Pay Gap and Is It Real?," Economic Policy Institute, October 20, 2016. https://www.epi.org/publication/what-is-the-gender-pay-gap-and-is-it-real/.

Green Carmichael, Sarah. "Why Walmart Expanded Parental Leave—and How to Convince Your Company to Do the Same," *Harvard Business Review*, March 1, 2018. https://hbr.org/2018/03/why-walmart-expanded-parental-leave-and-how-to-convince-your-company-to-do-the-same.

Gross, Elana Lyn. "How Paid Paternity Leave Can Help Close the Gender Pay Gap," *Forbes*, May 14, 2019. https://www.forbes.com/sites/elanagross/2019/05/14/how-paid-paternity-leave-can-help-close-the-gender-pay-gap/#31b97af450c1.

Guise, Stephen. *How to Be an Imperfectionist*. Selective Entertainment, 2015.

Hadary, Sharon, and Laura Henderson. *How Women Lead*. New York: McGraw-Hill Education, 2012.

Hancock, Adrienne B., and Benjamin A. Rubin. "Influence of Communication Partner's Gender on Language," *Journal of Language and Social Psychology* vol. 34(1), May 11, 2014. https://journals.sagepub.com/doi/abs/10.1177/0261927X14533197?papetoc=.

Hartley, Gemma. *Fed Up: Emotional Labor, Women and the Way Forward*. New York: HarperOne, 2018.

Harts, Minda. *The Memo: What Women of Color Need to Know to Secure a Seat at the Table*. New York: Seal Press, 2019.

Harvard Business Review. "We Deserve Better Than 'Attagirl,' " *Women at Work* (podcast), Season 2, Episode 4. https://hbr.org/podcast/2018/10/we-deserve-better-than-attagirl.

Harvard Business Review. "Why Are We Still Promoting Incompetent Men?," *HBR IdeaCast* (podcast), Episode 673. https://hbr.org/podcast/2019/03/why-are-we-still-promoting-incompetent-men.

Hauser, Christine. "Twitter's Ill-Timed 'Frat Party,' " *New York Times*, July 22, 2015. https://www.nytimes.com/2015/07/23/business/twitters-ill-timed-frat-party.html?_r=0.

Hauser, Fran. *The Myth of the Nice Girl*. New York: Houghton Mifflin Harcourt, 2018.

Heath, Kathryn, Jill Flynn, Mary Davis Holt, and Diana Faison. *The Influence Effect*. Oakland, CA: Berrett-Koehler Publishers, 2017.

Herrera, Tim. "3 Steps to Avoid Giving Biased Feedback," *New York Times*, April 8, 2018. https://www.nytimes.com/2018/04/08/smarter-living/give-better-feedback.html.

Hewlett, Sylvia Ann, Maggie Jackson, and Ellis Cose with Courtney Emerson. "The Sponsor Effect: Breaking Through the Last Glass Ceiling," Center for Work-Life Policy, December 2010. https://30percentclub.org/wp-content/uploads/2014/08/The-Sponsor-Effect.pdf.

Hewlett, Syliva Ann, and Maggie Jackson. "Vaulting the Color Bar: How Sponsorship Levers Multicultural Professionals into Leadership," Center for Talent Innovation, 2012. https://www.talentinnovation.org/_private/assets/VaultingTheColorBar-KeyFindings-CTI.pdf.

Hochschild, Arlie Russell. *The Managed Heart: Commercialization of Human Feeling*. Berkeley: University of California Press, 1983.

Hoey, J. Kelly. *Build Your Dream Network*. New York: TarcherPerigee, 2017.

Holt, Brianna. "Why Forced Arbitration Policies Are a Huge Red Flag for Women at Work," *Quartz*, September 19, 2019. https://qz.com/1711352/what-is-forced-arbitration-and-why-should-women-be-wary-of-it/.

Holzer, Harry J. "Paid Family Leave: Balancing Benefits and Costs," The Brookings Institution, January 30, 2017. https://www.brookings.edu/blog/social-mobility-memos/2017/01/30/paid-family-leave-balancing-benefits-and-costs/.

Huang, Jess, Alexis Krivkovich, Irina Starikova, Lareina Yee, and Delia Zanoschi. "Women in the Workplace 2019 McKinsey Report," McKinsey & Com-

pany, October 15, 2019. https://www.mckinsey.com/featured-insights/
gender-equality/women-in-the-workplace-2019.

Hunt, Vivian, Dennis Layton, and Sara Prince. "Why Diversity Matters,"
McKinsey & Company, January 2019. https://www.mckinsey.com/~/
media/McKinsey/Business%20Functions/Organization/Our%20Insights/
Why%20diversity%20matters/Why%20diversity%20matters.ashx.

Ibarra, Herminia. "A Lack of Sponsorship Is Keeping Women from Advancing
into Leadership," *Harvard Business Review*, August 19, 2019. https://hbr
.org/2019/08/a-lack-of-sponsorship-is-keeping-women-from-advancing
-into-leadership.

Ignatova, Maria. "New Report: Women Apply to Fewer Jobs Than Men, But
Are More Likely to Get Hired," *LinkedIn*, March 5, 2019. https://business
.linkedin.com/talent-solutions/blog/diversity/2019/how-women-find
-jobs-gender-report.

Institute for Women's Policy Research. "Employment, Education & Economic
Change," https://iwpr.org/issue/employment-education-economic-change/
pay-equity-discrimination/.

Institute for Women's Policy Research. "Narrow the Wage Gap Through Access to Good Jobs," *Pathways to Equity* (report). https://womenandgoodjobs
.org/.

Institute for Women's Policy Research. *Status of Women in the States* (report).
https://statusofwomendata.org/explore-the-data/employment-and
-earnings/employment-and-earnings/#StateStatutesThatAddresstheGender
WageGap.

Issid, Joe. "Does Gender Bias Play a Role During an Interview?," *Monster*.
https://www.monster.ca/career-advice/article/gender-role-during-a-job
-interview-ca.

Kabat-Farr, Dana, and Lilia M. Cortina. "Sex-based Harassment in Employment: New Insights into Gender and Context," American Psychological
Association, 2014. https://psycnet.apa.org/record/2013-27981-001.

Kaplan, Sarah. "Because It's 2017: Gender Equality as an Innovation Challenge," Rotman School of Management, 2017. https://www.rotman
.utoronto.ca/Connect/Rotman-MAG/Back-Issues/2017/Back
-Issues---2017/Fall2017-Inequality/Fall2017-FreeFeatureArticle-Kaplan.

Karpf, David. *Analytic Activism: Digital Listening and the New Political Strategy*.
New York: Oxford University Press, 2016.

Kerby, Sophia. "Pay Equity and Single Mothers of Color," Center for American
Progress, April 16, 2012. https://www.americanprogress.org/issues/race/
news/2012/04/16/11436/pay-equity-and-single-mothers-of-color/.

Keshner, Andrew. "This Is What Happens When Employers Can't Ask Job

Applicants About Salary History," *MarketWatch*, January 18, 2020. https://www.marketwatch.com/story/when-employers-cant-ask-about-salary-history-workers-can-see-double-digit-jumps-in-pay-2020-01-14.

Klaus, Peggy. *Brag! The Art of Tooting Your Own Horn Without Blowing It.* New York: Warner Business Books, 2003.

Knight, Rebecca. "When You Find Out a Coworker Makes More Money Than You Do," *Harvard Business Review*, March 7, 2016. https://hbr.org/2016/03/when-you-find-out-a-coworker-makes-more-money-than-you-do.

Knight, Sarah. *You Do You.* Boston: Little, Brown and Company, 2017.

Kolhatkar, Sheelah. "The Tech Industry's Gender-Discrimination Problem," *The New Yorker*, November 13, 2017. https://www.newyorker.com/magazine/2017/11/20/the-tech-industrys-gender-discrimination-problem.

Kostoula, Caterina. "How to Design Performance Reviews That Don't Fail Women," *Fast Company*, January 22, 2018. https://www.fastcompany.com/40518562/how-to-design-performance-reviews-that-dont-fail-women.

Kozan, Kayla. "Diversity Hiring: 6 Steps to Hiring More Diverse Candidates," Meeting Jobs, August 2, 2019. https://meetingjobs.com/diversity-hiring-6-steps-hiring-diverse-candidates/.

Krumrie, Matt. "The Right Way to Incorporate Diversity Hiring Goals and Strategies," ZipRecruiter (blog). https://www.ziprecruiter.com/blog/the-right-way-to-incorporate-diversity-hiring-goals-and-strategies/.

Kurtzleben, Danielle. "Lots of Other Countries Mandate Paid Leave. Why Not the U.S.?," *It's All Politics*, NPR, July 15, 2015. https://www.npr.org/sections/itsallpolitics/2015/07/15/422957640/lots-of-other-countries-mandate-paid-leave-why-not-the-us.

Lawler III, Edward E. *Reinventing Talent Management: Principles and Practices for the New World of Work.* Oakland, CA: Berrett-Koehler Publishers, 2017.

LeanIn.Org. "What Is Affinity Bias?," https://leanin.org/education/what-is-affinity-bias.

Leske, Lucy A. "How Search Committees Can See Bias in Themselves," *The Chronicle of Higher Education*, November 30, 2016. https://www.chronicle.com/article/How-Search-Committees-Can-See/238532.

Levanon, Asaf, Paula England, and Paul Allison. "Occupational Feminization and Pay: Assessing Causal Dynamics Using 1950–2000 U.S. Census Data," *Social Forces* vol. 88(2), December 1, 2009. https://academic.oup.com/sf/article/88/2/865/2235342.

Locker, Melissa. "Diversity in Business Really Does Boost Innovation, According to a New Study," *Fast Company*, January 12, 2018. https://www.fastcompany.com/40516536/diversity-in-business-really-does-boost-innovation-according-to-a-new-study.

Lorenzo, Rocío, Nicole Voigt, Miki Tsusaka, Matt Krentz, and Katie Abouzahr. "How Diverse Leadership Teams Boost Innovation," BCG, January 23, 2018. https://www.bcg.com/en-us/publications/2018/how-diverse-leadership-teams-boost-innovation.aspx.

Lytle, Tamara. "Closing the Gender Pay Gap," SHRM, June 4, 2019. https://www.shrm.org/hr-today/news/hr-magazine/summer2019/pages/closing-the-gender-pay-gap.aspx.

———. "Should HR Make Pay Public?" SHRM, September 1, 2014. https://www.shrm.org/hr-today/news/hr-magazine/Pages/0914-salary-transparency.aspx.

Mackenzie, Lori, and Shelley J. Correll. "Two Powerful Ways Managers Can Curb Implicit Biases," *Harvard Business Review*, October 1, 2018. https://hbr.org/2018/10/two-powerful-ways-managers-can-curb-implicit-biases.

Maldonado, Abby. "Diversifying Engineering Referrals at Pinterest," *LinkedIn*, January 15, 2016. https://www.linkedin.com/pulse/diversifying-engineering-referrals-pinterest-abby-maldonado/.

Manson, Mark. *The Subtle Art of Not Giving a Fuck*. New York: HarperOne, 2016.

McFeely, Shane, and Ben Wigert. "This Fixable Problem Costs U.S. Businesses $1 Trillion," Gallup, Inc., March 13, 2019. https://www.gallup.com/workplace/247391/fixable-problem-costs-businesses-trillion.aspx.

McGrew, Will. "Gender Segregation at Work: 'Separate But Equal' or 'Inefficient and Unfair.'" Washington Center for Equitable Growth, August 18, 2016. https://equitablegrowth.org/gender-segregation-at-work-separate-but-equal-or-inequitable-and-inefficient/.

McLaren, Samantha. "Why Referrals Might Be Hurting Your Diversity Efforts (and What You Can Do to Change That)," *LinkedIn,* April 3, 2018. https://business.linkedin.com/talent-solutions/blog/diversity/2018/why-referrals-might-be-hurting-your-diversity-efforts-and-what-you-can-do-to-change-that.

———. "8 Tips to Improve the Gender Diversity of Your Recruiting Pipeline," *LinkedIn*, May 28, 2019. https://business.linkedin.com/talent-solutions/blog/diversity/2019/8-tips-to-improve-gender-diversity-of-recruiting-pipeline.

Menendez, Alicia. *The Likeability Trap*. New York: Harper Business, 2019.

Miller, Alice. *The Drama of the Gifted Child*. New York: Basic Books, 1979.

Milli, Jessica, Yixuan Huang, Heidi Hartmann, and Jeff Hayes. "The Impact of Equal Pay on Poverty and the Economy," Institute for Women's Policy Research, April 5, 2017. https://iwpr.org/wp-content/uploads/2020/09/C455.pdf.

Moss Kanter, Rosabeth. "Some Effects of Proportions on Group Life: Skewed

Sex Ratios and Responses to Token Women," *American Journal of Sociology* vol. 82(5), March 1977. https://www.jstor.org/stable/2777808?seq=1.

Moss-Racusin, Corinne A., John F. Dovidio, Victoria L. Brescoll, Mark J. Graham, and Jo Handelsman. "Science Faculty's Subtle Gender Biases Favor Male Students," *Proceedings of the National Academy of Sciences of the United States of America* vol. 109(41), October 9, 2012. https://www.pnas.org/content/109/41/16474.

Murphy, Heather. "Picture a Leader. Is She a Woman?" *New York Times*, March 16, 2018. https://www.nytimes.com/2018/03/16/health/women-leadership-workplace.html.

National Partnership for Women & Families. "An Unlevel Playing Field: America's Gender-Based Wage Gap, Binds of Discrimination, and a Path Forward," April 2015. https:/www.nationalpartnership.org/our-work/resources/economic-justice/fair-pay/an-unlevel-playing-field-americas-gender-based-wage-gap-binds-of-discrimination-and-a-path-forward.pdf.

National Women's Law Center. "The Wage Gap: The Who, How, Why, and What to Do," September 2019. https://nwlc-ciw49tixgw5lbab.stackpathdns.com/wp-content/uploads/2018/10/The-Wage-Gap-Who-How-Why-and-What-to-Do-2019.pdf.

Newendorp, Taylor. *The Perfectionism Workbook*. San Antonio, TX: Althea Press, 2018.

Newman, Romy. "How to Start a Women's ERG," *Fairygodboss*, https://fairygodboss.com/career-topics/how-to-start-a-womens-erg.

The Nielsen Company (US). "African-American Women: Our Science, Her Magic," LLC, September 21, 2017. https://www.nielsen.com/us/en/insights/report/2017/african-american-women-our-science-her-magic/.

Nobel, Carmen. "How to Take Gender Bias Out of Your Job Ads," *Forbes*, December 14, 2016. https://www.forbes.com/sites/hbsworking-knowledge/2016/12/14/how-to-take-gender-bias-out-of-your-job-ads/#26e4fd5c1024c.

Nobscot Corporation. "How to Start a Corporate Mentoring Program," *Mentor Scout,* 2011. https://www.mentorscout.com/how-to-start-a-corporate-mentoring-program.cfm.

Oluo, Ijeoma. *So You Want to Talk About Race*. New York: Seal Press, 2018.

Oncken, Lindsay. "Policy Recommendation: Paid Family Leave," New America, *Better Life Lab* (blog). https://www.newamerica.org/in-depth/care-report/policy-recommendation-paid-family-leave/.

Orr, Marissa. *Lean Out*. New York: HarperCollins Leadership, 2019.

Pace, Cindy. "How Women of Color Get to Senior Management," *Harvard Business Review*, August 31, 2018. https://hbr.org/2018/08/how-women-of-color-get-to-senior-management.

The Paid Leave Project. "The Benefits to Your Business of Offering Paid Family and Medical Leave," http://www.paidleaveproject.org/the-playbook/assess/evaluate-the-business-benefits/.

The Paid Leave Project. "Industry Leaders Are Known to Hire and Retain the Best Talent Available," http://www.paidleaveproject.org/.

The Paid Leave Project. "Instructions to Craft a Winning Case for Paid Family and Medical Leave," http://www.paidleaveproject.org/the-playbook/persuade/craft-a-winning-case/.

Paid Leave US. "Paid Family Leave Frequently Asked Questions," 2020. https://paidleave.us/paidleave_faq.

Pan, Jessica. "Gender Segregation in Occupations: The Role of Tipping and Social Interactions," *Journal of Labor Economics* vol. 33(2), April 2015. https://www.journals.uchicago.edu/doi/10.1086/678518.

Passy, Jacob. "Men Exaggerate Their Importance at Work, While Women Do the Exact Opposite," *MarketWatch*, October 8, 2019. https://www.marketwatch.com/story/women-dont-engage-in-self-promotion-as-much-as-men-and-it-could-be-hurting-their-careers-2019-10-08.

Paycor. "Are Your Job Descriptions Driving Away Talent With Unconscious Gender Bias?," October 4, 2019. https://www.paycor.com/resource-center/gender-discrimination-in-job-descriptions.

PayScale, Inc. "The 2020 Gender Pay Gap Report Reveals That Women Still Earn Less for Equal Work," https://www.payscale.com/compensation-today/2020/03/the-2020-gender-pay-gap-report-reveals-that-women-still-earn-less-for-equal-work#:~:text=PayScale%20launches%20the%20Gender%20Pay%20Gap%20Report%20in,by%20the%20National%20Committee%20on%20Pay%20Equity%20.

Perez, Teresa. "Sponsors: Valuable Allies Not Everyone Has," PayScale, Inc., July 31, 2019. https://www.payscale.com/data/mentorship-sponsorship-benefits.

Powers, Anna. "A Study Finds That Diverse Companies Produce 19% More Revenue," *Forbes*, June 27, 2018. https://www.forbes.com/sites/annapowers/2018/06/27/a-study-finds-that-diverse-companies-produce-19-more-revenue/#5856e1e5506f.

Ridgeway, Cecilia L. *Framed by Gender: How Gender Inequality Persists in the Modern World*. New York: Oxford University Press, May 2011. https://www.oxfordscholarship.com/view/10.1093/acprof:oso/9780199755776.001.0001/acprof-9780199755776.

Robbins, Ted. *Time Management*. CreateSpace Independent Publishing Platform, 2016.

Robinett, Judy. *How to Be a Power Connector*. New York: McGraw-Hill Education, 2014.

Rose, Stephen J., and Heidi I. Hartmann. "Still a Man's Labor Market:

The Slowly Narrowing Gender Wage Gap," Institute for Women's Policy, November 26, 2018. https://iwpr.org/wp-content/uploads/2018/11/C474_IWPR-Still-a-Mans-Labor-Market-update-2018-1.pdf.

Rowe-Finkbeiner, Kristin. *Balancing Work and Family: What Policies Best Support American Families?: Hearing Before the Subcommittee on Workforce Protections*, 110th Cong. 49 (2007) (statement of Kristin Rowe-Finkbeiner, cofounder, MomsRising). https://books.google.com.ph/books?id=KAaSM43sbSIC&pg=PA24&dq=Kristin+Finkbeiner+systemic+failure&hl=en&sa=X&ved=2ahUKEwiuwJ-etJrqAhUXx4s-BHYsBDVYQ6AEwAHoECAMQAg#v=onepage&q=Kristin%20Fink-beiner%20systemic%20failure&f=false.

Roy, Katica. "How the Gender Pay Gap Cuts Through the U.S. Economy," *Fast Company*, January 8, 2020. https://www.fastcompany.com/90449297/how-the-gender-pay-gap-cuts-through-the-u-s-economy.

Rudman, Laurie A., and Kris Mescher. "Penalizing Men Who Request a Family Leave: Is Flexibility Stigma a Femininity Stigma?," *Journal of Social Issues* vol. 69(2), June 12, 2013. https://spssi.onlinelibrary.wiley.com/doi/full/10.1111/josi.12017.

Ruiz, Don Miguel. *The Four Agreements*. San Rafael, CA: Amber-Allen Publishing, 1997.

Rutherford-Morrison, Lara. "6 Little Ways the Pay Gap Hurts Women on a Daily Basis," *Bustle*, April 4, 2017. https://www.bustle.com/p/6-little-ways-the-pay-gap-hurts-women-on-a-daily-basis-47863.

Sanchez, Janis, and Donald D. Davis. "Women and Women of Color in Leadership: Complexity, Identity, and Intersectionality," *American Psychologist* vol. 65(3), April 2010. https://www.researchgate.net/publication/42637958_Women_and_Women_of_Color_in_Leadership_Complexity_Identity_and_Intersectionality.

Schaffer, Neal. *Understanding, Leveraging & Maximizing LinkedIn*. Booksurge Publishing, 2009.

Schoellkopf, Karen. "THE PROBLEM: Monoculture Is Bad for Business," *Hire More Women in Tech*. https://www.hiremorewomenintech.com/.

Schultz, Vicki. "Reconceptualizing Sexual Harassment," *Yale Law Journal* vol. 107(6), February 24, 1998. https://papers.ssrn.com/sol3/papers.cfm?abstract_id=61992.

Scott, Kim. *Radical Candor*. New York: St. Martin's Press, 2019.

Segal, Jonathan. "17 Tips for Anti-Harassment Training," SHRM, October 27, 2016. https://www.shrm.org/hr-today/news/hr-magazine/1116/pages/17-tips-for-anti-harassment-training.aspx.

Seiter, Courtney. "Why We've Stopped Saying 'Culture Fit' and What We're

Saying Instead," Buffer Inc., April 6, 2017. https://open.buffer.com/culture-fit/.

Sholar, Megan A. "The History of Family Leave Policies in the United States," Organization of American Historians, January 7, 2016. https://www.oah.org/tah/issues/2016/november/the-history-of-family-leave-policies-in-the-united-states/.

Single Mother Guide. "Single Mother Statistics," accessed February 16, 2020. https://singlemotherguide.com/single-mother-statistics/.

Smith, David G., Judith E. Rosenstein, Margaret C. Nikolov, and Darby A. Chaney. "The Power of Language: Gender, Status, and Agency in Performance Evaluations," Springer Nature, May 3, 2018. https://link.springer.com/article/10.1007%2Fs11199-018-0923-7.

Snyder, Kieran. "The Abrasiveness Trap: High-Achieving Men and Women Are Described Differently in Reviews," *Fortune*, August 26, 2014. https://fortune.com/2014/08/26/performance-review-gender-bias/.

Sostrin, Jesse. "To Be a Great Leader, You Have to Learn How to Delegate Well," *Harvard Business Review*, October 10, 2017. https://hbr.org/2017/10/to-be-a-great-leader-you-have-to-learn-how-to-delegate-well.

Stigler, George J. "Part 2: Investment in Human Beings," *Journal of Political Economy* vol. 70(5), October 1962. https://www.jstor.org/stable/i304799.

Stone, Douglas and Sheila Heen. *Thanks for the Feedback.* New York: Penguin Books, 2014.

Swanner, Nate. "Key to Closing Gender Pay Gap Is White Male 'Sponsors': Study," *Dice*, August 8, 2019. https://insights.dice.com/2019/08/08/gender-pay-gap-white-male-sponsors/.

Tallon, Monique. *Leading Gracefully.* Highest Path Publishing, 2016.

Tarr, Tanya. "How Citi Is Continuing to Level Set Equal Pay for Employees and Businesses," *Forbes*, January 22, 2020. https://www.forbes.com/sites/tanyatarr/2020/01/22/how-citi-is-continuing-to-level-set-equal-pay-for-employees-and-businesses/#73377fc11ed2.

Thompson, Karl. "What Percentage of Your Life Will You Spend at Work?," *ReviseSociology*, August 16, 2016. https://revisesociology.com/2016/08/16/percentage-life-work/.

Thorne, Heidi. *Time Management and Productivity*, 2017.

Tracy, Brian. *Time Management.* New York: AMACOM, 2018.

Traister, Rebecca. *All the Single Ladies.* New York: Simon & Schuster, 2016.

Travis, Dnika J., Jennifer Thorpe-Moscon, and Courtney McCluney. "Report: Emotional Tax: How Black Women and Men Pay More at Work and How Leaders Can Take Action," *Catalyst*, October 11, 2016. https://www

.catalyst.org/research/emotional-tax-how-black-women-and-men -pay-more-at-work-and-how-leaders-can-take-action/.

Tulgan, Bruce. *It's Okay to Be the Boss.* New York: Harper Business, 2007.

———. *The 27 Challenges Managers Face.* San Francisco: Jossey-Bass, 2014.

Tulshyan, Ruchika. "Sponsors Help Women Advance," *Diversity Woman*, 2020. https://www.diversitywoman.com/sponsors-help-women-advance/.

———. *The Diversity Advantage.* CreateSpace Independent Publishing Platform, 2016.

———. "How Managers Can Make Casual Networking Events More Inclusive," *Harvard Business Review*, October 22, 2018. https://hbr.org/2018/10/ how-managers-can-make-casual-networking-events-more-inclusive.

Tung, Irene, Yannet Lathrop, and Paul Sonn. "The Growing Movement for $15," National Employment Law Project, November 2015. https://www .nelp.org/wp-content/uploads/Growing-Movement-for-15-Dollars.pdf.

Twohey, Megan and Jodi Kantor. *She Said.* London: Penguin Press, 2019.

United States Congress. *Pay Equity: Equal Pay for Work of Comparable Value— Part II, Hearing Before the Subcommittees on Human Resources, Civil Service, Compensation, and Employee Benefits of the Committee on Post Office and Civil Service*, 97th Cong. 53 (1982). https://books.google.com.ph/books ?id=ncgHAAAAIAAJ&printsec=frontcover&dq=Pay+Equity:+Equal +Pay+for+Work+of+Comparable+Value:&hl=en&sa=x&ved=2ahUKE wiW95uRvprqAhUV_GEKHXUaB1QQ6AEwAXoECAMQAg#v =onepage&q=Pay%20Equity%3A%20Equal%20Pay%20for%20Work% 20of%20Comparable%20Value%3A&f=false.

U.S. Department of Labor, Wage and Hour Division. "Minimum Wage," https://www.dol.gov/agencies/whd/minimum-wage.

Wagner, Tyler. *How to Network at Networking Events.* Independently published, 2014.

Wang, Jim. "What a $359.17 Electricity Bill Taught Me About Negotiation," *Best Wallet Hacks*, October 23, 2018. https://wallethacks.com/what-electricity -bill-taught-me-about-negotiation/.

Washington Center for Equitable Growth. "Fact Sheet: Occupational Segregation in the United States," *Equitable Growth*, October 3, 2017. https:// equitablegrowth.org/fact-sheet-occupational-segregation-in-the -united-states/.

Washington, Zuhairah, and Laura Morgan Roberts. "Women of Color Get Less Support at Work. Here's How Managers Can Change That," *Harvard Business Review*, March 4, 2019. https://hbr.org/2019/03/women-of -color-get-less-support-at-work-heres-how-managers-can-change-that? referral=03758&cm_vc=rr_item_page.top_right.

Watkins, Michael. *The First 90 Days.* Boston: Harvard Business Review Press, 2007.

Wickre, Karen. *Taking the Work Out of Networking.* New York: Gallery Books, 2019.

Williams, Joan C. "Double Jeopardy? An Empirical Study with Implications for the Debates over Implicit Bias and Intersectionality," *Harvard Journal of Law & Gender* vol. 37, March 2014. https://repository.uchastings.edu/faculty_scholarship/1278/.

Williams, Joan C., and Marina Multhaup. "For Women and Minorities to Get Ahead, Managers Must Assign Work Fairly," *Harvard Business Review*, March 5, 2018. https://hbr.org/2018/03/for-women-and-minorities-to-get-ahead-managers-must-assign-work-fairly.

Williams, Joan C., and Rachel Dempsey. *What Works for Women at Work: Four Patterns Working Women Need to Know.* New York: New York University Press, 2014.

Wingfield, Nick, and Jessica Silver-Greenberg. "Microsoft Moves to End Secrecy in Sexual Harassment Claims," *New York Times*, December 19, 2017. https://www.nytimes.com/2017/12/19/technology/microsoft-sexual-harassment-arbitration.html.

Wittenberg-Cox, Avivah. "In Search of a Less Sexist Hiring Process," *Harvard Business Review*, March 17, 2014. https://hbr.org/2014/03/in-search-of-a-less-sexist-hiring-process.

Wong, Alia. "The U.S. Teaching Population Is Getting Bigger, and More Female," *The Atlantic*, February 20, 2019. https://www.theatlantic.com/education/archive/2019/02/the-explosion-of-women-teachers/582622/.

Woods-Giscombé, Cheryl L. "Superwoman Schema: African American Women's Views on Stress, Strength, and Health," *Qualitative Health Research* vol. 20(5), May 2010. https://www.ncbi.nlm.nih.gov/pmc/articles/PMC3072704/#R49.

Yurkiewicz, Ilana. "Study Shows Gender Bias in Science Is Real. Here's Why It Matters," *Scientific American*, September 23, 2012. https://blogs.scientificamerican.com/unofficial-prognosis/study-shows-gender-bias-in-science-is-real-heres-why-it-matters/.

Zahariades, Damon. *The Procrastination Cure.* Independently published, 2017.

———. *The 30-Day Productivity Plan.* Independently published, 2016.

Zhou, Julie. *The Making of a Manager.* New York: Portfolio, 2019.

INDEX

A Better Balance, 259
accountability, 23
Adichie, Chimamanda Ngozi, 3
Adkins, Rodney, 215, 216
allies, 179–82, 200, 269, 271
Anderson, Tracy, 150
apologetic language, 37
Arena, 272
Association for Women in
    Communications, 76
Avellino, Lia, 159

beta (alternative) plans, 214
Biaggi, Alessandra, 267–68
Big Friendship (Friedman and Sow),
    194
Black women, xx, 64–65, 145,
    166–67, 178
    emotional labor and, 161–66
    paid family leave and, 232
    self-care and, 150
    wage gap and, xv. *See also* women
    of color
body language, 80, 136
Booker, Nissa, 113–14
bosses, relationships with, 33, 42,
    144, 249
boundaries, setting, 159–61
"broken rung" barrier, 225
Brown, Brené, 159–60
budgeting, 188–89
Built By Girls Ventures (BBG), 84
Burchard, Brendon, 153
burnout, 146, 169
    breaking point of, 149–51
    warning signs of, 146–49
business cards, xiv, 78, 81, 82

calendars, 23, 49, 55, 93
Call Your Girlfriend podcast, 194

Career Horizons, 115
career paths, 14, 19, 22, 24
Center for American Progress, 259
Center for American Women in
  Politics (Rutgers University), 272
Center for Work-Life Policy, 196
CEOs, xiii, 4, 216, 233
Chamorro-Premuzic, Tomas, 5
childcare, 145, 230
Child Care Aware of America, 261
Clinton, Hillary, 267
collaborative environment, 16
comfort zone, stepping out of, 72
communication, effective, 206
community building, 19, 74, 92
  company culture, 36, 102, 103, 114
    diversity in management and, 225
  interviews and, 104–6
  toxic, 241
competitive environment, 16, 19, 36
Comstock, Beth, 81–83
conference speaker listings, 85
connectors, networking and, 94–98,
  103
Correll, Shelley, 183
cost-benefit analysis, 127
Cotel, Orli, 232
COVID-19 pandemic, 130, 145, 260
creativity, 22
criticism, fear of, 52–53
Csikszentmihalyi, Mihaly, 15
Cuomo, Governor Andrew, 266–67

deal breakers, 21, 103, 208
Dee, Ruby, 71
delegation, of tasks, 51, 55–57
diary, writing in, 35–36
Dickinson, Alexandra, 125
discrimination, x, 161, 168, 221, 239
  discovery of, 241–42
  emotional burden from, 167

microaggressions and, 163
  options for taking action about,
    243–47
diversity and inclusion, 105, 112,
  167, 225, 226–27
Dua, Nisha, 84, 87, 95, 98

Economic Policy Institute, 257
Eisenhower Matrix, 51
Eleanor's Legacy, 272
Emerge America, 272
emotional labor, xvi, 145, 161–66
Equal Pay Act (1963), 258
ERGs (employee resource groups),
  105, 226–28, 232
Eventbrite listings, 75
expectations, xix, 4, 15, 57, 170

Facebook, 75, 85, 88, 90
failure, reframing of, 34
Fair Workweek, 261–62
Fair Workweek Initiative, 262
Fairygodboss, 191
family leave, paid, 145, 222, 231,
  235, 250
  employees' petition for, 236
  policy change and, 259
  policy pitch template for, 233–34
Family Medical Leave Act (FMLA),
  230
feedback, 42, 66, 88, 162, 179, 210
  clients, from, 63
  critical, 33–35, 115
  getting buy-in and, 214
  necessity of, 52, 180–81
  positive and constructive, 57, 182
  soliciting of, 183–84
  from trusted sources, 51
Feelin' Good Money, 126, 138, 139
femininity, cultural ideal of, 38, 176
Ferris, Gerald, 195

financial crisis (2008), 145
financial security, 7, 8, 20, 127
flexibility, 20
flextime, 16
"flow," 15, 16, 22
Fonda, Jane, 150
Fortune 500 companies, 4
Friedman, Ann, 194
Frink, Dwight, 195
Fuck You Money, 126, 131, 139,
    140, 141, 249
full compensation ("full comp"),
    129–32

Galang, Maria Carmen, 195
gender: broken rung and, 225
gendering of jobs, 13
gender norms, 55–56, 145, 164
    imbalance of power and, xiii,
        30–31
    occupational segregation by, 208
    speakers at meetings, 205
    sponsors and, 190–91
    wage gap and, xv, xvii, 120, 122
Gilbert, Alison, 34
glass ceiling, 225
Glassdoor reviews, 106
graduate school, 29–30, 109
Granovetter, Mark, 92
growth, feedback and, 33, 34

habits, xix–xx
harassment, 187, 221
headhunters, 122
Healthy Families Act, 260
Heilman, Madeline, 164
Hellerer, Megan, 12, 24
High Performance Planner, 153
Hispanic women, xv, xx, 232
Hochschild, Arlie, 163
Horney, Karen, 12–13

How to Be a Power Connector
    (Robinett), 92
HR Dive, 257
HRuprise consulting firm, 169, 185,
    228

imposter syndrome, xix, 5, 6, 30, 68,
    101, 204
    deferential appearance and, 32
    experiments in vulnerability and, 42
    external circumstances and, 36
    plan for combatting, 39–40
    salary negotiation and, 131
    self-doubts and, 31–32
    "Tyranny of the Should" and, 13
    work-based identity and, 35
inequities, identifying, 167–69
influences, understanding of, 14
inner critic, 9, 10, 23, 54–55
Instagram, 68, 75, 85, 88, 89, 90–91,
    214
Institute for Women's Policy Re-
    search, 256
interests, digging into, 18, 21, 22
internships, 75
interviews, xix, 31, 113–15
    proactive outreach and, 104
    research to prepare for, 104–6
    storytelling and, 102
    Superpowers and, 110–12
    talking yourself up, 106–10

job applications, 101
journalism, 7, 9, 90

Klein, Jeff, 267
knowledge, 36–37, 112
Koch brothers, 267

Ladies Get Paid organization, xiii, xix,
    24, 61, 83

Ladies Get Paid organization *(cont.)*,
  civic engagement of members, 25
  launching of, 81, 94
  Money Scrunchie icon, 82
laws, updated, xx, 222, 255
leadership, 111, 198, 225, 236, 255
Lean In Foundation, 225
LifeLabs Learning, 206
LinkedIn, 76, 84, 85, 88, 89–90, 91,
  93
  job search and, 103, 109
  preparation for interviews and, 104
  salary negotiation and, 122
London School of Economics, 29, 42
Luna, Tania, 206

Maher, Carolyn, 209, 215
Managed Heart, The (Hochschild),
  163
managers, relationships with, 180–82,
  183–84, 213
  annual reviews and, 211
  conversations about discrimination,
  242
  dealing with difficult managers,
  184–89
maternity leave, 224, 231, 241. *See
  also* family leave, paid
Matthews, Gail, 188
meetings, speaking up in, 204–6
men: imposter syndrome and, 35
  networking and, xiii–xv, 73, 123
  occupational segregation and, 208
  office politics and, 195
  promotions and, 168, 177
  senior leadership dominated by, 225
  sponsors and, 190–91
  white men, 123, 163, 225
mentors, 8–9
meritocracy, xv
microaggressions, 163

micromanaging, 56, 57
middle management, xv
millennial generation, 145
minimum wage, 256
MomsRising.org, 221
money, xviii, 20, 116, 125
  policy change and, 267
  women's stories about, xvi–xvii
  writing down money goals, 188
monologue, internal, 54
mothers, 55, 65, 68
  discrimination and, 222
  ERGs and, 226–27
  Motherhood Penalty, 229–30, 231
  wage gap and, 168
motivations, reframing of, 58–61
Multhaup, Marina, 168
multitasking, 155–56

National Child Care Association,
  261, 262
National Employment Law Project,
  257
National Partnership for Women &
  Families, 259, 260
National Women's Law Center, 232,
  262
networking, 8, 17, 22, 25–26, 71, 72,
  98–99
  cold outreach, 83–88
  college alumni, 123
  community and, 74
  connectors and, 94–98
  etiquette of, 84, 90–91, 95, 98, 103
  event, 77–81
  expanding a network, 74, 76, 216
  finding your people, 74–76
  gender power imbalance and, xiii–
  xiv, 73
  new jobs filled through, 115
  opening lines for meeting people, 78

with peers, 193–95
relationships and, 91–93
social media and, 88–91
New Leaders Council, 272

Obama, Barack, 267
Ocasio-Cortez, Alexandria (AOC),
    25, 250, 267
office politics, 21, 195–201
overcommitment, 65–66
overwork, 46, 47–51, 64, 67
    balance and replenishing, 158–59
    focus on wellness and, 152–57
    lightening the workload, 155–57
    self-care and, 150–51
    setting boundaries and, 159–61
    therapeutic activities for, 151–52
    warning signs of burnout, 146–49

Paid Leave for the United States
    (PL+US), 232, 233, 259
Paid Sick Days, 260
patterns, finding, 18
Paycheck Fairness Act, 258
pay raises, 190, 203, 211, 250
peers, 193–95
peer-to-peer sharing, xviii
Pennebaker, James W., 36
people of color, 150, 162, 171, 226
perfectionism, xix, 5, 6, 13, 30, 67
    delegation as option against, 51,
        55–57
    growth and, 209
    letting go of, 60–61, 64, 68
    medical risk factors and, 60
    overwork and, 46, 47–51
    perspective and, 52
    reframing of motivations and,
        58–60
    rumination and, 52–55
    self-sabotage and, 33

unachievable standards and,
    46–47
performance, xv
    perfectionism and, 59
    "shoulds" mindset and, 54
performance reviews, 162, 224, 236,
    244
podcasts, 85
policy change, 233, 236, 255
    donating money to campaigns, 267
    in-person advocacy, 263
    phone call and letter templates,
        264–65
    policies for working women,
        256–62
    running for public office, 267–71
    social media and, 266–67
    training programs for, 272
"portal people," 92–93, 94, 123
power, xvii, xviii, xix, 175, 222, 247
    change from the people and, 255
    women's representation in positions
        of, 5
praise and recognition, 20
pregnancy, 223
priorities, determining, 21–22
prioritizing, 49, 51, 71, 156
problem-solving, 18
productivity, 171, 227
promotions, xvii, 5, 168, 175–76,
    194, 203
    advocating for yourself, 210–13
    broken rung and, 225
    denial of, 229
    gender differences and, 177
    positioning yourself for, 207
public speaking, xvii, 19, 62–63, 205

racism, 135, 145
recruiters, 8, 104
reinvention, case study in, 24–25

relationships, building, 177, 216, 217
relationships, cultivating, 91–93
remote working, 16
resilience, 43, 53
reviews, annual, 210, 211, 243
Rhimes, Shonda, 175
Rising Strong (Brown), 159–60
Robinett, Judy, 92
role models, 8
Rowe-Finkbeiner, Kristin, 221
Run for Something (organization),
    272

salary history ban, 257
salary negotiation, xviii, 71, 101,
    117–18, 140–41, 175, 211
  anxiety and, 133–34
  bottom line and, 126, 128
  choosing a range of numbers,
    126–28
  Double Bind and, 135–36, 164
  full compensation and, 129–32
  market value and, 119–22
  planning and, 136–40
  self-advocacy and, 102
  shifting mindset for, 118–19
  talking to people about, 122–25
Sanders, Bernie, 267
schedule flexibility, 129, 130
scope, establishing, 49
self-care, 10, 150–51
self-doubt, 31
Self-Enhancement Bias, 55
self-esteem, 60
self-flagellation, 33, 34, 60
self-worth, xviii, 31, 54
sexism, x, 135, 178, 191, 243
She Should Run (nonprofit
    organization), 268, 272
Shine Theory, 194
"shoulds" mindset, 13, 22, 23, 54

Simard, Caroline, 183
skills, learning, 23, 179, 207
Skype, 31, 87, 116
Sobierajski, Leta, 82
social anxiety, 77
social media, 41, 63, 88–91
  policy change and, 267–71
  STAR Method and, 108
Society for Human Resource
    Management, 257
Sow, Aminatou, 194
space, taking up, 37–39
sponsors, finding, 190–93, 229
STAR Method, 107, 108–10
strengths, 16–17, 19
success, xix, 7, 8, 63
  definition of, 4, 9
  delegation and, 57
Superpowers, 110–12
Superwoman Schema (Woods-
    Giscombé), 64–65
sustainability, 19, 48, 172, 229

Take Your Kids to Work Day, 227,
    233
Taking the Work Out of Networking
    (Wickre), 93
technology: 24/7 work environment
    and, 144
  as double-edged sword, 170
TheLi.st, 25–26
time management, 49, 50
#TimesUp, 255
Toomey, Taryn, 150
town halls, xvi, xviii, 82, 263
Twitter, 81, 85, 88, 89, 90, 168,
    266

Universal Child Care and Early
    Learning Act, 260–61
upward mobility, 221

values, motivating, 20
VoteRunLead, 272
vulnerability, experiments in, 40–43

wage gap, xv, xvii, 120, 122, 168, 222, 249
    occupational segregation and, 208
    paid family leave and closing of, 231
    policy change and, 256. *See also* discrimination
Wall Street, as boys' club, 240
Walters, Barbara, 7
Wang, Jim, 189
Weaver, Rebecca, 169–70, 185, 187, 228
webinars, 23
We Should All Be Feminists (Adichie), 3
Whitney, Susan, 179, 190, 207
whole-body breaks, 52
Wickre, Karen, 93
Williams, Joan, 168
women: cultural messaging about, 3
    housework/childcare and, 55–56

"ideal" girl or woman, 3–4, 6, 32
    as majority of college graduates, xv
    marginalized status of, xx
    masculinized power suits, 176
    networking and, xiii–xv
    occupational segregation and, 208
    "Old Boys Network" and, 73
women of color, xvi, 135, 145, 167, 194, 221
    emotional labor and, 163–64
    in finance industry jobs, 246
    office politics and, 196
    in systems engineering, 179. *See also* Black women
Women's Campaign School (Yale University), 272
Woods-Giscombé, Cheryl L., 64–65
work-life balance, 16, 19, 21, 22, 106, 208
workload, 12, 27
"work wife," 163
writing therapy, 36

Youngquist, Matt, 115

ABOUT THE AUTHOR

Claire Wasserman is a thought leader, speaker, and entrepreneur. She is the founder of Ladies Get Paid, a global community that champions the professional and financial advancement of women. Claire has traveled the country, teaching thousands of women how to negotiate millions of dollars in raises, start businesses, and advocate for themselves in the workplace. Claire was named one of *Entrepreneur* magazine's 100 Most Powerful Women for her work inspiring a new generation of female leaders and she is a highly sought-after expert for Fortune 500 companies working to improve diversity, equity, inclusion, and belonging within their organizations.

CONTINUE THE CONVERSATION

I hope you enjoyed reading *Ladies Get Paid* as much as I enjoyed writing it! But this is so much more than a book; Ladies Get Paid is a global network of thousands of women who come together to learn, lift one another up, and make collective change.

Continue the conversation by joining us at ladiesgetpaid.com. I also encourage you to check out the Institute for Higher Learning, our video library with hundreds of hours of career development and financial education.

Stay in touch with me on Instagram @ladiesgetpaid and keep me posted on all your progress. I know you'll go far! Now go get paid!